The Rise of the Gothic Novel

Maggie Kilgour

London and New York

First published 1995
by Routledge
11 New Fetter Lane, London EC4P 4EE

Simultaneously published in the USA and Canada
by Routledge
29 West 35th Street, New York, NY 10001

© 1995 Maggie Kilgour

Typeset in Baskerville by LaserScript, Mitcham, Surrey
Printed and bound in Great Britain by
Mackays of Chatham PLC, Chatham, Kent

British Library Cataloguing in Publication Data
A catalogue record for this book is available from the British Library

Library of Congress Cataloging in Publication Data
Kilgour, Maggie
The rise of the Gothic novel/Maggie Kilgour.
p. cm.
Includes bibliographical references and index.
1. Horror tales, English – History and criticism.
2. Gothic revival (Literature) – Great Britain.
3. English fiction – History and criticism. I. Title.
PR830.T3K5   1994
823′0872909 – dc20   94-27075

ISBN 0–415–08181–5
ISBN 0–415–08182–3 (pbk)

Contents

Acknowledgements

Like Mary Shelley, I am often asked what a nice girl like me is doing with a bunch of ghouls like this. So I have had to think about why I like brooding on sensational, grotesque, gruesome stories, and digging up the past. As this book will show, it would be appropriate for me to trace my present pursuit back to some trauma in early childhood, or, perhaps even better, the *lack* of trauma in early childhood. That could account too for my having wasted the best years of my life in a darkened theatre, watching Dracula rise from the dead – again and again and again. From that depth, my development into an academic was obviously inevitable. As the medievalist and writer of gothic stories, M.R. James, especially showed, all scholarship is a necromantic art, in which we bring the dead back. Part of the appeal for me of this kind of literature is the way in which it so graphically embodies the desire to hold on to the past, to strive against loss and mortality. At the same time, however, the fact that it often does so in crude and parodic forms seems to suggest a useful caveat for criticism, and, more broadly, for an age which sees itself as progressive to the point of being 'postmodern,' but which obsessively resurrects and recycles everything, from dinosaurs to bell-bottoms and Elvis.

It is also tempting for me to claim that I wrote this book in the grip of an irresistable impulse, and therefore am not responsible for the consequences. However, *Frankenstein* provides a sobering warning of the dangers of repudiating one's creation, and so I acknowledge this thing of darkness mine. At the same time, there are many people whose help and encouragement I have depended upon. I am again grateful to the Social Sciences and Humanities Research Council of Canada for their support. I want to thank my series of Igors, who dug up the ghastly bits and pieces from which

Acknowledgements

I assembled my textual body – Steven Bruhm, Lisa Brown, Sue Laver, Tara Walker, and Laura Killian. My very ungothic Australian relations, the Herci, Bennies, and Grants, cheered me up so much that it made getting back to my tower of filthy creation extremely difficult. Mary Grant's exuberance for life and literature was especially distracting, but also inspiring. Talia Rodgers, Tricia Dever and everyone at Routledge led me through the labyrinthine passage of publication with care, kindness, and good humour. With her usual alacrity, Megan Williams conjured up something nice and nasty for the cover. The rest of my thanks go to the usual suspects, who in their various weird ways have inspired me as I toiled away: Hugh Roberts (whose brains are always delicious to pick), Rachel Gamby, Chris Heppner, Ian 'the Barbarian' Duncan, and my own gothic double, Lisa Darrach. Brian Trehearne deserves a special medal for heroic valour and sheer patience, for repeatedly releasing me from my entrapment in gothic fantasy, reminding me that there is a difference (most of the time) between art and life. I regret deeply, however, that my muse Kit, the Montoni of the budgie world and *rara avis*, did not live to tear to atoms the final draft of this manuscript:

> exequias ite frequenter, aves!
> ite, piae volucres, et plangite pectora pinnis
> et rigido teneras ungue notate genas;
> horrida pro maestis lanieter pluma capillis,
> pro longa resonent carmina vestra tuba!
>
> (Ovid, *Amores* II. vi. 2–6)

Part I

1 The Nature of Gothic

One of the powerful images conjured up by the words 'gothic novel' is that of a shadowy form rising from a mysterious place: Frankenstein's monster rising from the laboratory table, Dracula creeping from his coffin, or, more generally, the slow opening of a crypt to reveal a dark and obscure figure. This iconography has haunted various critical representations of the rise of the genre. The imagery supports psychoanalytical critics' contention that the gothic reflects the return of the repressed, in which subconscious psychic energy bursts out from the restraints of the conscious ego. The emergence of the gothic in the eighteenth century has also been read as a sign of the resurrection of the need for the sacred and transcendent in a modern enlightened secular world which denies the existence of supernatural forces, or as the rebellion of the imagination against the tyranny of reason. Recent historical studies have positioned the genre more specifically in relation to the rise of the middle class and the novel proper, with which that class has been identified, since Ian Watt especially. In general, the gothic has been associated with a rebellion against a constraining neoclassical aesthetic ideal of order and unity, in order to recover a suppressed primitive and barbaric imaginative freedom. Until recently therefore, the gothic novel has often been treated also as a kind of generic missing link between the romance and the novel, a very low road to Scott, whose rise is a deviation in the evolutionary chain that leads from Enlightenment to Romanticism. Manifesting prematurely, and therefore understandably somewhat crudely, the emerging values of romanticism – an interest in the bizarre, eccentric, wild, savage, lawless, and transgressive, in originality and the imagination – the gothic itself is a transitional and rather puerile form which is superseded by the more mature 'high' art of the superior Romantics, such as Coleridge, Keats, and, especially, Byron who both realises and renders redundant the gothic hero–villain. Like so many of its hero–villains, its development is one of rapid rise and fall, which occurs roughly between 1760 and 1820.

This developmental model plays an important part both in critical discussions of the rise of the gothic and in the novels themselves. However, one of the factors that makes the gothic so shadowy and nebulous a genre, as difficult to define as any gothic ghost, is that it cannot be seen in abstraction from the other literary forms from whose graves it arises, or from its later descendants who survive after its demise, such as the detective novel and horror movie. It feeds upon and mixes the wide range of literary sources out of which it emerges and from which it never fully disentangles itself: British folklore, ballads, romance, Elizabethan and Jacobean tragedy (especially Shakespeare), Spenser, Milton, Renaissance ideas of melancholy, the graveyard poets, Ossian, the sublime, sentimental novelists (notably Prevost, Richardson, and Rousseau), and German traditions (especially Schiller's *Robbers* and *Ghost-Seer*). The form is thus itself a Frankenstein's monster, assembled out of the bits and pieces of the past. While it therefore can at times seem hopelessly naive and simple, it is, at its best, a highly wrought, artificial form which is extremely self-conscious of its artificiality and creation out of old material and traditions. The narratives of Walpole, Radcliffe, Maturin, Stoker, as well as Shelley, thematise their own piecemeal construction, drawing attention to the relation of the story and unfolding of the plot. Gothic creation thus suggests a view of the imagination not as an originating faculty that creates ex nihilo, but as a power of combination. As one charitable reviewer noted in relation to Matthew Lewis's 'borrowings' from other texts (which later critics have occasionally, though not always accurately, identified as plagiarism): 'the great art of writing consists in selecting what is most stimulant from the works of our predecessors, and in uniting the gathered beauties in a new whole, more interesting than the tributary models. This is the essential process of the imagination. . . . All invention is but new combination.'[1] Gothic creation is a Frankensteinian process, as described also by Mary Shelley in her 1831 preface to her own textual monster: 'Invention, it must be humbly admitted, does not consist in creating out of a void, but out of chaos; the materials must, in the first place, be afforded; it can give form to dark, shapeless substances, but cannot bring into being the substance itself.'[2]

Gothic criticism often inverts this creation of a whole from fragments: what the writer puts together, the critic pulls apart. It seems easier to identify a gothic novel by its properties than by an essence, so that analysis of the form often devolves into a cataloguing of stock characters and devices which are simply recycled from one text to the next: conventional settings (one castle – preferably in ruins; some gloomy mountains – preferably the Alps; a haunted room that locks only on the outside) and characters (a passive and persecuted heroine, a sensitive and rather ineffectual hero, a dynamic and tyrannical villain, an evil prioress, talkative servants). However, this dismemberment of the text seems often justified by narrative incoherence, which has been the subject of much critical complaint, and generally leads to the denigration of the form for its lack of aesthetic unity. Made up of these assorted bits and pieces, gothic novels often seem to disintegrate into fragments, irrelevant digressions, set-pieces of landscape description which never refer back to the central point. Such a tendency towards dismemberment may be encouraged by the fact that they also often look to lyric poetry and painting as models for their own mode of representation. At times the gothic seems hardly a unified narrative at all, but a series of framed conventions, static moments of extreme emotions – displayed by characters or in the landscape, and reproduced in the reader – which are tenuously strung together in order to be temporised both through and into narrative, but which do not form a coherent and continuous whole.

Given its corporate identity, it may not be surprising that the gothic seems also a confused and self-contradictory form, ambivalent or unsure about its own aims and implications. Criticism has reflected these contradictions. Some modern critics have wanted to assert its psychological complexity; Robert Hume claimed that 'Robert Lovelace is a simpler character than Lewis's Ambrosio', a somewhat outrageous statement which seems to reflect a desire to vindicate the form according to inappropriate criteria.[3] Others have agreed with J.M.S. Tompkins that the gothic is simplistic in its representation of character, which it subordinates to plot, scenery, and moralising. According to Tompkins: 'The fates of the human beings merely illustrate the nature of these places, while they themselves make the story and brood over it. The intricate plots of the romances are mainly a working-out of the suggestions of mountain scenery and Gothic architecture.'[4] Critics who agree on this point, however, still debate its implications. Elizabeth Napier argues that this focus on surfaces reveals that the gothic, far from being psychologically profound, is a shallow and superficial form.[5] According to Robert Keily, however, the subordination of person to place enables the gothic to explore 'the whole concept of individual identity', to show 'human personality as essentially unstable, inconsistent'.[6] William Patrick Day similarly reads it as reflective of a fragmented fable of identity, while for Robert Miles it is a site, a 'carnivalesque' mode which represents 'the subject finding itself dispossessed in its own home, in a condition of rupture, disjunction, fragmentation'.[7] Recent criticism has often focused on the gothic's fragmentation as a response to bourgeois models of personal, sexual, and textual identity, seeing it as a Frankensteinian deconstruction of modern ideology.[8]

Ian Watt, however, argues that superficiality is due to the displacement of complexity from characters onto the readers' response to the situations presented,[9] as the gothic's main concern is not to depict character but to create a feeling or effect in its readers by placing them in a state of thrilling suspense and uncertainty. From its origins, the gothic has been defined in terms of this peculiar and palpable effect upon its audience. As a result, it has also frequently been involved in discussions concerning the relation of art to life, aesthetics to ethics. With its cast of extreme characters, unnatural settings and perverse plots, the gothic played a significant part in late eighteenth-century debates over the moral dangers of reading. Such debates were of a partially political origin, in England looking back to Milton's argument in *Areopagitica*, a text much cited in the eighteenth century. From the seventeenth century on, with the rise of literacy and the increase of the press, reading became a focal point in debates over authority and self-determination; indeed, it became identified with self-determination. Originating in the Protestant ideal that every man had the right to read the scripture for himself, a right viewed with some concern in the seventeenth century with the rise of dissenting movements (which sometimes even extended that right to women), the idea that to read for oneself was the property of the self-governing individual permeated discussions of both literature and politics. At the same time, however, there was a mistrust of the reader's ability to handle this heavy responsibility, and a wariness of the potentially pernicious influence of literature on a broad but naive market. The spread of literacy, the growth of a largely female and middle-class readership and of the power of the press, increased fears that literature could be a socially subversive influence. Prose fiction was particularly suspect: romances, for giving readers unrealistic expectations of an idealised life, novels for exposing them to the sordidness of an unidealised reality.

As a hybrid between the novel and romance, the gothic was accused on both accounts. The gothic was seen as encouraging a particularly intimate and insidious relationship between text and reader, by making the reader identify with what he or she read. As one contemporary reviewer said of Radcliffe: 'it may be true that her persons are cold and formal; but her readers are the virtual heroes and heroines of her story as they read.'[10] According to Scott as well, the purpose of the gothic author was 'to wind up the feelings of his reader till they become for a moment identified with those of a ruder age'.[11] Ideally, this identification served a moral purpose, as it allowed readers to exercise safely and so educate their emotions; the danger was when the means became an end in itself. To many early concerned critics, gothic novels were the unlicensed indulgence of an amoral imagination that was a socially subversive force. The possibility that the gothic represented simply a fairy-tale world created by an imagination, an artistic aesthetic realm that was completely irrelevant and detached from the social order and norms, made it more, rather than less, threatening. The escapist imagination was denounced as corruptive of family values, as, when uncontrolled by reason, it rendered the vulnerable pro-verbial 'young person' unfit for real life. The art that is completely fanciful, an autonomous creation that does not refer to reality, offers a tempting alternative to the mundaneness of everyday life. It was feared that readers of fictions, seduced by the enticing charms of an illusory world, would lose either their grip on or their taste for reality: 'the false expectations these wild scenes excite, tend to debauch the mind, and throw an insipid kind of uniformity over the moderate and rational prospects of life, consequently adventures are sought for and created, when duties are neglected and content despised.'[12] Too much mental stimulation of the sensibilities was seen as producing insensibility and apathy in real life. As Coleridge warned, novel-reading may be 'especially injuri-ous to the growth of the imagination, the judgment, and the morals, especially to the latter, because it excites mere feelings without at the same time ministering to an impulse to action . . . they afford excitement without producing reaction'.[13] Imagination and appetite are too closely connected, and reading itself a way of feeding destructive and anti-social desires. The ill consequences of reading works which fill 'the mind with extravagant thoughts and too often with criminal propensities'[14] are dramatised in numer-ous gothic stories in which the heroine is the victim of her own imagination and sensibility, indulged in reading, through which she loses the ability to differentiate between art and life.[15]

Some of the most powerful critiques of the force of the gothic appear within the gothic, which internalised external criticism, both in stories such as those described above, and in tales of works of art that take on lives of their own. As I will discuss further (see pp. 85–7; 156–8), in its various versions of the familiar Pygmalion myth, the gothic seems to both represent and punish the imagination's power to realise its own desires. It therefore seems also to denounce precisely the transgressive qualities with which it was associated. While to earlier conservative moralists the gothic's offer of an imaginative retreat from reality was seen as a potentially amoral subversion of social order, to many modern critics this, contradictorily, has proved it to be a reactionary, socially conservative form. In the Radcliffean model, especially, the imagination is indulged through suspense, only to be ultimately contained, imprisoned by the final authority of morality, in which the good and bad are separated out by a poetically just system of rewards and punishments. The gothic appears to suggest that the inevitable can only be pleasurably, and fictitiously, deferred for a time, as the domestic sphere is the only appropriate end of a woman's adventures: whether that woman be the heroine or the reader herself, who, the thrilling adventure of reading over, closes the book and returns to her daily duties. The gothic thus both represents in the story of its heroine and offers to its readers a momentary subversion of order that is followed by the restoration of a norm, which, after the experience of terror, now seems immensely desirable.[16] Reading is thus a dangerously conservative substitute for political and social action, offering an illusory transformation to impede real change by making women content with their lot, and keeping them at home – reading.

Like the carnivalesque, the gothic appears to be a transgressive rebellion against norms which yet ends up reinstating them, an eruption of unlicensed desire that is fully controlled by governing systems of limitation.[17] It delights in rebellion, while finally punishing it, often with death or damnation, and the reaffirmation of a system of moral and social order. However, the fact that the endings are often, as Robert Keily notes,[18] unsatisfactory when compared to the delicious experience of the middle of the text, might in itself suggest a radical, antiteleological, model for reading, in which closure, which necessarily involves some restabilisation of categories, is deprivileged. For Sir Walter Scott, the notorious dissatisfaction of Radcliffe's endings could not diminish our pleasure in the rest of the text, and 'the impression of general delight which we have received for the perusal remains unabated'.[19] The dissatisfaction of the moral at the end in fact forces us to focus on the aesthetic pleasure of the middle.

Some recent critics have claimed further that in its potential as a vehicle for female anger the gothic provides a 'plot of feminine subversion'.[20] Its escape from the real world has a deeper moral purpose, as distance enables literature to become an indirect critique of things as they are; in Punter's nicely gothic description, the gothic is 'not an escape from the real but a deconstruction and dismemberment of it'.[21] The female gothic itself is not a ratification but an exposé of domesticity and the family, through the technique of estrangement or romantic defamiliarisation: by cloaking familiar images of domesticity in gothic forms, it enables us to see that the home *is* a prison, in which the helpless female is at the mercy of ominous patriarchal authorities. For Kenneth Graham, therefore, the gothic generally: 'was as rebellious in letters as its contemporary parallel in France was in politics. It challenged fundamental notions of aesthetics and psychology.'[22]

More critics argue, however, that whatever radical and subversive implications the gothic might have are radically limited by its own inconsistencies. Coral Ann Howells attributes the contradictory nature of the gothic to the fact that: 'Gothic novelists didn't know what to do with their own feelings of frustration and rebelliousness. . . . Their fiction is both exploratory and fearful. They are not always totally in control of their fantasies, for having opened up new areas of awareness which complicate life enormously, they then retreat from their insights back into conventionality with the rescue of a heroine into happy marriage and the horrible death of a villain.'[23] For Robert Keily, 'Gothic fiction was not only about confusion, it was written from confusion'.[24] Terry Lovell argues further that its irresolution exposes the conflicts within bourgeois ideology that it is supposed to hide, a conflict between morality and aesthetics, work and pleasure.[25] Similarly, for Wylie Sypher, the ambiguity of the gothic is created by a tension between its reactionary moral and revolutionary aesthetic values, both of which, however, are bourgeois creations. The gothic therefore reveals 'the naked contradictions intrinsic in bourgeois romanticism', but only through 'a revolt so radically inhibited that it failed to be in a deep social sense creative'.[26] Its ambiguity reflects tensions it cannot solve. For Hume, this makes it secondary to Romanticism, which asserts the power of the synthetic imagination to reconcile and resolve all contradictions; the gothic imagination, in contrast, cannot transform or transcend the everyday world: it 'has no such answers and can only leave the "opposites" contradictory and paradoxical', ending in 'only unresolvable moral and emotional ambiguity'.[27] For Day, however, the gothic exposes the gothic reality of modern identity, and by failing to represent an adequate solution it forces its readers to address them in real life, thus (ideally) using literature to encourage social change.[28] In her rejection of such recent assumptions that the form is deep and significant, which she connects to a current post-romantic ideal-isation of fragmentation, Napier argues, however, that the gothic represents a flight from meaning into a quest for sensations. Its self-contradiction and critiquing reveal only that it is an irre-sponsibly escapist form marked by 'profound uncertainty about its genuine status and intent', which lacks the guts to confront its own moral and aesthetic implications.[29]

The gothic seems a puzzling contradiction, denounced and now celebrated for its radical imaginative lawlessness, feared for its encouragement of readers to expect more from life than is real-istic, and also for its inculcation of social obedience and passivity. Revolutionary or reactionary? An incoherent mess or a self-conscious critique of repressive concepts of coherence and order? Apolitical or a direct product and artistic equivalent of the French Revolution? Transgressive and lawless or conformist and meekly law-abiding? Psychologically deep in its representation of char-acters or motives, or totally superficial in its interest in mere appearances and coverings? While at its origins, a concern with the social role and effects of reading made the gothic a debated genre, current critical interest in the politics of literature has turned it into a 'contested castle' [30] that is both attacked and defended for the secret it supposedly conceals in its hermeneutical dungeon.

2 Past and Present

Since Ian Watt, the rise of the British novel proper has been tied to the emergence of Protestant bourgeois culture. The novel's focus on character as the motive, and causality as the form, for narrative is seen as an extension of middle-class faith in indi-vidualism, self-determination, 'getting ahead', reason, autonomy, and progress.[31] The gothic's relation to the class that, for the most part, produced and consumed it has seemed more convoluted, involving a kind of gothic doubling.[32] The gothic is part of the reaction against the political, social, scientific, industrial, and epistemological revolutions of the seventeenth and eighteenth centuries which enabled the rise of the middle class.

Like Romanticism, the gothic is especially a revolt against a mechanistic or atomistic view of the world and relations, in favour of recovering an earlier organic model. The gothic is symptomatic of a nostalgia for the past which idealises the medieval world as one of organic wholeness, in which individuals were defined as members of the 'body politic', essentially bound by a symbolic system of analogies and correspondences to their families, societies, and the world around them. This retrospective view of the past serves to contrast it with a modern bourgeois society, made up of atomistic possessive individuals, who have no essential relation to each other. While the medieval individual was defined by his relation to other groups and the world outside of himself, modern identity is defined in terms of autonomy and independence.[33] Relations are not organic but mechanistic, based on scientific laws of cause and effect and sheer self-interest, which prompt the artificial construction of a society seen now as based on a 'social contract'. While in the feudal world the individual will had been restrained by external systems, in the modern world, authority is transferred to the autonomous and self-regulating individual. The belief in the ability of the individual to govern himself rationally is necessary for the modern liberal definition of freedom as the absence of external restraints. It is a logical extension of the Protestant faith in individual conscience,[34] which we will see later in Godwin pushed into a philosophy of anarchism, in which all external systems of regulation are unnatural and evil.

As we will see with Godwin also, however, the gothic extends the Protestant tradition of self-scrutiny into a critique of Protestant bourgeois values. Its potential to serve as an attack on dominant modern notions of identity has increased its current popularity. As a corporate hybrid genre made up through relations with other forms, it suggests a 'relational model' as an alternative to the modern view of autonomous identity. Moreover, it frequently attacks, especially, the modern liberal assumption that the individual is a self-regulating autonomous entity who is able to govern his own passions rationally without the help, or hindrance, of external restraints. The location of authority within the individual, rather than in external systems, is suspected of leading to rampant and anti-social individualism, as is most clearly shown in satires of religious enthusiasm and non-conformity, such as Hogg's and

11

Brockden Brown's. The gothic villain is frequently an example of the modern materialistic individual taken to an extreme, at which he becomes an egotistical and wilful threat to social unity and order: even Dracula, who is obviously a holdover from a foreign past, is, as Harker notes with admiration, a good modern business-man, who 'would have made a wonderful solicitor'.[35]

The gothic is thus a nightmare vision of a modern world made up of detached individuals, which has dissolved into predatory and demonic relations which cannot be reconciled into a healthy social order. It shows the easy slide of the modern Cartesian mind from autonomy and independence into solipsism and obsession, depict-ing the atomistic individual as fragmented, and alienated from others and ultimately from himself. In the gothic, 'normal' human relationships are defamiliarised and critiqued by being pushed to destructive extremes. Incest in particular, both in the gothic and for the later Romantics, suggests an abnormal and extreme desire (a violation of natural familial ties) that is antithetical to and subversive of social requirements. At the same time as it opposes the needs of modern society, it is also an exaggerated form of the relations they require, a parody of the modern introverted nuclear family.[36] Individualism further creates a broader conflict between individual desire, frequently idealised as natural and authentic, and social duty, often denounced as artificial and hypocritical, a conflict which is exaggerated in the gothic, and replayed especially in terms of sexual relations. Most commonly, gothic novels revolve around a battle between antithetical sexes, in which an aggressive sexual male, who wants to indulge his own will, is set against a passive spiritual female, who is identified with the restrictions of social norms. With its simplistic black and white division of good and evil figures, the gothic seems to suggest that the reward of modern change is the emergence of a world made up of alienated obsessed individuals, who can relate to each other only as enemies. Self-government by reason is exposed as the rule of pure appetite; genteel, harmonious, bourgeois relations conceal deadly opposi-tions and struggles between victors and victims.

Attacking a dehumanising modern world, the gothic is thus a part of the rise of medievalism, manifested in works such as Hurd's *Letters on Chivalry and Romance*, which attempted to defend 'gothic' art and romance on its own merits, and so to recover the 'world of fine fabling' succeeded by that of 'good sense'.[37] What was new about this nostalgia for the past, compared to the earlier Renaissance revival of the classical and foreign dead, was its focus on recovering a *native* English literary tradition. The gothic revival thus played an important part in the development of both political and literary nationalism.[38] While most critics have tended to position the gothic in relation to the French Revolution, it was originally a part of the legacy of the English Revolution of 1688. Throughout the eighteenth century, as agitation for government reform increased, writers were preoccupied with defining exactly what had occurred at that time: whether a new social order had been created, or England had returned to its 'old Constitution'. According to Robert Walpole, 1688 had marked a revolution which had freed England from an original state of gothic tyranny:

> To bring the government of England back to its first principles, is to bring the people back to absolute slavery: the primitive purity of our constitution was, that the people had no share in the government, but were the villains, vessels, or bondsmen of the lords, a sort of cattle bought and sold with the land . . . our Modern constitution is infinitely better than the Ancient Constitution . . . the New England, or England since the Revolution, is vastly preferable to Old England.[39]

Walpole identified himself with the middle-class forces of enlightened progress that saw themselves as having liberated Britain from a dark age of feudal slavery.

However, according to the more common Whig view of history, before the Norman conquest Anglo-Saxon Britain had been in an advanced state of freedom. While to some eighteenth-century radicals, tradition and freedom might seem antithetical, to a Whig like Burke, they were the same: the British tradition *was* freedom, lost in 1066 through, significantly, a *French* invasion, partially regained with the Magna Carta, and wholly regained in 1688. That Revolution was only revolution in its original sense – a return to an original state of being.[40] Change was the recovery of an ongoing tradition, if one sometimes suppressed by oppression, which identified past and present.

The gothic's appearance at this time suggests this political interest, and the concern with reinforcing a mythology of an unbroken British past and tradition of freedom. Studies of the word 'gothic' have tended to position it in relation to a shift in aesthetic values, also evident in the reversal of meaning in the word 'Romantic': during the eighteenth century both move from originally pejorative connotations of savagery and barbarism, to signify a valuable imaginative freedom, thus heralding the Romantic aesthetic revolt against the tyranny of classicism and Enlightenment reason. [41] During the eighteenth century both positive and pejorative connotations co-existed. But the word was used also for the antithetical political purposes of condemnation and praise: to depict both an oppressive feudal past and a golden age of liberty. As the term could still be applied to aesthetic primitivism, it was also used to denounce the British past as one of barbaric oppression. However, as Samuel Kliger noted, the modern use of the word 'gothic' (the sense in which it becomes detached from the original Goths, or a more general meaning of barbarism) begins to appear first in the seventeenth century, where, through an etymological confusion between Goth and Jute, or Gete, it is connected specifically to the imaginary ancient constitution of Britain.[42] Gothic, that is, Anglo-Saxon, political freedom is contrasted with classical (especially Roman and later French neoclassical) tyranny to create a myth of a continuous British inheritance of freedom. From the seventeenth century on, the gothic is thus associated with native political freedom based on 'the true old Gothick Constitution' [43] which resists tyrannical foreign laws. The association of the gothic with liberty is continued by later nineteenth-century medievalists, such as Ruskin, who identified the gothic with the creative imagination, freedom of expression, as opposed to classical servility and modern mechanical reproduction. It is a peculiarly British characteristic, a sign of a national inherent love of freedom, liberty, that differentiates the country from servile foreign countries (especially, of course, France), and which is present even during times of tyranny (such as under William I or Robert Walpole).

While the term gothic could thus be used to demonise the past as a dark age of feudal tyranny, it could also be used equally to idealise it as a golden age of innocent liberty. Its meaning was the territory for a political battle between the ancients and the moderns over the nature of the past and its relation to the present. It was at the centre of a British version of its own history as the story of the fall: a myth of alienation from and return to an original state of harmony and innocence.[44] Such myths have a long tradition in England. The Reformation was imagined as a recovery of the original, pure form of Christianity, before it had been corrupted by the false (Catholic) systems of mediation that stood between a man and his God; while Protestantism was obviously not a purely English phenomenon, this aspect of it certainly suggests one reason why it appealed to the imagination of a country that has as one of its major legends the story of the once and future king, Arthur, whose return is prophesied. The legend of Arthur, which has been constantly resurrected by British writers, was itself a potential subject for Milton's epic; his shift to the story of *Paradise Lost* may be only an expansion from a purely national to a more universal version of the same story of loss and return. As Robert Keily has noted, a similar impulse underlies the rhetoric around the rise of the novel, which was held up as being 'to the romance what the Reformation had been to poetry, a purification and return to unadorned truth'.[45] The use of the myth of the ancient constitution throughout the eighteenth century is a manifestation of a recurrent British argument that a better future is to be found by recovering the past. Present evils may be cured by returning to the purity of the past, through a Machiavellian return to first principles.[46] The gothic is thus haunted by a reading of history as a dialectical process of alienation and restoration, dismembering and remembering, a version of the secularised myth of fall and return, which, as M.H. Abrams showed, is central to Romanticism.[47] The fragmentation and estrangement of the gothic thus both reflects a modern alienated and estranged world made up of atomistic individuals, and suggests the hope of recovering a lost organic unity.

3   The Sublime and the Odd

As a means of recovering a world of freedom, lost through the rise of the modern world, the gothic looks backwards to a kinder simpler paradise lost of harmonious relations that existed before the nasty modern world of irreconcilable opposition and conflict. It thus becomes easily allied with Rousseauian primitivism, in which the past is seen as closer to nature than the present, associated with the corrupting and artificial influence of society. While for Rousseau that past is irretrievable, the gothic tries to use its necromantic powers to raise it. However, such a past is always obviously an idealised myth, made to fit the needs of the present – which may also be one reason why so many of the 'relics' found in the eighteenth century were forgeries. An idealised past is constructed in order to deconstruct a degenerate modernity; Clara

15

Reeve prefaced her *Memoirs of Sir Roger de Clarendon* with a statement of the moral purpose in reviving history:

> to give a faithful picture of a well-governed kingdom, where-
> in a true subordination of ranks and degrees was observed,
> and of a great prince at the head of it.
>
> The new philosophy of the present day avows a levelling
> principle, and declares that a state of anarchy is more beauti-
> ful than that of order and regularity. There is nothing more
> likely to convince mankind of the errors of these men, than
> to set before them examples of good government, and warnings
> of the mischievous consequences of their own principles.[48]

In the works of the odd couple of Horace Walpole and Edmund
Burke, the revival of the past is a means of revolting against a
debased commercial and mechanical modern world, in which the
dismembering of an already divided and fragmented atomistic
present enables an organic whole gothic past to be put back
together.

It seems appropriate that the genealogy of this genre begins
with an idiosyncratic text, written by a truly eccentric individual,
who hovered on the class border between bourgeoisie and aristocracy. It is fitting, too, that the first gothic novel was written by the
son of Robert Walpole, the figure of authority for much of the
early eighteenth century, whose government was denounced by
Bolingbroke as the source of modern corruption that was threatening the tradition of British liberty re-established by the Glorious
Revolution. His son escaped from the politics he believed had
destroyed his father, into a gothic world he constructed for himself
at Strawberry Hill out of bits and pieces of the past. Macaulay, who
detested everything Walpole stood for, described him as 'an unhealthy and disorganised mind'; 'the most eccentric, the most
artificial, the most fastidious, the most capricious of men. His mind
was a bundle of inconsistent whims and affectations. His features
were covered by a mask within a mask'.[49] Walpole was a mass of
contradictions: a Whig who flaunted his hatred of authority (keeping
a copy of the Magna Carta and the warrant for the execution of
Charles I beside his bed), who yet, as Macaulay put it, was 'a
gentleman-usher at heart', who 'liked revolution and regicide only
when they are a hundred years old' and who during the French
Revolution was 'frightened into a fanatical royalist and became
one of the most extravagant alarmists of those wretched times'.[50]

What Macaulay objected to most in Walpole was the sheer perversity of the man: his total inversion of 'normal' values and standards of behaviour and taste, in which 'serious business was a trifle to him, and trifles were his serious business'.[51] Walpole rebelled against the aesthetic standards of the times, claiming the artistic superiority of Soame Jenyns over Pope and Swift. Furthermore: 'with the Sublime and the Beautiful Walpole had nothing to do, but . . . the third province, the Odd, was his peculiar domain.'[52] In writing his gothic *Castle of Otranto* he claimed to write as a revolt against all critical rules:

> I have not written the book for the present age, which will endure nothing but cold common sense . . . this is the only one of my books with which I am myself pleased; I have given reins to my imagination till I became on fire with those visions and feelings which it excited. I have composed it in defiance of rules, of critics, and of philosophers.[53]

However, like its author, the text is a hybrid made up of conflicting impulses: an eccentric individual's whim that yet indicts unrestrained egotism; a lawless pre-romantic work rebelling against limits, which in fact obsessively abides by the laws it claims to break, observing the neoclassical dramatic unities, so that, as the first preface says: 'Every thing tends directly to the catastrophe.'[54]

The Castle of Otranto has often been seen as indicative of Walpole's reactionary nostalgia, his longing to escape into an idealised past, later embodied in Strawberry Hill. The known past is more secure than the changing present: 'Old castles, old pictures, old histories, and the babble of old people make one live each into centuries that cannot disappoint.'[55] David McKinney has shown how Strawberry Hill was constructed also to idealise Walpole's family, giving it a central position in an idealised gothic past and a relation, especially to the ancient constitution which he claimed, contra Bolingbroke, that his father had preserved.[56] His gothic world, both architectural and fictional, wasn't a mere retreat from politics, but a place where politics were transformed into art. Furthermore, also like his museum of curiosities, his fiction is an attempt to create something new from the past; to return to older models for relations as a means of creating a new and truly original narrative form. The very name 'gothic novel' which was ultimately given to the form he created is an oxymoron that reflects its desire to identify conflicting impulses: both towards newness, novelty, originality, and towards a return to nature and revival of the past. Walpole's text offers a myth of reconciliation of past and present, which suggests the past can be revived in a way that will be empowering and liberating for the present, freeing it from modern aesthetic and political forms of oppression.

Like Walpole's gothic play, *The Mysterious Mother*, the novel is a highly oedipal work, no doubt in part reflecting his relation to his own formidable and authoritative father. As a version of history it is closer to the view of Bolingbroke than that of Robert Walpole.[57] The novel introduces some of the most basic gothic ingredients: characters – the Miltonically satanic hero or fallen angel, with his complementary selfless and passive female counterpart, the bland hero who will inevitably turn out to be the rightful heir, the selfless victimised heroine; setting – the castle with its secret buried in its past that will finally emerge to determine the direction of the future, the portrait and other works of art that mysteriously come to life; plot – a story of usurpation, concerned with the issues of succession and inheritance, which flirts with the possibility of incestuous relations, but ends with the rightful distribution of persons and property. The development of the story juxtaposes Manfred's attempt to perpetuate his illegitimate line (both narrative and familial) into the future, with its final fragmentation: the annihilation of one false line with the recovery of the true one.

Walpole's form sets the pattern for later writers, who work with techniques of interruption, deferral, ellipsis, framing, to slice stories into bits and pieces and disrupt superficial narrative unity or linearity. In Walpole the structural and thematic fragmentation of the line of Manfred's narrative mirrors the breakdown of his succession and of himself as a character: he is increasingly incoherent and unable to get to a point.[58] The story opens with the death of his son Conrad, on the day that was both his birthday and the occasion of his wedding that was designed to secure the succession. Birth, marriage, death – the three crucial events that are supposed to mark the narrative of a life and organise it into temporal sequence – occur simultaneously, thus flamboyantly introducing at the genre's very inception the problem of constructing continuous narrative sequence, a problem that has haunted the static and disjointed gothic form. Moreover, to start off the story with a big bang that literalises the themes of fragmentation and collapsing, Conrad is grotesquely squashed by a gigantic helmet that suddenly and mysteriously (if one can call such a crudely bizarre event mysterious) falls from nowhere. The origin of the story is the breaking of the genealogical line, which forces Manfred to find new ways of restoring it. The death of his son causes Manfred to try to take his place, to be in effect his own heir, realising a somewhat inverted or perverted oedipal fantasy of self-perpetuation. This attempt to secure his line against a prophecy that obscurely predicts its overthrow has, however, disastrous consequences. Through the dynamics that will become typical of the gothic, the more Manfred tries to assert his individual control over fate, the more he loses control; as he loses his inability to pull his ideas together into a coherent sentence, he also loses his ability to order the reality around him into a plot that suits his dynastic desires. He is finally the victim of total chance, which causes him to be the author of the destruction of his own plans, as he accidentally kills his own daughter.

As later gothic novels also show, however, such chances are always strictly predetermined. In Walpole's tale, cause and effect seem both opposed, as actions have ludicrously disproportionate consequences, and yet rigidly bound together, as past actions relentlessly effect the present. As Manfred's own story and family falls apart, the pieces of a gigantic statue to which the helmet that killed Conrad belongs gradually come back together, as the helmet turns out to be a grotesquely literal synecdoche both for the real owner of the titular castle of Otranto and for the structure of the plot. Against the disintegration of Manfred's story, its splintering into isolated and incoherent atoms, occurs the piece by piece re-membering of this statue, whose parts are restored into a new whole, which marks the recovery of an original, pure past. Manfred's literally poisonous line is shown to originate in the murder of a master by his servant. This act of usurpation is suggestive of the gothic's ambivalent representation of servants, which I will be discussing further later (pp. 62–3; 180–4 esp.): while Walpole associates them with Shakespeare's comic figures, they also reflect a contemporary anxiety about changing class relations, in particular, the basis of the master–servant bond in a new commercial world. At the end of Walpole's text, the rightful noble heir, Theodore, is recovered, and his marriage with Isabella (Conrad's fiancée, upon whom Manfred had incestuous dynastic designs) consolidates his rule and produces a new social order. The poisonous servile line is totally eradicated – ultimately, and rather neatly, by itself, since it is through Manfred's crimes that his children are murdered, thus proving the moral offered by the fictitious editor of the first edition that 'the sins of fathers are visited on their children' (*Otranto*, p. 18). Moreover, the establishment of a new order is also a return to an original one: past and present join together when the original owner, Alphonso the Good, who was poisoned by Manfred's ancestor, descends at the end to recognise his look-alike heir. A false line and system of authority is broken down and replaced by a new one, which turns out, however, to be true because even older – the original, uncontaminated order.

In some ways this is a tidy way of suddenly resolving, in a highly oedipal text, the potential conflict between past and present, or guilt about the representation of the overthrow of a tyrannical father, by showing the father to have been a usurper all along. Theodore's claim is through his *mother*, a fact which prevents him from being a rival for his newly discovered father, who has become a spiritual 'Father', the priest Jerome. The glorious, though not totally bloodless, revolution that takes place in the text turns out to be a recovery of the rightful dynastic line. The story thus enacts Walpole's own desire to create a narrative line that will enable him to bring past and present together into an aesthetic whole:

> to blend the two kinds of romance, the ancient and the modern. In the former, all was imagination and improbability: in the latter, nature is always intended to be, and sometimes has been, copied with success. Invention has not been wanting; but the great resources of fancy have been dammed up, by a strict adherence to common life. But if, in the latter species, Nature has cramped imagination, she did but take her revenge, having been totally excluded from old romances.
>
> (ibid., p. 21)

As Bishop Hurd had also complained, the modern novel is ruled tyrannically by dry realism, which banishes the fertility of the imagination; in the past, however, the opposite was true, as the imagination had too unlicensed a rule. Rather than choosing one form, Walpole wants to find a balance between mimetic and fanciful forms of representation, in order to unite fruitfully past and present. His work is a hybrid form, born of the yoking of opposites.[59] In this, he claims that it is something totally new. Yet he de-emphasises his claim for originality, instead falling back on the very basis of British law and tradition, precedent, and takes as a model for his mixing (specifically of comedy and tragedy) the august authority of Shakespeare: 'I might have pleaded that, having created a new species of romance, I was at liberty to lay down what rules I thought fit for the conduct of it: but I should be more proud of having imitated, however faintly, weakly, and at a distance, so masterly a pattern, than to enjoy the entire merit of invention, unless I could have marked my work with genius, as well as with originality', and so he insists that he will 'shelter my own daring under the canon of the brightest genius this country, at least, has produced' (ibid., p. 25).

Shakespeare often appears as a kind of patron saint of imaginative freedom for the gothic, a voice from a golden age before the tyranny of neoclassicism with its rules and unities set in. For Walpole, too, he is the symbol of *British* aesthetic freedom who is to be defended against the threat of tyrannical French rules dictated by Voltaire.[60] However, hiding behind the precedent of a past great man is typical of the kind of guardedness and indirection, the obfuscation of authority, that is frequently found in the gothic. Walpole first published his book as an original Renaissance work, discovered in Italy, which he was merely editing. The pretense that the author is merely an editor is of course a common device of the time, used, as in Richardson, often to create an impression of authenticity. While this may have been, further, a ploy to protect the author, uncertain as to how his strange new work would be received by readers, it also exploited the contemporary fascination with things resurrected from the past. Something totally new and original is first presented disguised as something old: a mode of presentation common also to the numerous fakes and forgeries that proliferated during this time. In a time when originality was beginning to emerge as a value, the artistic counterpart to individualism, there is a striking countermovement amongst authors precisely to deny their own originality.

As we are now well aware, the burden of originality creates an anxiety of influence, a rivalry between past and present; its repudiation, however, can produce an impression of non-conflictual relations between past and present. The denial of authority was common in the middle ages, where it has been read as a sign of the individual's identification with a tradition through which he defined himself.[61] To identify oneself with other authors can itself be a way of rejecting competition and individualist values and recovering idealised benign relations associated again with a historical and

21

literary past. At a more self-interested (and thus individualist) level, of course, the abnegation of authorial responsibility is a clever tactic in a form that is morally as well as aesthetically suspect. Even when he later acknowledged the text as his own work, Walpole located its origin in subconscious forces beyond his control, thus sowing the seeds for later psychoanalytical readings. The text came to him in a dream, and practically wrote itself:

> Shall I confess to you, what was the origin of this romance? I waked one morning, in the beginning of last June, from a dream, of which all I could recover was that I had thought myself in an ancient castle (a very natural dream for a head like mine filled with Gothic story), and that on the upper-most banister of a great staircase I saw a gigantic hand in armour. In the evening I sat down, and began to write, without knowing in the least what I intended to say or relate. The work grew on my hands. . . . In short I was so engrossed with my Tale, which I completed in less than two months.[62]

Gothic writers will often claim that their stories came to them in dreams, and were written not only about but *from* demonic compulsion. As I have already suggested, too, critics have often tended to doubt gothic writers' abilities to control their impulses or even material – which flowed into them either from their subconscious or, more often, Germany – thus undercutting the author's authority. [63] With the striking exception of Radcliffe, I will argue that the gothic author often seems a passive vehicle, a rather crude version also of the Romantic artist described by Shelley as 'an instrument over which a series of external and internal impressions are driven, like the alternations of an ever-changing wind over an Aeolian lyre, which move it by their motions to ever-changing melody'.[64] One of the consequences of this strategy of self-effacement, however, is that it encourages a transference of authority and responsibility from the writer to the reader. While the eighteenth century is often identified as marking the birth of the modern author, it also anticipates his recently announced death, through an increasing shift from author to reader as a centre of attention, and hero or heroine of the act of interpretation.

In his self-representation as an author, Walpole represents himself as part of a tradition rather than an originator, and an aristocratic amateur rather than the bourgeois literary labourer he truly was.[65] We will see this image of the author revised in Radcliffe and Lewis, who also hover between middle- and upper-class models for their own authority. But Walpole's accounts of the origins of his text suggest a characteristic yoking together of contradictory motives: it was both sheer self-indulgence, an expression of nothing but his own eccentric individuality, and a rebellion against modern conventions and expectations, *including* individuality. As a literary species it certainly looked at first like one which, like poor Conrad, was nipped in the bud; with few exceptions, notably Clara Reeve who claimed Walpole as her rightful, if somewhat erring, literary father, the gothic looked as though it rose and fell at the same time. Despite its engagement of contemporary issues, it might have been an aesthetic dead end, a one-shot eccentric mutation on the literary evolutionary line, if the terrifying events of the 1790s had not made it an appropriate vehicle for embodying relevant political and aesthetic questions. While the nature of the past, and its relation to the present, was debated throughout the eighteenth century, it gained new life with the French Revolution, as the Terror proved fertile for a literature of terror. In an England obsessed with the question of parliamentary reform and agitation for social changes, the abrupt and total change that occurred in France seemed both exhilarating and terrifying, and to require a complete rethinking of the basis of all systems of order.[66] This was partially because this spectacle, as well as raising the danger of contamination from abroad, raised again and more pressingly the spectre of its own past: the Civil War and Glorious Revolution. The gothic displaced anxieties at home onto places geographically and temporally remote, at the very time that, inversely, the British were reading the Revolution of 1789 through the Revolution of 1688, understanding the foreign present in terms of the domestic past.

In his famous address to the Revolution Society in 1789, Richard Price saw the two events (as well as the American Revolution) as both analogous and part of a continuous chain of cause and effect:

> After sharing the benefits of one Revolution, I have been spared to be a witness to two other Revolutions, both glorious. And now methinks, I see the ardour for liberty catching and spreading; a general amendment beginning in human affairs; the dominion of kings changed for the dominion of laws, and the dominion of priests giving way to the dominion of reason and conscience.
>
> Be encouraged all ye friends of freedom, and writers in its

defence! The times are auspicious. Your labours have not been in vain. Behold kingdoms, admonished by you, starting from sleep, breaking their fetters, and claiming justice from their oppressors! Behold, the light you have struck out, after setting AMERICA free, reflected in FRANCE, and there kindled into a blaze that lays the despotism in ashes, and warms and illuminates EUROPE![67]

Price's apocalyptic imagery suggest how, for the radicals, what was happening was seen through biblical terms as the imminent realisation of heaven on earth, the true recovery of not just the ancient constitution but paradise itself, which the seventeenth-century revolution had begun but failed to achieve, as political illumination was now spreading through the world.

Price's speech is most famous now for being the pretext for Burke's rebuttal in his *Reflections*, in which he argued that there could be no comparison between the two types of events, and also therefore no comparison between Britain and France. 1688 was an end, not a beginning, a deviation not a rule, that was necessary only:

> to preserve our *ancient*, indisputable laws and liberties and that *ancient* constitution of government which is our only security for law and liberty. . . . The very idea of the fabrication of a new government is enough to fill us with disgust and horror. We wished at the period of the Revolution, and do now wish, to derive all we possess as *an inheritance from our forefathers*. Upon that body and stock of inheritance we have taken care not to inoculate any cyon alien to the nature of the original plant. All the reformations we have hitherto made have proceeded upon the principle of reverence to antiquity.[68]

The English Revolution was good because it aimed at the preservation of the past, the reinforcement of continuity and tradition. In contrast, the French Revolution was an attempt to break all links between past and present. It was thus a totally novel form of social change, an overthrow of natural order whose inevitable result would be a return to 'Barbarism' (*Reflections*, p. 84) and chaos:

> the French revolution is the most astonishing that has hitherto happened in the world. The most wonderful things are brought about, in many instances by means the most

absurd and ridiculous, in the most ridiculous modes, and apparently by the most contemptible instruments. Everything seems out of nature in this strange chaos of levity and ferocity, and all sorts of crimes jumbled together with all sorts of follies.

(ibid., p. 9)

A sign of revolutionary chaos is Price's confounding of 1688 and 1789:[69]

These gentlemen of the Old Jewry, in all their reasonings on the Revolution of 1688, have a revolution which happened in England about forty years before and the late French revolution, so much before their eyes and in their hearts that they are constantly confounding all the three together. It is necessary that we should separate what they confound.

(ibid., p. 15)

For Burke, the two events are in fact poles which must be distinguished: the first, as a model for natural and organic change and order, the second, for artificial and mechanistic change and disorder. English change is not revolutionary but evolutionary, an organic development, analogous to natural growth and the laws of inheritance, which ensures unbroken succession and so maintains the continuity of tradition. The naturalness of this model is proved in Burke's logic by its correspondence to the model of change found in the universe itself:

Our political system is placed in a just correspondence and symmetry with the order of the world and with the mode of existence decreed to a permanent body composed of transitory parts, wherein, by the disposition of a stupendous wisdom, molding together the great mysterious incorporation of the human race, the whole, at one time, is never old or middle-aged or young, but, in a condition of unchangeable constancy, moves on through the varied tenor of perpetual decay, fall, renovation, and progression. Thus, by preserving the method of nature in the conduct of the state, in what we improve we are never wholly new; in what we retain we are never wholly obsolete.

(ibid., p. 30)

Society is therefore an ongoing process: 'a partnership not only between those who are living, but between those who are living, those who are dead, and those who are to be born' (ibid., p. 85). The *Reflections* is Burke's attempt rhetorically to recreate that partnership. By playing on his readers' 'natural' emotions, speaking as 'we English' and shifting constantly between 'I' and 'we', the individual private author (who claims his opinions are only his own) becomes the voice of the people. Through the use of allusions, too, he demonstrates that the isolated individual needs grounding in tradition; the present cannot be naturally or healthily imagined in abstraction from the past, any more than the individual can be conceived of as stripped of social relations down to a bare essence. The author therefore presents himself as an example of an individual working within a tradition, boasting not of his originality but of the fact that he says what everyone 'naturally' feels, and that further: 'I am unable to distinguish what I have learned from others from the results of my own meditation' (ibid., p. 87). He is a remnant from a medieval world, in which one is defined by interdependent relations with others rather than in vulgar bourgeois competition with them. For Burke, the individual is only truly free when bound to others, connected through tradition, conventions, and prejudice. The modern conflict between individual desire and social duty is therefore an illusion produced by misguided ideals of individualism. Complete individual freedom, without internal or external restraints, is madness, as we need limits to be truly human. Chivalric subservience and hierarchy did not degrade but exalt its members, through 'that generous loyalty to rank and sex, that proud submission, that dignified obedience, that subordination of the heart which kept alive, even in servitude itself, the spirit of an exalted freedom' (ibid., p. 66). The chivalric order emerged out of a dark age because it sublimated the most barbaric human feeling into the most civilised, transforming human nature into a work of art and thus realising its highest potential.[70] Humans need to feel the existence of a power that transcends individuality, a power Burke earlier described as the sublime: 'whilst we contemplate so vast an object, under the arm, as it were, of almighty power, and invested upon every side with omnipresence, we shrink into the minuteness of our own nature, and are, in a manner, annihilated before him.'[71] The limits of human knowledge prove the existence of greater forces which control individual will and freedom: 'Dark and inscrutable are the ways by which we come into the world. The instincts which give rise to this mysterious process of Nature are not of our making'.[72] Government is itself a mystery whose foundations are hidden by a 'politic well-wrought veil' (*Reflections*, p. 17), which we cannot simply rip away.

For Burke's radical opponents, such coverings are human constructs, examples of superstition used as a vehicle for political oppression. Paine picked up on Burke's image of the veil to parody it, turning monarchy into an empty fraud that reason can easily expose:

> I compare it to something kept behind a curtain, about which there is a great deal of bustle and fuss, and a wonderful air of seeming solemnity; but when, by accident, the curtain happens to be open, and the company see what it is, they burst into laughter.[73]

Similarily, for Wollstonecraft, government is a feudal system perpetuated by an empty mystery, which enlightened reason can easily see through: 'Its throne is built across a dark abyss, which no eye must dare to explore, lest the baseless fabric should totter under investigation'; if reason examined prejudices, 'how men would smile at the sight of the bugbears at which they started during the night of ignorance, or the twilight of timid insecurity.'[74] As Price's speech had indicated, such writers drew upon a radical, originally biblical and apocalyptic rhetoric, to represent their own overthrowing of the ancient forces of darkness through the modern revelatory power of progress and reason. By exposing and demystifying old superstitious systems, the radicals believed they could effect a secular revelation and revolution that would lead to social and personal freedom.

In the *Reflections*, however, Burke's strategy is to demystify the supposed demystifiers, whom he denounces as stripping the world not of empty systems but of its human meaning through their inhuman and violent acts of abstraction. He mistrusts the modern premise that knowledge begins in abstraction, with the stripped Cartesian self who accepts nothing on the authority of those who came before and who must always think for himself, an ideological imperative reinforced by Protestantism's mistrust of both political and religious systems of mediation and emphasis upon self-reliance. He therefore attacks enlightenment attempts to detach individuals or ideas from traditions, conventions, history, contexts, and prejudices, in order to distil human nature down to the

'nakedness and solitude of metaphysical abstraction' (ibid., p. 7).
Burke's famous description of Marie Antoinette reduces the enlightenment pretense of stripping the artificial veneer from the
world to the gothic violation of the persecuted female.[75] It is the
epitome of a dehumanising world in which:

> All the decent drapery of life is to be rudely torn off. All the
> superadded ideas, furnished from the wardrobe of a moral
> imagination, which the heart owns and the understanding
> ratifies as necessary to cover the defects of our naked, shiver-
> ing nature, and to raise it to dignity in our own estimation,
> are to be exploded as a ridiculous, absurd, and antiquated
> fashion.
>
> (ibid., p. 67)

The attempt to separate art from life is as disastrous as the artificial
division of past and present. Human nature is defined by what is
superfluous over mere nature. Both society and artifice are natural
to mankind: 'For man is by nature reasonable, and he is never
perfectly in his natural state but when he is placed where reason
may be best cultivated and most predominates. Art is man's nature'
(*Appeal*, p. 105).

Burke thus contrasts the past which turned savagery into the
basis of civilisation, with a present in which a veneer of light and
reason hides the darkness and sheer barbarism which is now
erupting and uncontainable. Promethean 'illuminators of the world'
(ibid., p. 82) have created the 'solid darkness of this enlightened
age' (*Reflections*, p. 213). The Revolution is the horridly and
violently logical consequence of the transition, encouraged by the
radical middle class for their own interests,[76] from a world based
on natural organic ties between social members to an artificial
one, based on pure abstraction, a 'mechanic philosophy' (ibid., p.
68) in which relations are reduced to those of cause and effect.
The French Revolution destroyed all natural methods of creating
social and individual coherence, and tried to set up false systems
based on philosophical abstractions. For all of its apparent idealism,
such a system is based on the lowest possible view of human nature,
in which it is identified with total self-interest: the creation of
paper money, a valueless currency that also indicates the country's
financial emptiness, serves Burke as a symbol for a meaningless
and crassly materialistic, artificial system of social representation.
The modern world is a shrunken one: 'the age of chivalry is gone.

That of sophisters, economists, and calculators has succeeded; and the glory of Europe is extinguished forever' (ibid., p. 66). An older system of relations, based on natural family ties, has been replaced in the modern world by merely commercial links, the organic body politic transformed into a mechanistic social contract made up of humans defined essentially as atomistic 'possessive individuals'. The Revolution is an artificial entity, a grotesquely unnatural body politic, fabricated by a conspiratorial band of illuminati, the models for many gothic villains, who, like Frankenstein, have created what he will later call 'that nameless thing', 'that monstrous thing', which was 'produced . . . ready-made and ready-armed, mature in its birth, a perfect goddess of wisdom and of war, hammered by our blacksmith midwives out of the brain of Jupiter himself' (*Appeal*, pp. 17, 18, 22). The result is an inverted natural world, in which normal family relations are disordered. The safe sphere of the home becomes an uncanny place of alienation:

> They destroy all the tranquillity and security of domestic life; turning the asylum of the house into a gloomy prison, where the father of the family must drag out a miserable existence, endangered in proportion to the apparent means of his safety; where he is worse than solitary in a crowd of domestics, and more apprehensive from his servants and inmates, than from the hired blood-thirsty mob without doors, who are ready to pull him to the lantern.[77]

Burke represents the Revolution in terms of the gothic imagery of grave robbing, parents dismembering their children and children dismembering their parents (*Reflections*, pp. 84, 146).[78] In a world of alienated individuals, people only meet as victors and victims. Like Victor Frankenstein, the creators of the Revolution have set in motion a force that ultimately they will not be able to control; Burke predicts that: 'A violent spirit is raised, which the presiding minds after a time find it impracticable to stop at their pleasure, to control, to regulate, or even to direct' (*Appeal*, p. 119).

As Walpole and Burke show, the gothic is involved in the eighteenth-century debates over the proper relation between past and present, which were essential to the emergence of a modern middle-class Protestant model for both individual and national identity. Like Burke, the gothic resists this emergence, attacking an enlightened present which represents itself as heroically rising from and overthrowing a barbaric past. Horace Walpole's myth of recovery thus subverts his father's narrative of British history as a radical revolution. As the present mythologises itself as detached from its own dark origins, the gothic turns it into a world of complete detachment and alienation, and looks back to a past antithetically identified with organic unity, a world in which, as Walpole and Burke suggest, past and present are essentially related. By reviving the dead, recalling to life an idealised past, the gothic tries to heal the ruptures of rapid change, and preserve continuity. It offers the kind of refuge from modern isolation that Coleridge found in the gothic cathedral:

> On entering a cathedral, I am filled with devotion and awe; I am lost to the actualities that surround me, and my whole being expands into the infinite; earth and air, nature and art, all swell up into eternity, and the only sensible impression is that 'I am nothing'.[79]

For Coleridge, the gothic and the sublime break down the opposition between subject and object, impressing 'the beholder with a sense of self-annihilation; he becomes as it were, part of the work contemplated'.[80] The gothic returns us to a world in which the divisions of modern life seem transcended, a world before the burden of individuality and originality – a world in which there are therefore no individuated 'characters', in which plots and effects are themselves conventional, formulaic, and predictable.

The gothic thus originates in a sense of historical difference, and the desire to transcend it by recovering a lost past. However, what it increasingly demonstrates is the disappearance of historical difference. The potential solution reproduces the problem, as the restoration of original unity itself turns into the monstrous merging and confusion of differences which Burke used to describe both the Revolution and the modern world order. Readers have always noted and complained of the gothic's loose and inaccurate use of history. Recalled to life, the past is brought back to critique the present, so that the feudal tyrant is really the modern egoist in historical dress. The paradox of this is, however, that the revived past cannot be an alternative to the present for it is a nightmare version of it. This contradictory recovery of the past appears both in the gothic's own choice of setting, and in various common plots in which the dead return. The return of Alphonso at the end of *The Castle of Otranto* suggests one positive model for the return of the past. In another common gothic narrative, the past is represented by a parent, long thought dead, but in fact imprisoned in a subterranean vault (an image with obvious significance for any psychoanalytically inclined reader), whose release empowers the hero or heroine, helping them to discover their true identity. As we will see later, this motif is common in the female gothic, as, after Radcliffe's *Sicilian Romance*, 'the experienced reader of Gothic Romance hesitates to believe in the death of anybody, especially if it be a parent or a wife'.[81] But Radcliffe's romantic family reunion hides its darker oedipal subtext, Schiller's *Robbers*, in which the return of the dead, both father and son, does not avert but causes tragedy. Furthermore, the 'undead' parent can also be represented by a force such as Dracula, both a rapaciously possessive individual and a remnant from an older world whose constant self-resurrection threatens the identity of the future. Dracula is the demonic version of the English myth of return, an infernal once and future king Arthur, as well as an anti-Christ who offers a literal resurrection of the dead. Attacking the present, the gothic ends up also parodying its own enterprise. For Walpole, the dismembering of a corrupt present necessarily reveals a re-membered and pure past. From the late nineteenth century on, however, the gothic dead have increasingly returned in fragmented forms that are not re-membered, like the mutilated corpse in W.W. Jacobs' classic short story, 'The Monkey's Paw'. The past comes back not to critique or reform the present, but to deform and destroy it.[82] As we will see, the gothic is better at dismemberment than re-memberment, at parody than the construction of an alternative, which is appropriate: according to Christopher Wren, 'The *Goths* were rather destroyers than builders'.[83]

4   Everything that Rises Must Converge

be sure to preserve his [the child's] tender Mind from all Impressions and Notions of *Sprites* and *Goblins*, or any fearful Apprehensions in the dark. This he will be in danger of from the indiscretion of Servants, whose usual Method it is to awe Children, and keep them in subjection, by telling them of *Raw-Head* and *Bloody Bones*, and such other Names, as carry with them the Idea's of some thing terrible and hurtful, which they have reason to be afraid of, when alone, especially in the dark. . . . Such *Bug-bear* Thoughts once got into the tender Minds of Children, and being set on with a strong impression, from the Dread that accompanies such Apprehensions, sink deep, and fasten themselves so as not easily, if ever, to be got out again; and whilst they are there, frequently haunt them with strong Visions, making Children dastards when alone, and afraid of their Shadows and Darkness all their Lives after.[84]

As Paulson has argued, Burke's representation of revolution involves a reworking of his discussion of the sublime.[85] The Revolution becomes a monstrous realisation of the elements associated with the sublime – mystery, a loss of boundaries, and confusion of differences. Part of its terror for Burke lies in its parody through literalisation of his own aesthetic ideal, which makes it his own gothic double, his art come to demonic life.

As has been often noted, gothic landscapes and imagery also owe much to Burke's discussion of the sublime. However, the sublime further informs the gothic's narrative principle of prolonged suspense. Conscious of the delicious aspects of suspense and the disappointing nature of certainty, gothic narratives, often interminably long, create a tension between a desire to prolong and defer the inevitable and an impulse towards the revelation of all mysteries, between the indulgence of curiosity and its satisfaction.[86] While gothic narratives move towards the revelation of the mystery, they also defer it, taking a narrative scenic route in which one has time to admire the impressively sublime scenery along the way. As I suggested earlier, the suspense of the plot, rather than the final moment of revelation, is the focus of attention, and revelation is itself often either bathetic or disastrous. It is telling that Mrs Radcliffe, the mistress of suspense, creates endings that almost universally disappoint. In so doing, they seem to suggest a contradiction between a moral principle, expounded in the conclusion, and an aesthetic one, created through suspense; or between what Freud would call a reality principle, which pushes the narrative forward to get to the truth, the moment of revelation, and a pleasure principle, which attempts to defer this moment, to enjoy the aesthetic experience of suspense itself.[87] The typical gothic plot tends to delay narrative development through digressions, interruptions, infolded tales, interpolated poems, etc., which move the narrative backwards as well as forwards.

While the novels thus also seem to exemplify a Burkean model for change, identifying narrative past and present, the general effect is often to create a sense of stasis, and non-development. Burke himself, of course, was accused of desiring a static world of perpetuated tradition, in which historical development was arrested in the feudal era. The gothic revival has also been described as a form of regression; the genre has often been treated, usually implicitly, as an immature form, a throwback to an earlier stage of the literary tradition which rises in infantile resistance to the grand progress of the novel proper towards the maturity of realism. Gothic authors too are often described as children – Lewis and Shelley were of course both adolescents, child prodigies really, when they wrote their most famous works, but neither matured much artistically and Lewis, like Beckford before him, was described as a perpetual boy. Gothic readers also are often described, if not by the authors then by critics, as children or at best teenagers; Addison said that ghost stories appeal because they remind us of childhood – although Edith Birkhead thought that fairy tales were best for small children and gothic novels should be the next stage in our development as adolescents.[88] Scott noted how attackers of the gothic saw the fad as:

> evil signs of the times, and argued a great and increasing degradation of the public taste, which, instead of banqueting as heretofore upon scenes of passion, like those of Richardson, or of life and manners, as in the pages of Smollet and Fielding, was now coming back to the fare of the nursery, and gorged upon the wild and improbable fictions of an overheated imagination.[89]

Reading such novels was seen as an impediment to moral growth. The novels themselves, moreover, often show various forms of regression or arrested development: Beckford's Vathek is a big baby, absorbed in his own voracious appetites, the perpetually youthful Dorian Gray keeps the painting that ages in his place in his old nursery, while Stoker's Dracula, according to his nemesis Van Helsing, 'In some faculties of mind he has been, and is, only a child',[90] a figure clearly stuck in his own version of Freud's oral phase. Gothic heroines seem notoriously infantile and passive, while gothic villains exemplify a contradiction Paul Cantor identifies in Victor Frankenstein who is both a 'Faustian figure, daring to undertake a superhuman task' and yet also 'a little boy, hoping to prolong forever the experience of his childhood, in which he can live within the private world of his fantasies, unburdened by the duties of adult life'.[91]

The gothic interest in the child is of course a manifestation of a broader interest in individual as well as historical past which appears at this time. Since Locke especially, thinkers had become increasingly interested in childhood as a state of development, both separate from and vitally formative of adulthood, our personal past out of which we evolve as individuals. The idea of childhood was in transition, undergoing a gradual revolution from the older view that the child is born corrupt, needing to be redeemed through education, to the Rousseauian ideal, in which the child is born innocent and corrupted later by society. In the latter view, childhood was idealised as a time of innocence and freedom, an individual paradise that is lost with maturation and the attainment of individual identity and its responsibilities. The child is, further, the essential individual, anarchic, asocial, unruly – Jane Eyre is introduced as a revolutionary rebelling against an unjust tyranny – and so a version of the noble savage who is free from the restraining and distorting conventions of society. The freedom of childhood was therefore opposed to the slavery of adulthood in the same way that the natural freedom of the individual was antithetical to the society. At the same time, however, childhood came to be seen as the cause that determined later identity. For Locke especially, childhood is the time in which we acquire the habits that rigidly determine our characters as adults. Childhood is thus the opposite of adulthood, but it is also its determinant, through the individual causal or genealogical sequence which reconciles opposed developmental stages by making the child father to the man.

In Locke's *Some Thoughts Concerning Education,* the formation of society told in the *Two Treatises on Government* is recapitulated in the development of the child. While human society is based on individual self-control, self-control must first be learned, taught by means of external controls that the child later internalises. The child is the primal individual, neither good nor evil, but a *tabula rasa* to be written on, who must be socialised in order to be made compatible with social needs and order. Locke's child begins as an outsider, compared to 'Travellers newly arrived in a strange Country, of which they know nothing' (*Education,* p. 184), who is brought inside the social order by education. This process is literalised by Rousseau in his critique and fulfilment of Locke in *Emile*, in which the child grows up outside of society, and is only gradually educated so that he can enter into it actively. In turn the social order enters him, as he internalises its rules and conventions to become self-governing. For Locke, development thus also replays at an internal level the historical narrative of the development of the middle class first through and then against the past aristocracy: from feudalism to self-government, external to internal authority. The parent is a temporary ruler who guides the child only until he is able to control himself through the exercise of his reason. Children, born free, naturally love to dominate and control others; they must be taught self-control, denial, to reject immediate satisfaction for a greater deferred gratification, 'to *resist* the importunity of *present Pleasure or Pain*, for the sake of what Reason tells him is fit to be done' (ibid., p. 111), in order to become rationally self-governing and so free self-determining individuals. Self-denial must be taught by repetition and habit, rather than abstract rules, for humans are essentially imitative 'Camelions' (p. 126); children should be coaxed and not beaten, their energies sublimated not repressed. Tyrannical parental authority backfires, creating either a servile whimp or a rebellious and sneaky churl, as '*slavish Discipline* makes a *slavish Temper*' (p. 113). Education is thus a delicate business, in which the parent must exercise constant care, remembering always that 'The little, and almost insensible Impressions on our tender Infancies, have very important and lasting Consequences' (p. 83). Maturation is a dangerous process; the journey 'from a Boy to a Man . . . is the most hazardous step in all the whole course of Life' (p. 152).

Dancing and music provide Locke with an image for the individual's internalisation of social conventions and traditions which ultimately enables him to move naturally, giving ' a freedom and easiness to all the Motions of the Body' (p. 252): 'the Carriage is not as it should be, till it is become Natural in every Part; falling, as Skillful Musicians Fingers do, into Harmonious Order without Care and without Thought' (p. 151). Nature is transformed into art, in an image that looks backward to Castiglione's ideal of *sprezzatura* and forward to Yeats's dancer, indistinguishable from his dance, for whom life and art have become one. Locke's works are, however, full of counter stories about individuals, who were scarred for life by various pernicious formative influences, becoming social rejects. As the quotation at the beginning of this section shows, Locke constantly denounces servants as improper teachers for children, who read them ghost stories at an early age. He is sure that such stories have a particularly adverse effect on impressionable minds, producing timid and superstitious characters.[92] Moreover, maturation is threatened by forces from within as well as without: while self-government is achieved by the exercise of reason, character is deformed by the subversive faculties of the imagination and association, which parody reason. Where reason logically puts pieces of knowledge together, these faculties form unnatural combinations of things in ways that deform character, creating not a gentleman but an eccentric. In the *Essay*, as an example of the dangerous power of association and because of 'the pleasant oddness of it', he tells the story of the poor pathetic fellow who, having learned to dance in a room in which there was a trunk, forever associated dancing and trunks, and so could only dance under rather limited and peculiar circumstances.[93]

Reflecting a rise of interest in eccentrics and abnormal states of mind, the gothic expands on the stories in the margins of Locke's texts, focusing on children who do not grow up, or who become eccentrics, whose development is not teleological but caught in a repetition compulsion like that of Dracula, who, constantly resurrected, 'continue to do the same thing again every time, just as he have [*sic*] done before'.[94] Like many other villains, Dracula is a parodic version of the romantic child, Wordsworth's boy of Winander, whom death preserves from change. For the Romantics, moreover, art is able to recover the paradise lost of childhood and the artist is a version of the child; to say that art returns us to our youth is a term of praise not disparagement, as in André Breton's remark concerning the gothic: 'A work of art worthy of its name is one which gives us back the freshness and emotions of childhood.'[95] The gothic both represents and distorts the Romantic artist's attempt to recover an earlier stage of individual development, childhood, which is idealised, like the gothic middle ages, as a time of symbiotic unity and oneness with the world before the alienation of adulthood set in.

The gothic thus constructs a distorted version of the *Bildungsroman*'s narrative of normal maturation. Psychoanalytical readings have argued that the narrative structure of the novel proper is generally oedipally, and therefore teleologically, oriented: a linear structure with a discrete beginning, middle, and end, propelled by causality, moving towards closure which involves the establishment and resolution of contradictions told in Freud's story of development.[96] Like its ancestor the romance, the gothic has been associated with the pre-oedipal, oral, phase, and thus with the failure of normal maturation.[97] In its structure, settings, and characters it presents a view of an identity which has not evolved triumphantly into a Lockean unified person, but remains trapped in the past, fragmented, incoherent, and divided.

The rise of the gothic thus suggests a resistance to the ideas of rising, progress, and development, either historical or individual, which lead to the attainment of individuation and detachment. It suggests that the present can never detach itself from the past: the gothic from its precursors, the adult from his childhood self, the Protestant middle class from the Catholic aristocratic ancestors it demonises. Furthermore, in its elimination of autonomy as the goal of development, it raises questions about both personal identity and sexual identity. Some recent discussions of the gothic have identified two traditions of the gothic, one male and one female (which basically means Radcliffe).[98] The two forms reflect the way in which the modern redefinition of sexual relations, based on the idea of the separate spheres, turns the goals of the development of the sexes into antitheses. While the male moves through the standard *Bildungsroman* towards personhood and individuation, the female is never independent, and achieves her goal by entering into a new relation through marriage. Male identity, thus, is based on autonomy, while female identity, which in many ways resembles Burke's model, is conceived of as essentially relational.

In the gothic these two gender positions are pushed to extremes, both in representation of character and in narrative structure. In the tradition of the male gothic the focus of the narrative is on the individual as satanic revolutionary superman, who is so extremely alienated that he cannot be integrated into society. The basic narrative form is linear, causal, propelled by a genealogical imperative, a story of succession involving conflict based on oedipal or fraternal rivalry. In contrast, the female pattern has a circular form that works to eliminate conflict and radical discontinuity.[99] In the female version of development, the female individual is usually brought safely into a social order which is reaffirmed at the end. The male plot is one of teleological development towards detachment; the female, one of repetition and continuity. Whereas female writers explore ways of reconciling individual interests with demands of society, for male authors the focus is on the impossibility of such a compromise. The male hero achieves what is commonly seen as the goal of male development: autonomy; the female heroine what is commonly seen as her lot: relationship. Thus male identity is also created through rivalry, and oedipal conflict with precursors, and female through identification with precursors, particularly with the mother.[100] Each extreme is achieved, however, at a price, as autonomy turns out to be incompatible with relationships, and produces total isolation, while relationships seem to preclude autonomy: the fact that the heroines of Radcliffe and her followers seem totally interchangeable suggests that individuality is denied the properly socialised female. The first implies that individuality makes society impossible (Burke's nightmare), the second that society makes individuality impossible.

These two traditions, divided by gender, suggest – superficially – polar political implications. In terms of their endings, the male gothic seems revolutionary, the story of a rebel who resists the pressures of society that would repress individual desire, while the female seems reactionary, allowing us to indulge our imaginations safely because preaching the joys of ultimate conformity. The male gothic follows a revolutionary aesthetic, often associated with romantic art which defamiliarises and alienates reality in order to make us see it anew. The gothic extends this further when, by focusing on an eternally alienated individual, it refuses to allow us to return complacently to a safe 'norm'. The female, inversely, suggests a bourgeois aesthetic, as it creates a circle of defamiliarisation and estrangement followed by the re-establishment of conventional life.[101] In the female gothic, the private world is turned temporarily into a house of horrors; the domestic realm appears in distorted nightmare forms in the images of the prison, the castle, in which men imprison helpless passive females, angels in the house, whose spirituality may be pushed, as in the case of Walpole's Matilda, to an extreme. But this transformation cannot serve as an exposé of the fundamental reality that the bourgeois home is a gothic prison for women, for at the end of the text life returns to a normality that is ratified by its difference from the nightmare counterpart. The gothic forms of domesticity evaporate, enabling the heroine to return to the real version, now purified of its contaminated forms, so that women's continuing incarceration in the home that is always the man's castle is assured.

In my grouping of readings of individual texts, I have taken these divisions between male and female, radical and reactionary gothic, as provisional boundaries, in order to show, however, the gothic dynamics and doubling between them which complicate neat black and white polarities of gender or politics. In the next section, I look at the pair of Godwin and Wollstonecraft as examples of an apparently radical and progressive gothic, which attempts to use the tools of the past against themselves. The next and rather odd couple of Radcliffe and Lewis would seem, in contrast, to exemplify a gothic that is used for a conservative agenda. However, while Godwin and Radcliffe may seem to suggest the neatly antithetical nature of the two traditions, male/radical, female/reactionary, Wollstonecraft and Lewis suggest their interdependence. Both between the novels and within the novels, revolution and reaction, rising and falling, are, as Burke said, part of a single process, a dynamics of gothic creation, best dramatised by Mary Shelley's *Frankenstein*, a work which provides such a lovely image for the form itself.

My discussions will involve some of what Peter Brooks has called 'reading for the plot': analyses of the gothic's construction of narrative out of the bits and pieces of conventions, characters, events, landscapes. How the authors put things together – their use of sequence, order, the relations which they establish between their characters, places, and events – relates to larger aesthetic and social questions of the proper relationships between parts and wholes.[102] Timothy Reiss has described the emergence of a modern world view as involving the replacement of an organic medieval model, in which relations between things are seen in terms of analogy or a system of correspondences, with a mechanistic one, in which relations are described in terms of cause and effect.[103] In its turn to the past, the gothic often conflates the two: as causality seems inadequate in a world in which origins cannot be known, analogy can become a determining, and overdetermining, force.

Such overdetermination seems apparent in the frequently incestuous relationship between individual texts, which turns the gothic tradition into an oddly reflexive genealogical line, impelled and impeded by family resemblance. The gothic is an extremely allusive form that is self-conscious of its own literary relations. As I suggested earlier, intertextuality is one way of imagining reconciliation: of resisting a growing interest in individualism, novelty, originality, a personal and textual identity defined against others, in constant oedipal conflict with them, in favour of an older, communal model for identity as a collaborative effort. Some of the most important sources drawn upon by the gothic – Schiller's *Robbers*, Milton's Satan, Shakespeare's *Hamlet* and *Macbeth* – provide models for explorations of themes such as inheritance, usurpation, oedipal conflict, fraternal rivalry, incest. By invoking such sources, the gothic both suggests its own 'anxiety of influence', its fears about its own rightful place in the English literary line, and tries to assuage it, by showing it can choose its own fathers. The act of choosing selectively from tradition gives the impression that the present can bring the past back on its own terms.

One of the most omnipresent spectres called back in the gothic is that of Milton, whose version of the myth of fall and redemption, creation and decreation, is, as *Frankenstein* again reveals, an important model for gothic plots. For Burke, Milton is the great artist of the sublime, who exploits ambiguity and uncertainty to its highest effect. Eighteenth-century writers also inherited from Milton his 'great myth of a lost garden of innocence, and in his recurrent related themes of freedom, choice, and responsibility, his celebration of marriage'.[104] His popularity was reinforced in 1688, when he became associated with the Glorious Revolution as a part of the recovery of British freedom. Along with Locke he was toasted by the radicals and Commonwealthmen of the 1790s, hailed as a representative of a native tradition of poetry that was associated with the continuing struggle for political freedom and the right to self-determination. While Milton himself becomes an important image for a tradition of British liberty, his Satan provided an important model for (among other things) the gothic villain: the individual who fights against an oppressive tradition, the revolutionary oedipal son, who not only rebels against but also denies his father, claiming absolute originality with the insistence that he is 'self-begot, self-rais'd' (*Paradise Lost* V, 860). For Godwin, and the Romantics, Milton's Satan is a noble revolutionary figure: 'a manly radical asserting himself against the tyranny of absolute government', 'a being of considerable virtue. . . . He bore his torments with fortitude, because he disdained to be subdued by despotic power.'[105] He is the tragic individual, whose grandeur is increased by the fact that his quest is doomed by a predetermined fate. Moreover, as the prototype for the gothic version of the individual, he suggests the illusory nature of individuality. Individuality is itself a literary convention, an imitation of the forbidding 'original' Milton. Milton's Satan merges with Schiller's Karl Moor and other types of the noble robber or outlaw as an archetype of

the individual alienated from society because of society's inherent
evil. Furthermore, through romantic readings of Satan as a figure
for Milton himself, he anticipates a gothic identification of an
author with a satanic figure. Writers like Lewis, Beckford, and
Wilde – who claimed that his fate was 'foreshadowed and prefigured
in my art'[106] – identified themselves with their gothic villains. As we
will see, if the gothic identifies reader and text, it also often
assumes a peculiarly intimate relation between author and text.
Victor Frankenstein is the perfect image of the gothic artist whose
conscious attempt to detach himself from his work (as Walpole
had denied his authorship) itself turns his creation into his gothic
double.

In the gothic, this epitome of a native literary and political
tradition is oddly paired with a foreign counterpart. As Milton
became identified with the glorious British Revolution, which
Whigs claimed fulfilled his Republican ideals, Rousseau became
seen as the symbolic literary father of the French Revolution. For
Godwin, as we will see, Rousseau was a hero who not only stripped
himself naked in his *Confessions*, but exposed the artificial means
by which society corrupted the essentially good individual. Burke,
of course, loathed Rousseau, whom he saw as a seeker after novelty
and notoriety, a criminally irresponsible father, who exemplified
'deranged eccentric vanity',[107] licensing irresponsibly anti-social
behaviour and mythologising the artist as satanic loner, noble outlaw,
victim of society. To others, he was also an example of the man
whose good intentions had evil consequences, a Frankensteinian
creator, who unwittingly unleashed amoral literary and social
forces. Like Milton's Satan, Rousseau provides a link between the
gothic villain and the Romantic artist as revolutionary, the outsider
and outcast, who rejects all conventions, social and literary, and
seeks freedom from determining traditions that are seen as in-
hibiting individualism. The artist is in fact the ideal individual,
whose natural desires alienate him from a hypocritical society that
resents his revelation of its underlying truths. While *Emile* builds on
Locke to tell the story of an isolated individual who is trained to
enter the community, Rousseau's own story is that of the member
of the community who becomes exiled: 'The most sociable and
loving of men has with one accord been cast out by all the rest' and
become 'a monster'.[108] His individuality and, he claims, independence isolate him from others with whom he can have no community
as they are mere 'automata, entirely governed by external impulses'

(*Reveries*, p. 127). Ironically, however, while withdrawal from a society that demands conformity is the individual's only means of preserving his uniqueness, it also reveals its loss, as he becomes a passive victim, deprived of the very autonomy he claimed distinguished himself from them. Rousseau abnegates all responsibility for his actions – 'At least I am not to blame' – because he has been reduced to helplessness:

> I should regard all the details of my fate as the workings of mere necessity, in which I should not seek to find any intention, purpose, or moral cause, that I must submit to it without argument or resistance since these were useless, that since all that was left to me on earth was to regard myself as a purely passive being, I should not waste the strength I needed to endure my fate in trying to fight against it.
>
> (ibid., pp. 128–9)

Rousseau is the model for both Romantic artist and gothic villain, the individual at odds with society because of his individuality, who yet has no power of self-determination or self-control.

Rousseau's personal story is central to a gothic fall through which an essentially social being becomes alienated (and ultimately completely paranoid), in which, too, activity becomes passivity, autonomy a state of being an automaton, power becomes weakness, freedom slavery. The gothic world seems a revolutionary one in a literal sense, in which one thing becomes its opposite. The development of the genre, its own rapid rise and fall, suggests this circle. Politically, it begins as a conservative reaction against a progressive and radical middle class; as that class establishes itself as the new status quo, the revolutionary possibilities of the form appear, so that today it may be read as subversive of bourgeois norms. What once made it seem regressive makes it now appear progressive, a foreshadowing of twentieth-century concerns. Its formal progress, however, is the reverse. In 1764, with Walpole, it is a new, original, novel and radical genre; by the end of the century it has already begun to degenerate into stale stereotypes. The unconventional form that breaks the rules became a new conformity with relentlessly predictable conventions and tediously reliable effects. Perhaps this degeneration into conventionality is the inevitable fate of a form that depends on suspense; once its patterns are known it dwindles into merely mechanical formulae. Not all gothic novels after the 1790s are dreadful, of course, and there have been some masterpieces since in which authors have managed to revive and revitalise the old forms. But the rapidity with which a revolutionary literary form became reactionary seems astonishing, even to a twentieth century in which the speed of change has increased to the point at which almost any invention is instantaneously redundant, in which radical movements often rapidly establish themselves as new and sometimes monstrous orthodoxies, and in which the past is revived before it has had a decent burial.

Part II

Part II

1 Godwin and the Gothic of Revolution

It may seem somewhat perverse to begin a discussion of the gothic with a thinker who is more easily associated with the forces of light than those of darkness. William Godwin appears to be Burke's antithesis: a man who believed in individualism, the power of science, human perfectibility through progress, the evil of all external restraints and of all forms of concealment, and that the truth has only to be revealed to make men free. The relationship between the conservative and the anarchist thinkers plays a major role in Godwin's works, especially his most famous ones, *Enquiry Concerning Political Justice* and *Caleb Williams*, in which Godwin responds to and critiques the formidable influence of Burke. For Godwin, Burke was the defender of old systems of gothic tyranny, which supported 'the influence of superstitious awe' that is 'a cloak for oppression'.[1] Such artificial systems would simply dissolve when their true nature was revealed: 'the chains fall off of themselves when the magic of opinion is dissolved' (*Political Justice*, p. 149). The enlightenment thinker's aim is to expose mysteries, the illusory systems of suspense that keep humans in the dark and thus powerless, empowering them to think freely for themselves. Godwin thus could be read retrospectively as a prototype for the deconstructer of ideological systems, who shows how human constructs disguised as natural are a means of oppression; in his own time, however, he became a model for the gothic villain, the rational philosopher, who uses reason itself not only to reveal society's evils, but to conceal his own sinister interests.

Like other works by writers including Wollstonecraft and Paine, *Political Justice* was written in reaction to Burke's *Reflections on the Revolution in France*.[2] Where Burke defends the sublime obscurity of forms of government, Godwin begins by assuming that government is an object of scientific study to be taken apart and analysed rationally. For Burke, science and philosophy are twin evils, forces of abstraction, that have torn the old organic world order apart in the name of an inhuman idealism. Science is associated with radical industrial change which is dehumanising an older way of life, alienating the individual from both society and himself. For Godwin, however, it is precisely philosophy and science that will recreate the world, and lead the way to a higher form of human existence. In this again, Godwin is the descendent of seventeenth-century radicalism, which saw scientific, religious, and social reform

47

as all connected. Science was the tool of a revolutionary middle class which imagined itself as the spirit of change in the world, advancing towards an apocalyptic conquest of nature and superstition.[3] For Godwin, therefore, society needs itself to be analysed scientifically, on the model of 'taking to pieces a disordered machine, with a purpose, by reconstructing it, of enhancing its value' (*Political Justice*, p. 576). And so, as he later urges: 'Men of genius must rise up, to show their brethren that these evils, though familiar, are not therefore the less dreadful, to analyse the machine of human society, to demonstrate how the parts are connected together, to explain the immense chain of events and consequences, to point out the defects and the remedy. It is thus only that important reforms can be produced.'[4] Reformation is thus envisaged as an act of scientific analysis which will take apart and thus inevitably free us from the old systems of oppression.

The goal of this analysis is ultimately to free the essentially good and independent individual from false social restraints that inhibit his freedom and autonomy. Godwin's thinking is influenced by two traditions: a domestic one of radical dissenting Protestantism, into which he was born, and a foreign one of the French philosophes and Rousseau, which he acquired through reading.[5] Godwin combines and pushes these twin sources into the realm of political anarchism, in a belief in the absolute priority of the individual over all systems or social groups. For Godwin, we are all essentially independent:

> Man is a being who can never be an object of just approbation, any further than he is independent. He must consult his own reason, draw his own conclusions and conscientiously conform himself to his ideas of propriety . . . it is necessary that every man should stand by himself, and rest upon his own understanding.
>
> (*Political Justice*, p. 198)

External systems are pernicious because they undermine our essential independence, compromising by various insidious means our unique identity. Thus Godwin attacks all form of external influences: eating together, cohabitation, marriage. His main target, however, is all government institutions, which, designed to enable people to come together, in fact make that impossible, by imposing a false and reductive homogeneity that annihilates individual identity. For Godwin, Burke's belief in the individual's construction through tradition is a mystification of the means by which systems infiltrate and take over our identities, through forms of 'seduction' (ibid., p. 256). External systems of authority are forms of disguised violence, comparable to gothic demonic possession, invasions of our privacy and individuality. They further inhibit 'the piercing search of truth upon the mysteries of government' (ibid., p. 256). Because the government is set apart from us as an external system of power we are not supposed to investigate, it gains an insidious force over us. Through its networks of mystification – the law, class system, national education, organised religion – the government uses obscurity to oppress our intellects and keep us weak and dependent. Moreover, the tendency of all institutions is to reduce us to a machinelike conformity, to prevent all progress by making us acquiesce to a tradition that is merely disguised ancestor worship. While human nature is progressive, governments are regressive, impeding the natural movement of history:

> Incessant change, everlasting innovation, seem to be dictated by the true interests of mankind. But government is the perpetual enemy of change. . . . Their tendency is to perpetuate abuse. Whatever was once thought right and useful they undertake to entail to the latest posterity. They reverse the genuine propensities of man, and, instead of suffering us to proceed, teach us to look backward for perfection. They prompt us to seek the public welfare, not in alteration and improvement, but in a timid reverence for the decisions of our ancestors, as if it were the nature of the human mind always to degenerate, and never to advance.
>
> (ibid., p. 252)

However, at the same time as government is always an evil, society is essentially good, as 'human beings are formed for society' (p. 757). We are all bound together, though by the impartial law of justice rather than by Burke's natural emotional ties which, for Godwin, are poisoned by self-interest. Every individual is part of a network of connections, as: 'Everything in the universe is linked and united together. No event, however minute and imperceptible, is barren of a train of consequences' (pp. 108–9), and so 'no man stands alone, and can pursue his private conceptions of pleasure, without affecting, beneficially or injuriously, the persons immediately connected with him, and through them, the rest of the world' (p. 392).

While for Burke, the bonds that link humans together in a great chain of being are organic, for Godwin, they are mechanistic, a chain of causes and effects that link us all together. For Godwin, the mechanistic predictability of the world guarantees rational order: if the universe did not behave in a regular and comprehensible fashion, there would be no stable basis for human action. But the doctrine of Necessity obviously creates a problem for the question of human freedom. Humans are joined together as 'parts of one great machine . . . driven forward by impulses over which they have no real control'.[6] While, according to Hazlitt, Godwin 'had the happiness to think an author the greatest character in the world',[7] and while he insists on our essential autonomy, he also claims that people are not the true authors of their actions, as they are caught in a deterministic chain of Necessity: 'Man is in no case, strictly speaking, the beginner of any event or series of events that takes place in the universe, but only the vehicle through which certain antecedents operate' (p. 351), and so 'we perpetually annex erroneous ideas to this phrase, that we are the authors. Though mind be a real and proper antecedent, it is in no case a first cause, a thing indeed of which we have in no case any experimental knowledge. Thought is the medium' (p. 376). While individuals are in one sense the *cause* of society, they are also the *effect* of it, being the product of their environment and circumstances. Throughout all his works, Godwin constantly returns to the ways early influences and education determine character because of the fact that: 'the actions and dispositions of mankind are the offspring of circumstances and events, and not of any original determination that they bring into the world', as 'Man is in reality a passive, and not an active being' (pp. 97, 354). Appropriately, his own early Calvinist origins, from which he never detached himself despite his rebellion against religion, determined his own later ideas of determinism and the impossibility of free will; through a process typical of enlightenment and romantic secularisation, he translated spiritual forces into scientific terms.

Humans thus seem to be in a paradoxical situation. Godwin both values individualism, thinking for oneself, yet constructs a model for human nature which seems to make it impossible. However, freedom within this apparently deterministic and mechanistic system lies in the relentless and rational scrutiny of our own motives:

the perfection of the human character consists in approaching as nearly as possible to the perfectly voluntarily state. We ought to be upon all occasions prepared to render a reason of our actions. We should remove ourselves to the furthest distance from the state of mere inanimate machines, acted upon by causes of which they have no understanding.

(pp. 127–8)

Again Godwin draws upon his religious inheritance, turning the Protestant tradition of self-surveillance into a scientific process of self-analysis. For Godwin, as for his heir Freud, self-scrutiny can make us free. While external systems of monitoring oppress us, internal self-awareness liberates us from the powerful force of custom and habit, and makes involuntary actions subject to volition. Although we are not authors of ourselves, we can be our own readers, as interpretation not creation is the means of liberation.

Through reading, scrutinising our own actions, we gain control over actions which would otherwise be determined by forces outside of ourselves. Interpretation is also the basis of morality, which depends upon our understanding of our own causes, our motives, and our effects: 'morality itself is nothing but a calculation of consequences' (p. 114). Furthermore, it is a source of power, as *Political Justice* concludes with the eerily Frankensteinian prophesy that by gaining control of our own involuntary actions we will learn to control further our own bodies and 'obtain an empire over every articulation of our frame' (p. 774), thus conquering the natural world which has previously frustrated the progress of mankind. Power begins at home: self-control and self-regulation will ultimately produce a total dominion over nature; rational self-knowledge and self-mastery may lead to an apocalyptic world of self-regulating individuals who are therefore a race 'of men and not of children' (p. 776), in which, too, 'the mind will one day become omnipotent over matter' (p. 770).

Political Justice thus counters Burke's depiction of an ideal medieval world through a turn to an equally ideal future in which the gothic systems Burke reveres have completely dissolved. Once these systems dissolve, and the shackles of government are exploded, individuals will come together freely and honestly, in a new society based on equality, sincerity, and open communication, in which the truth will be revealed through a rational and secular apocalypse:

51

Every man will commune with his neighbour. Every man will
be eager to tell, and to hear, what the interests of all require
them to know. The bolts and fortifications of the temple of
truth will be removed. The craggy steep of science, which it
was before difficult to ascend, will be levelled. Knowledge will
be generally accessible. Wisdom will be the inheritance of
man.

(p. 290)

Just as Burke's work is an attempt to recreate the world he fears is
being lost, Godwin's also offers a model for the utopia he
anticipates. It demonstrates that the truth is clear, obvious, capable
of being conveyed in direct plain language by one man to another:
'Sound reasoning and truth are capable of being so communi-
cated: Truth is omnipotent: The vices and moral weakness of man
are not invincible: Man is perfectible, or in other words susceptible
of perpetual improvement' (p. 140). The truth is seen and naturally
preferred when the false media that the government imposes
between us are removed, allowing us to see things as they are. The
text itself is an attempt to create a transparent medium, for conveying the objective truth in simple and accessible language.[8] The
work has an apocalyptic goal of stripping away false systems, ideas,
Burkean prejudices that blind us from seeing the truth and impede
the true sincere relations between freely thinking and self-
regulating individuals, in order to create a revelation in the reader
that would help an ongoing revolution.

Writing in 1792, Godwin therefore saw the time as one of crisis,
when 'The condition of the human species at the present hour is
critical and alarming' (p. 783). For Burke, the events in France
were a catastrophe whose consequences threatened the entire
world order. In contrast, the message Godwin offers is reassuring.
His voice of reason responds to Burke's in a way that makes Burke
seem emotional, hysterical, a reactionary extremist, whose terror is
motivated by an inability to comprehend the necessity of progress
in human life. For Godwin, any external crisis of authority caused
by the destruction of old political systems is assuaged by his insistence on the authority within each of us which makes all external
systems superfluous. Men are naturally impartial, objective, benevolent, and love the truth. We have been seduced into error by
the systems, but fortunately, our errors are not irrevocable. Our
bad habits can be easily reformed through the reason which allows

us to see and change the errors of our ways. The reformation of society involves only a simple act of mental revelation, so that extreme forms are unnecessary. Even more, the extremes of repression and revolution are twin evils, caught in their own web of cause and effect. The attempt to prevent change only causes violent reactions in the form of revolutions. However, such human attempts to institute change artificially also backfire, generating a new tyranny, as they interfere with the natural processes of change unfolding in the universe under the banner of Necessity; Godwin himself is not the author or agent of change, but rather its herald. Between the two extremes of repression (with which he associates Burke) and revolution, between 'those friends of antiquity, and those friends of innovation, who, impatient of suspense, are inclined violently to interrupt the calm, the incessant, the rapid and auspicious progress which thought and reflection appear to be making in the world' (p. 261), Godwin offers in his text a *media via* of gradual illumination: 'The unfettered progress of investigation', whose 'advances are gradual, and each step prepares the general mind for that which is to follow' (p. 785). Reading itself becomes the first stage in the revolution, changing the mind of the reader by revealing the truth. It is only when grounded in that internal private transformation that change can, and indeed must, naturally spread outside to the external public world. The ultimate goal of this gradual evolution is to heal the present opposition between individual and society created by the government systems which simultaneously stand apart from people and invade their lives and even selves. Society and the individual would be not opposed but reconciled, as a healthy society would be one consisting of free individuals whose individuality was upheld, who did not merge into a machinelike conformity as, through the constant process of interpretation, they exercised their reason.

Caleb Williams, or Things as They Are has often been read as a kind of accommodation of Godwin's philosophical abstractions – to which Burke objected – to the popular reader.[9] It develops his theoretical claim that literature can be a political force, leading to social freedom. Literature has a powerful influence even upon those who do not read; as he wrote later:

> I cannot tell what I should have been, if Shakespear or Milton had not written. The poorest peasant in the remotest corner of England, is probably a different man from what he

would have been but for these authors. Every man who is changed from what he was by the perusal of their works, communicates a portion of the inspiration all around him. It passes from man to man, till it influences the whole mass.

(*Enquirer*, p. 140)

Reading and writing play important parts both in this novel and in Godwin's work in general.[10] Godwin is aware, however, of the dangers of reading in its undermining of individual thought. When we read, we think not like ourselves, but like another. So he notes in *Political Justice* that, 'All formal repetition of other men's ideas seems to be a scheme for imprisoning, for so long a time, the operations of our own mind. . . . Every man that reads the composition of another suffers the succession of his ideas to be, in a considerable degree, under the direction of his author' (*Political Justice*, p. 760). Later, in the *Enquirer*, he notes how in the act of reading one loses oneself in another: 'When I read Thomson, I become Thomson; when I read Milton, I become Milton. I find myself a sort of intellectual camelion, assuming the colour of the substances on which I rest' (*Enquirer*, p. 33). For Godwin, however, this is how reading fulfils the demands of morality that we put ourselves in the place of another, without undermining our essential individuality. The imagination is thus a moral force.[11] In the *Enquirer* in particular, Godwin picks up Milton's argument in *Areopagitica* (without, however, acknowledging this influence) to defend the importance of reading as a form of self-determination.[12] To read is to be human: 'Literature, taken in all its bearings, forms the grand line of demarcation between the human and the animal kingdoms' (*Enquirer*, p. 31). Moreover, reading is a preparation for life, a way of encountering others while learning to see through them (ibid., pp. 143–4). He attacks the anti-intellectual argument that 'a persevering habit of reading, kills the imagination, and narrows the understanding; that it overloads the intellect with the notions of others and prevents it from digesting them, and, by a still stronger reason, prevents it from unfolding its native powers', which he argues has gained popularity recently only because, 'It favours one of the most fundamental passions of the human mind, our indolence' (ibid., p. 356). He agrees that 'if the systems we read, were always to remain in masses upon the mind, unconcocted and unaltered, undoubtedly in that case they would only deform it', but replies that that is not the case, 'if we mix our own reflections with what we read; if we dissect the ideas and arguments of our author' (ibid., pp. 364–5), which is what all judicious and rational readers do. Thinking like another teaches us to think for ourselves, as: 'the study of other men's writings, is strikingly analogous to the invention and arrangement of our own' (ibid., p. 364). Reading is thus the basis for proper social relations, in which individuals can come together without losing their identities. It is the model for positive – as non-authoritarian – influence, an act in which readers, even while being influenced, are encouraged to think for themselves. It therefore also represents the progress of civilisation, in which thinkers build upon the work of one another. Finally, reading is power: 'He that loves reading, has every thing within his reach. He has but to desire; and he may possess himself of every species of wisdom to judge, and power to perform' (ibid., p. 31). Art can lead directly to control over life.

From his early childhood, Godwin had been a voracious reader who longed for fame. Raised to be a minister, a conflict over authority appropriately caused him to abandon this work and to become, what he admired most, an author. *Political Justice* made him instantly famous, perhaps leading him to be even more ambitious in his plans for *Caleb Williams*. In his preface to the 1832 edition, Godwin located the origins of his story in a desire to create a new and original work; he claimed to remember thinking to himself: 'I will write a tale, that shall constitute an epoch in the mind of the reader, that no one, after he has read it, shall ever be exactly the same man that he was before.'[13] While according to Godwin's philosophical beliefs, other authors were not in control of their own meaning, Godwin seemed sure he was. As David McCracken notes: 'as an author he believed himself to have an uncommon grasp of the newly revealed philosophic truth and to be able to determine and incorporate in his own work what would truly be the best tendency for men.'[14] His work was to be a truly unique and revolutionary novel, which would create a revolution in the reader.

However, while aiming at original creation, Godwin also mentioned that as preparation he read the works of others:[15]

it was ever my method to get about me any productions of former authors that seemed to bear on my subject. I never entertained the fear, that in this way of proceeding I should be in danger of servilely copying my predecessors. I imagined that I had a vein of thinking that was properly my own, which would always preserve me from plagiarism. I read other authors, that I might see what they had done, or more properly, that I might forcibly hold my mind and occupy my thoughts in a particular train, I and my predecessors travelling in some sense to the same goal, at the same time that I struck out on a path of my own, without ultimately heeding the direction they pursued.

(*Caleb Williams*, p. 339)

The creation of *Caleb Williams* becomes itself a model for an ideal literary society in which the free individual is able to encounter the ideas of others without losing his individuality: seeing how others think helps rather than impedes thinking for oneself. Literary relations produce not the conformity of sterile copying, but the individuality of new and original creations.

Part of its originality, moreover, lies precisely in its combination of other forms.[16] Reflecting Godwin's reading at that time, it brings together elements of the Jacobin novel, psychological study, fictional autobiography, *Bildungsroman*, fictionalised philosophy, sentimental novel, and the detective novel. This eclectic and eccentric combination of genres is typical of the gothic's assimilation of available forms. However, as a gothic novel, too, *Caleb Williams* is original. Its action takes place in the domestic present, rather than in a remote foreign past; there is no persecuted heroine, in fact there are few women at all (and the fact that Godwin could pull off a story without any explicit love interest was itself a feat), as the main relations are between men. Unlike the more expected baggy and loose form of a gothic novel, the text's structure is tight, unified, and relentlessly teleological, working towards the final outcome foreseen from the very beginning when the narrator introduces himself. Its most obvious gothic properties are its depiction of a disastrous quest for forbidden knowledge, and its representation of a relation between a pursuing oppressor and his pursued victim. For Godwin, the gothic is already a recognisable literary form, whose conventions are appropriate for social criticism. It can be used to expose the present domestic evil that we miss when projecting our attention and imaginations onto the safely distant regions abroad. The English expression of shocked horror at the tyranny of the crumbling French *ancien régime* is pure hypocrisy, considering the true nature of British liberty:

Thank God, exclaims the Englishman, we have no Bastille!
Thank God, with us no man can be punished without a
crime! Unthinking wretch! Is that a country of liberty where
thousands languish in dungeons and fetters? Go, go, ignorant fool! and visit the scenes of our prisons! witness their
unwholesomeness, their filth, the tyranny of their governors,
the misery of their inmates! After that, show me the man
shameless enough to triumph, and say, England has no
Bastille!

(*Caleb Williams*, p. 181)

For Godwin, the reassuring contrast between French tyranny and
British liberty (a staple of Burkean conservative arguments) dis-
solves. The source of gothic terror in Caleb is therefore not a
supernatural agent, but 'things as they are', the British social
system which, through a variety of insidious means, destroys the
naturally good individual. Godwin's creation of a domestic gothic
claims the gothic's critical potential for a revolutionary attempt to
dismantle old systems of oppression and recover a tradition of
freedom. By drawing upon the gothic form for this purpose,
Godwin suggests a way of achieving such a revolution by turning
his enemies' own weapons, mystery and suspense, against them.

As a writer of fiction, Godwin appears to maintain the objectivity
and coolness that marked him as a philosopher. He later stated
that, 'All talent may perhaps be affirmed to consist in analysis and
dissection' (*Enquirer*, p. 49), and claimed that his own particular
novelistic talent was an ability to analyse motives: 'the thing in
which my imagination revelled the most freely, was the analysis of
the private and internal operations of the mind . . . and laying bare
the involutions of motive' (*Caleb Williams*, p. 339). Like the philosopher, the novelist is interested in analysing the causes and
origins of human actions, using fiction to reveal the source of
'things as they are'.

The construction of fiction is, therefore, a form of scientific
analysis. According to his later recollection, in developing the plot
Godwin began with the end first, imagining a situation involving 'a
series of adventures of flight and pursuit; the fugitive in perpetual
apprehension of being overwhelmed with the worst calamities, and
the pursuer, by his ingenuity and resources, keeping his victim in
a state of the most fearful alarm' (ibid., p. 337). Starting with this
gothic situation of antagonism, Godwin proceeded backwards,

reasoning from effect to cause, and using the narrative to describe the series of events that produced the final situation. He believed that by working in this fashion, 'An entire unity of plot would be the infallible result' (ibid., p. 337). The plot thus seems tightly unified in its own pursuit of causes and effects. Its unfolding towards a tragic end announced in its opening sentence suggests the workings of a mechanistic and determined world which propel the individual.

The story, told by Caleb himself, begins as a vindication of his own right as an individual, an attempt to publish his own innocence and clear his reputation by telling the truth about himself which has been distorted by false representations. He begins, chronologically, by going back to the beginning to tell his early life. Throughout his career, Godwin, like Wollstonecraft, argued the vital importance of early upbringing and education.[17] In 1784 he proposed to open his own school, believing that proper education was the basis of social change: 'Let the most oppressed people under heaven once change their mode of thinking, and they are free . . . our moral dispositions and characters depend very much, perhaps entirely, upon education.'[18] Although he believed that men could change, he also saw early education as a major determinant of character. His novels depict individuals whose characters become fixed by their upbringing in ways which ultimately isolate them from society. Early habit becomes compulsive behaviour, which the individuals themselves are unable to control.

The determining habit of Caleb's early life is his curiosity, as his poor but honest parents give him a good education which stimulates his mind. For Godwin, curiosity is a sign of genius, which he defines as, 'a spirit of prying observation and incessant curiosity' (*Enquirer*, p. 13). Curiosity is a progressive impulse, which leads us to transcend limits: 'Curiosity is one of the strongest impulses of the human heart. To curiosity it is peculiarly incident, to grow and expand itself under difficulties and opposition. The greater are the obstacles to its being gratified, the more it seems to dwell, and labour to burst the mounds that confine it' (ibid., p. 131).[19] Curiosity is a sign of ambition and promise; the curious youth's mind 'may be expected to be incessantly at work, pursuing enquiries, accumulating knowledge, observing, investigating, combining' (ibid., p. 153).

In some of these early signs of promise, the character of the young Caleb is strikingly similar to that of the young Godwin, who described himself as a voracious reader, 'penetrated with curiosity and a thirst after knowledge'.[20] As Hazlitt noted, the novel creates a complex system of identification between author, character, and reader, as 'the reader identifies himself with the author; and the secret of this is, that the author has identified himself with his personages'.[21] Caleb is a great reader of books of both philosophy and romance, though it is significantly the latter which particularly influence him, as 'They took possession of my soul' (*Caleb Williams*, p. 4). Moreover, like the novelist, he is interested in analysis: 'I was desirous of tracing the variety of effects which might be produced from given causes' (p. 4). From the beginning Caleb is set up as a version of the author himself, a seeker after knowledge, who dissects the sources of human action.

Caleb's name suggests other ways in which he functions as a double for Godwin. In Numbers 13, Caleb is one of the spies sent by Moses to check out the land of Canaan. The other spies, overcome by their own cowardice, report falsely that the land is already occupied by giants, and council a hasty retreat; Caleb alone is brave enough to tell Moses the truth and advise him to enter into the Promised Land. For this intrepidity, Caleb is rewarded by a promise that he will enter into the Promised Land. Such a subtext replays Godwin's own apocalyptic goals, his concern with showing readers how to enter a promised land that they, fearful like the other spies, are unable to see, blinded by systems of oppression which make them see the present possessors as larger than they truly are.[22]

However, the fact that Caleb's Old Testament precursor was a spy has a more ambiguous resonance for a radical writing in the 1790s, when, as part of the crackdown on radical movements, the government invasion of privacy was intensified by the use of paid servants to spy on masters.[23] At the time of the publication of the text, spying was associated less with liberation than with the perpetuation of systems of oppression through complete domestic surveillance. Moreover, Caleb Williams is a different kind of spy from his Old Testament precursor; his subject is not a promised land but another human being, whose personal territory he invades. Through these actions he distorts Godwin's ideals, entering into a relation with Falkland in which Godwinian friendship and conversation is perverted, and knowledge of another, the desire for intimacy, is turned into an act of aggression. As the author's goal is to dissect character to expose motives, Caleb becomes a fiendish author, a psychological spy and torturer who, by vivisecting every action and word, aims at a demonic revelation.

In Caleb, therefore, the radical desire for revelation and revolution through science becomes a gothic quest for knowledge, and thus a version of the fall. In retrospect, Caleb will claim that he was motivated by an unhealthy compulsion, 'a mistaken thirst of knowledge' (ibid., p. 133), 'an infantine and unreasonable curiosity' (p. 144), for a knowledge that is not useful but rather poisonous.[24] Like that of another Old Testament precursor, Eve, his quest for forbidden knowledge is a rebellion against the act of forbidding itself:

> To do what is forbidden always has its charms, because we have an indistinct apprehension of something arbitrary and tyrannical in the prohibition. To be a spy upon Mr. Falkland! That there was danger in the employment served to give an alluring pungency to the choice . . . a kind of tingling sensation not altogether unallied to enjoyment. The farther I advanced, the more the sensation, was irresistible. . . . The more impenetrable Mr. Falkland was determined to be, the more uncontrollable was my curiosity.
>
> (pp. 107–8)

Mystery creates the desire to expose it: as Godwin had argued, repression is the cause of revolution, though the revolution it generates will itself impede true change. Unlike Eve, however, Caleb's transgression here is not of an external injunction set down by an omnipotent God, but of the moral order of the universe, which requires both reverence for the privacy of others and self-scrutiny, analysis of our own motives so that we can act responsibly and calculate the consequences of our actions. Caleb does not consider until too late the use he would make of the knowledge he desires, nor its consequences. Moreover, once Caleb begins spying he claims he has no power to control his own actions. His fixed habits control him, preventing him from thinking about the consequences of what he is doing and so, according to Godwin's scheme of things, of acting both independently and morally. He is in the power of a habit which appears to him as a form of demonic possession; he describes himself thus: 'I have been hurried along I do not know how. I have always tried to stop myself, but the demon that possessed me was too strong for me' (p. 119).

Character becomes fate, as Caleb fails to take authority and control over his own actions, so that he and the narrative seem impelled. The author claims he is caught in a narrative beyond his control, in which, 'Incident followed upon incident in a kind of breathless succession' (p. 131).

Caleb is thus an ambiguous figure, made up of contradictory impulses – part revolutionary author, part passive victim of circumstances and his own character. Again his name suggests this doubleness. It means both bold and dog – suggesting how Caleb combines both daring and servility. For Godwin, the dog is a type for Miltonic 'excremental whiteness', the negative goodness based on ignorance rather than rational choice: 'My dog seems attached to me; but change his condition, and he would be as much attached to the stupidest dunce, or the most cankered villain. His attachment has no discrimination in it; it is merely the creature of habit' (*Enquirer*, p. 9).[25] True to the contradictions of his proper name, Caleb's attitude towards Falkland is manic depressive, as he swings from a sadistic sense of having power over him, to an insistence on masochistic self-abnegation. Shortly after an episode in which Caleb uses candour sneakily to try to trap Falkland into revealing his secret, Falkland suddenly turns directly upon him, demanding that he reveal his secret purpose. Caleb responds in a characteristically melodramatic and hysterical fashion, by throwing himself at Falkland:

> For God's sake, sir, turn me out of your house. Punish me in some way or other, that I may forgive myself. I am a foolish, wicked, despicable wretch. . . . Do with me any thing you will. Kill me if you please. . . . Sir, I could die to serve you! I love you more than I can express. I worship you as a being of a superior nature. I am foolish, raw, inexperienced, – worse than any of these; – but never did a thought of disloyalty to your service enter into my heart.
>
> (*Caleb Williams*, pp. 119, 121)

The modern spy suddenly collapses back into the feudal servant.

The conflation suggests, further, how Caleb's attempts to know Falkland distort Godwin's own belief in knowledge as scientific analysis which aims at human empowerment through the revelation of truth. In this, Godwin is the heir of Bacon, who contrasted this modern model of objective knowledge, in which the subject is detached from its object, with earlier medieval forms of knowing, which were based on a religious act of submission, the complete identification through subjection of the knower to the known.[26] For Bacon and his followers, modern science liberated humans from this idolatry, and from the blind worship of superstition which disempowered them. In Caleb, however, the scientific and the religious, the modern and the medieval models for knowledge and relations, are part of a continuum linking extremes. The desire for mastery reverts into a need for subservience, as scientific knowledge regresses back into the superstition and ancestor worship out of which it emerged. The desire for power is paired with, and perhaps generates, the desire for the abnegation of power, a relinquishment of all authority, and indeed individuality.

Caleb is thus entangled in a master–slave dialectic, which also reflects his own position as Falkland's servant. As I noted in relation to Walpole, the figure of the servant is central to the gothic, partially because the bond between master and servant was being redefined in response to social changes, especially urbanisation. While increasingly becoming a purely commercial bond, it still retained elements of the old feudal system, in which loyalty and love bound men. Mr Collins is a feudal retainer, faithfully devoted to his master, and Caleb himself has a more affective than economic relation with his employer, expecting Falkland to act as his father more than his employer. For Burke, the transformation of the old feudal retainer into the paid employee epitomised the degeneration into a purely economic society. Loyalty is destroyed by self-interest, as, 'every servant may think it, if not his duty, at least his privilege, to betray his master'.[27] For Godwin, however, the treacherous, spying servant was associated with the government's attempt to prevent any change. Like Locke, moreover, Godwin has a deep distrust of servants, whom he sees as epitomising the way class destroys individuality. The servant cannot be considered an individual because he lacks economic independence: 'His great standing rule is to conform himself to the will of his master. His finishing perfection is to change himself into a mere machine.... He is destitute of the best characteristics of a rational being' (*Enquirer*, p. 210). The servant is thus the epitome of the individual dehumanised by society.

As the system reduces servants to subhuman machines, it inversely elevates the upper class to the level of superhuman gods. Through reserve and self-mystification, the appropriation of Burke's rhetoric of sublimity, the aristocracy keeps the lower class in a state of:

suspicion on one side, and infatuation on the other . . . in perpetual vibration, between rebellious discontent and infatuated credulity. Sometimes they suppose their governors to be the messengers and favorites of heaven, a supernatural order of beings; and sometimes they suspect them to be a combination of usurpers to rob and oppress them.

(*Political Justice*, pp. 503–4)

From the perspective of the lower class, their superiors are both gods and demons, an ambivalent perspective manifested in Caleb's view of Falkland. Falkland's constant ubiquity, his ability to be everywhere at once, suggests his godlike power from the very start. Caleb's transgression confirms him in the role of the vengeful punishing God of the last part of the text, who reminds Caleb of his omnipotence: 'You little suspect the extent of my power. . . . You might as well think of escaping from the power of the omnipresent God, as from mine!' (*Caleb Williams*, p. 144). However, the elevation of a man to the status of a god proves to be as equally dehumanising as the degradation of the human to the servile machine. By the end of the text, Falkland has lost all semblance of humanity, and becomes an allegorical devil, 'like nothing that had ever been visible in human shape' (ibid., p. 280), a cartoon version of not God but Milton's Satan.[28]

The effect of a class society is therefore to divide high and low, while condemning them to the identical fates of dehumanisation. For Godwin, the upper and lower classes, master and servant, are gothic doubles of each other, poles whose opposition hides a more profound identity. Caleb and Falkland are, further, a complex conflation of the relations of master/slave, father/son, hero/worshipper, and copy/imitator. They are even husband and wife – the sexual implications of Caleb's 'curiosity' have often been noticed, and Godwin himself later pointed out the similarity between his tale and that of Bluebeard's wife.[29] The Richardsonian subtexts suggest the complexity of the subterranean sexual dynamics: while, in the original ending, Caleb turns into Clarissa after her rape, in the first part of the text he plays the part of a symbolic rapist, who tries to penetrate Falkland. In its confusion of opposites, the relation between Caleb and Falkland has often been read as a prototype for the gothic double, later used more explicitly by writers such as Hogg, Stevenson, and Poe.[30]

Caleb's identification with Falkland is suggested by the domination of his own narrative by that of his master; after the brief first chapter, the story of Caleb Williams turns immediately into that of Falkland:

> To the reader it may appear at first sight as if this detail of the preceding life of Mr. Falkland were foreign to my history. Alas, I know from bitter experience that it is otherwise. My heart bleeds at the recollection of his misfortunes as if they were my own. How can it fail to do so? To his story the whole fortune of my life was linked; because he was miserable, my happiness, my name, and my existence have been irretrievably blasted.
>
> (ibid., p. 10)

The narrative veers abruptly from the straight and narrow path of Caleb's progress through life, and goes backwards into the past. This movement appears to disrupt the unity and the rather mechanical chronological unfolding of the story by digression. The two narratives are, however, tied together rigorously, both by cause and effect (as according to Caleb, Falkland's tragedy is the cause of his own) and by analogy.[31] The tale of Falkland's origins provides a parallel story of development to that just given by Caleb, which emphasises both the distance and proximity between the two characters. Falkland, too, is a product of his circumstances and class position. Early in life, he was influenced by his reading in 'the heroic poets of Italy' from which 'he imbibed the love of chivalry and romance' (ibid., p. 10), the veneration of honour and reputation that is his ruling passion. Whereas Caleb, like Godwin himself, wants to see into the heart of things, Falkland is concerned with keeping up appearances, with retaining social and literary traditions. In this, and in his veneration for the age of chivalry, his resemblance to Burke is clear.[32] His representation is telling of Godwin's complex attitude towards Burke. In many ways, Falkland is a sympathetic figure – gifted, sensitive, and gracious. Compared to the repulsive, boorish, and despotic Tyrrel, he is a benevolent tyrant, who acts responsibly on the principle of *noblesse oblige* and attempts to use his authority to aid those weaker than himself – Emily Melville, the Hawkins. Ironically, however, Falkland's attempts backfire as he destroys those he meant to help. Good motives have evil consequences that their author could not control. Falkland's fate not only foreshadows that of Caleb, but those of Godwin's later heroes. Godwin's stories of development follow the model of Rousseau, to show how the good individual, who desires relations with others, ultimately becomes an exile.

The identification between the two men is intensified by the inversion of their roles that takes place when, in a parody of Godwinian sincerity, Caleb finally breaks down Falkland's reserve and makes him reveal the truth. Paradoxically, it is when his secret is hidden that Falkland is in Caleb's power; when his secret is revealed, the power system changes. The truth does not make Caleb free but delivers him into Falkland's power as, with Falkland's revelation of his guilt, the relation between the two, victim and victor, detective and criminal, pursuer and pursued, is reversed. Now instead of Caleb watching Falkland, he will be watched himself, and scrutinised not by a friend but by a hostile enemy to whom, however, he is bound completely, as he finds himself with: 'All my actions observed; all my gestures marked. I could move neither to the right nor the left, but the eye of my keeper was upon me. He watched me' (ibid., p. 143). Caleb becomes confined to Falkland's home that becomes for him a 'dungeon'. Moreover, the wealthy Falkland has more effective means of surveillance than Caleb ever had, as what gives the aristocracy its divine omnipotence and omniscience is the law.[33]

The central part of the text is a direct and didactic attack on the legal system which, as in *Political Justice,* is the opposite of true justice (which resides in individuals and not in institutions), and supports prejudice and superstition. It is a system of political and linguistic misrepresentation, in which sublime obscurity is a means of political oppression that perpetuates a stagnant tradition. Ostensibly created to reveal the difference between guilt and innocence, the law is used by the powerful to confuse them. Moreover, as Caleb learns later, when he falls among thieves, it prevents all hope of human change and reformation. The leader of the group, Mr Raymond, is an example of the just outlaw forced into his position by an unjust society. Moreover, the law *keeps* him where he is; though he would like to return, he cannot:

Alas, Williams. . . . It is now too late. Those very laws, which by a perception of their iniquity drove me to what I am, preclude my return. God, we are told, judges of men by what they are at the period of arraignment, and, whatever be their crimes, if they have seen and abjured the folly of those crimes, receives them to favour. But the institutions of

countries that profess to worship this God, admit no such
distinctions. They leave no room for amendment. . . . What
then can I do? Am I not compelled to go on in folly, having
once begun?

(ibid., pp. 227–8)

The law is the artificial and gothic form of Godwinian Necessity,
which is used to perpetuate the status quo by seeing all behaviour
as deterministic, all error irrevocable. It refuses to admit the
possibility of individual change, and so successfully prevents the
possibility of social change.

With its own obsessive repetition compulsion, the text shows the
way in which 'things as they are' are perpetuated by a legal system
which prevents all change and crushes the individual: Emily
Melville, the Hawkins, Brightwel, Mr Raymond, Caleb himself.
Like Godwin himself, however, Caleb seeks to escape from this
system of oppression. Believing in his own essential independence,
he first seeks a stoic solution; isolated in prison, he attempts to turn
isolation into a good, in which his mind achieves freedom from its
external circumstances.[34] However, one extreme again produces
the next; stoic self-sufficiency is followed by a craving for friendships:

The pride of philosophy has taught us to treat man as an
individual. He is no such thing. He holds, necessarily, indi-
spensibly, to his species. He is like those twin-births, that have
two heads indeed, and four hands; but if you attempt to
detach them from each other, they are inevitably subjected
to miserable and lingering destruction.

(ibid., p. 303)

Our need for others makes us hideous monsters, but as Caleb
discovers, to be cut off from all others is to be equally monstrous.
The recognition that his own story is like that of others begins the
transformation of personal bitterness into political consciousness,
a realisation and loathing of 'things as they are':

I thought with unspeakable loathing of those errors, in consequence of which every man is fated to be more or less the
tyrant or the slave. I was astonished at the folly of my species,
that they did not rise up as one man, and shake off chains so
ignominious and misery so insupportable. So far as related to
myself, I resolved, and this resolution has never been entirely
forgotten by me, to hold myself disengaged from this odious

scene, and never fill the part either of the oppressor or the
sufferer.

(ibid., p. 156)

Oppression produces the social awareness that can overthrow it, as
Caleb's insight into the structure of society prompts his indignation and a desire to reject all relations based on power. A
growing sympathy for those who share his plight creates in him a
need both to become a part of a true community and to escape the
vicious dynamics of society as it is.

The problem is that given things as they are, there isn't really
any way in which these private feelings can be translated into
public action. In the world of the text there are only two roles
available, tyrant and slave, which is to say Falkland and Caleb, roles
that are both absolutely opposed and intimately identified. Caleb's
attempt to form relations in the latter half of the text are clearly
repetitions of his original relation with Falkland. Increasingly he
seeks a parent – Mrs Marney, Mr Spurrel, Laura, finally Mr Collins,
whom he addresses as father – as a means of recovering his original
relation with Falkland. However, even these substitutions are impossible. Flying from Falkland, Caleb finds his reputation precedes
him, so that he is always rejected by the alternative communities he
attempts to enter. His appeals for love and sympathy are rejected
when his identity is discovered, for he is seen as an unnatural
'monster with whom the very earth groaned!' (ibid., p. 249), who
has repaid a benefactor's kindness not with gratitude but betrayal.
Caleb is outcast from all intercourse, the domestic and family life
he seeks, and becomes paranoid that encounters will inevitably
involve betrayal:

> I shrunk from the vigilance of every human eye. . . . I was shut
> up a deserted, solitary wretch in the midst of my species. I
> dared not look for the consolations of friendship; but, in-
> stead of seeking to identify myself with the joys and sorrows
> of others, and exchanging the delicious gifts of confidence
> and sympathy, was compelled to centre my thoughts and my
> vigilance in myself.

(ibid., pp. 255–6)

He has become like Falkland now, suspicious that others will
discover his secret. His intense, overconnected relation with
Falkland has made him an exile from all other forms of relations,

67

especially domestic ones; persecuted, he is forced into satanic isolation, in which his only relation with an other outside of himself is with the wrathful God he has offended.

Alienation is therefore not even a guarantee of individuality, as Caleb comes to resemble Falkland. The crucial difference is that he is forced to endure what the other had chosen for himself. Isolation is thus both a mark of individuality, and yet a sign of its loss. As the text's narrator Caleb first appears as the author of his own story and the reader of Falkland's, who uses his interpretive skills as a means of asserting power and his own identity over another. But with the revelation of Falkland's secret the situation is reversed, as the wealthy aristocrat has the power to usurp the identity and narrative of the poor servant. Exposed, Falkland turns into an all-powerful author whose alternative version of Caleb's character and story usurps the place of the truth. The inversion of power relations gives Falkland narrative authority over Caleb, who finds himself suddenly bound up in someone else's plot over which he has no control, and in which he is increasingly reduced to a purely fictitious figure. Caleb watches in horror as his life is appropriated and converted into popular myths and narratives about the infamous criminal Kit Williams: 'I had gained fame indeed, the miserable fame to have my story bawled forth by hawkers and ballad-mongers, to have my praises as an active and enterprising villain celebrated among footmen and chambermaids' (ibid., p. 274). His public identity is no longer his own property but has been taken over by the agents of the infernal author, Falkland, who has trapped him and isolated him through forms of misrepresentation.[35] He is alienated not only from society but from himself. Caleb's story thus seems an inverted *Bildungsroman* in which development marks the obliteration rather than construction of individual identity. The last third of the text is a series of episodes of flight and pursuit, in which Caleb becomes a Protean shapeshifter assuming different false forms. In its repetitive structure the plot reproduces the force of Caleb's own compulsive behaviour which has cost him his individuality. All characters function as doubles of each other, and all can be reduced to a single story showing how the individual becomes an outcast from society. Ironically, whereas for Rousseau exile is the only means of preserving individual identity, for Caleb it signals its loss.

At the end of the novel, however, Caleb attempts to recover his identity and his right to tell his own story and to give the true authorised version of his own life. From being a reactionary force, mechanically responding to Falkland's oppression, he attempts to turn into a revolutionary figure who takes control of and claims authority for his own actions. While Caleb's downfall appears to begin with his early reading of romances, his attempt at freedom comes when he tries to become an author. The text moves therefore towards becoming a *Kunstlerroman*, the story of how Caleb the character became Caleb the author. He becomes 'fully determined to publish those astonishing secrets, of which I had hitherto been the faithful depository; and once for all to turn the tables upon my accuser' (ibid., p. 275), believing that revelation will put an end to the vicious circle of persecution, re-establish the categories of guilt and innocence in their proper places, and so turn law into justice. Caleb approaches Falkland as a revolutionary, who will conquer the systems of the world not through violence but through his pen:

> I will use no daggers! I will unfold a tale – ! I will show thee for what thou art, and all the men that live shall confess my truth! . . . I will tell a tale – ! The justice of the country shall hear me! . . . These papers shall preserve the truth: they shall one day be published, and then the world shall do justice on us both. . . . It is not to be endured that falsehood and tyranny should reign for ever. . . . With this engine, this little pen I defeat all his machinations; I stab him in the very point he was most solicitous to defend!
>
> (ibid., pp. 314–15)

Publication of a narrative will be the cause of social revolution. With his revelation of Falkland's guilt, Caleb believes he will recover his innocence. The text moves towards a closure in which an ambiguous situation is to be clarified, resolved by the reassertion of simple black and white categories, through a literary change that is also an act of political change.

The original ending which, according to Godwin, had been the beginning of his story, upholds the opposition with which the story began. The two characters do not change; having acted like machines conditioned to do one thing from the beginning they continue on their course, so their hostility is never resolved. Locked between these two antithetical but identical positions, the narrative comes to a dead end in which Caleb disintegrates into madness. Like Manfred, and more closely Clarissa, whose behaviour after her rape is clearly the model here, Caleb becomes totally incoherent, his speech falling into pieces that mirror the fragmentation of his own identity under the continuing oppression of Falkland. The text itself falls apart, suggesting that when opposites are maintained, narrative closure cannot be achieved.

Possible reasons for Godwin's revisions have been speculated upon.[36] The original ending is effective in terms of the text's purpose of social criticism; it gives a grand finale to drive home how things as they are dehumanise individuals, as the fragments conclude with Caleb calling himself 'a stone' (ibid., p. 334). Loss of authorial control is equated with a complete loss of human identity. But the fragmentation of the ending also suggests Godwin's own loss of authorial control – as he is suddenly possessed by the plot of Richardson. His end thus demonstrates at two levels a world in which individual agency and authority are impossible: we are all constructed by forces, literary as well as social, outside of our control.

The published ending gives authority back to both Caleb and Godwin himself. The text moves from things as they are, to things as they might be, showing a revolution in which the two characters, previously locked into rigid opposition because of society, exert their powers as free agents to move beyond their determined positions. In the first part of the final confrontation, the roles return to their original form, as Caleb is the pursuer, Falkland the pursued. But this inversion seems to be potentially the kind of revolution Godwin had abhorred in *Political Justice*, in which the oppressed turns into the oppressor, the revolutionary becomes in turn a tyrant, so that the power system is inverted but unchanged. At the moment, however, that Caleb publishes his innocence, he realises his own guilt. Attempting to use the perverted system of the law against his enemy has made him equally unjust. Moreover, the sight of Falkland's corpse-like condition suddenly makes him aware of the consequences that his actions have had for someone other than himself. Ironically, Falkland himself has become living proof of Godwin's anarchist arguments for the superfluity of the law: no external system could have punished the individual more effectively than he has himself. Protestant self-scrutiny (also known as the conscience and super-ego) has naturally imposed the political justice which society neglected;[37] as Freud would later show, internal surveillance is more brutal than any spy system. Moreover, as Caleb gains power over his rival and takes the superior position once more, he feels not hatred and bitterness towards Falkland but pity. In turn, he awakens sympathy in Falkland who suddenly sees the errors of *his* behaviour and the goodness of Caleb. The two previously self-enclosed individuals suddenly recognise each other. As a result, in the final moments of the confrontation the system of domination and vicious circle of victimisation appear not futilely inverted but totally transcended through the power of sympathy and the emergence of mutual love.

The text thus suddenly swerves towards a kind of conversion narrative in which, too, the death of the 'old man' necessary for the birth of the 'new' occurs on a literal level. The exchange between father and son in which they bless each other takes place just before the death of Falkland, at which point Caleb's whole purpose in life changes: 'Why should my reflections perpetually centre upon myself? self, an overweening regard to which has been the source of my errors! Falkland, I will think only of thee' (ibid., p. 325). On the surface, Caleb appears to have moved from egotism to altruism in his relation with Falkland, and so redefined their relation from antagonistic opposition to sympathetic identification. He has realised what Godwin will later call the primary rule of morality: 'that of putting ourselves in the place of another' (*Enquirer*, p. 298). Previously obsessed with his right to be the author of his own life, he suddenly defines himself as the narrator of an other's:

> I began these memoirs with the idea of vindicating my character. I have now no character that I wish to vindicate: but I will finish them that thy story may be fully understood; and that, if those errors of thy life be known which thou so ardently desiredst to conceal, the world may at least not hear and repeat a half-told and mangled tale.
>
> (*Caleb Williams*, p. 326)

An imaginative and moral revolution appears to have taken place which has dissolved the old power systems that the original ending left intact.

However, if the first ending can imagine no relation between the two poles, the second, despite its appearance of harmonious reconciliation and its aesthetically, morally, and psychologically satisfying resolution, seems to raise a complementary problem. While Caleb claims to have no character left, in one sense he has assumed the character of Falkland. While the 'old man' dies, the 'new man' lives to tell his story. With the death of the father, a

71

succession has taken place, as Caleb takes over Falkland's story. The conflict between men is resolved only when one is eliminated; any crisis of relations is solved by the fact that there is no longer an other to relate to. Oedipal rivalry has not been overthrown but satisfied, in a fantasy through which Caleb's original desire for an intense and ambivalent identification with Falkland is both fulfilled and idealised by the pretense of sympathy and benevolence made possible by the death of the father. He has become his father, stepping into the place, which means narrative, of his predecessor by giving up his claim to his own identity and story. The new ending thus neatly and economically satisfies both his desire to have control over Falkland and his desire to abnegate himself completely before him.

While the text thus seems to chart the development of the character Caleb into the author of his own story, at the end we are left wondering whose story 'Caleb Williams' is. In her *Life of William Godwin*, Mary Shelley noted how the text supported antithetical readings and class positions: 'those in the lower classes saw their cause espoused, & their oppressors forcibly & eloquently delineated, while those of higher rank acknowledged & felt the nobleness, sensibility and errors of Falkland with deepest sympathy.'[38] Many early readers saw Falkland as the true hero of the tale, and Caleb simply, as the arch-conservative Montague Summers dismissively denounced him, as a 'nosey young blackguard'.[39] As Kenneth Graham has argued, the double ending only emphasises the polar world of the text, divided by its two heroes, two prefaces (each offering a different yet plausible interpretation of the author's aim), and two titles.[40] The titular annunciation that this will be the story of Caleb Williams is complicated by the subtitle, *Things as They Are*, with its resonances of Jacobin slogans. To call the work *Caleb Williams* is to create an identification between text and individual, an identification common in the novel proper, in which character is the cause of narrative. One could argue then that 'things as they are' are the product of the obsessed mind of an isolated individual. But one could equally read the relation between the two titles as suggesting that that individual is not the cause but effect of the state of things. The identification of the two titles leaves them suspended in a circular web in which cause and effect, like the pursuer and pursued, are interchangeable.

The text has often been read as an indictment of society's destruction of individuals by isolating them and alienating them from themselves and others. Society undermines autonomy to create social automatons, like Caleb himself who is described by Mr Collins as: 'a machine: you are not constituted, I am afraid, to be greatly useful to your fellow man; but you did not make yourself; you are just what circumstances irresistibly compelled you to be' (ibid., p. 310). Both Caleb and Falkland, servant and master, are equally victims of a social order that has infiltrated them through their education and experiences.

The fates of both characters would thus seem to extend and develop the role of Burke in *Political Justice*. Hearing of Burke's death while revising *Political Justice*, Godwin added a footnote which represented Burke as the epitome of the individual as fallen angel, born good but infiltrated and thus corrupted by society. Burke himself is transformed ironically into the Rousseauian and Godwinian individual, a tragic example of the way in which the government wastes the potential of the superior class as well as the lower, a man who in defending prejudice has become its 'dupe' (*Political Justice*, pp. 788–9). Like Falkland, Burke is an individual who has lost his individuality in the traditions with which he identified and from which he can no longer distinguish himself, and ends up possessed completely by the demonic forces of ideology. Yet for Godwin, Burke's own rhetoric reveals its fallaciousness; the mystifier unconsciously gives himself away in the act of publication:

> at the same time that he tells us, we should cherish the mistake as mistake, and the prejudice as prejudice, he is himself lifting the veil, and destroying his own system. While the affair of our superiors and the enlightened is simply to impose upon us, the task is plain and intelligible. But, the moment they begin to write books, to persuade us that we ought to be willing to be deceived, it may well be suspected that their system is upon the decline.
>
> (ibid., p. 504)

But if Burke's attempt to conceal reveals, Caleb's attempts to reveal end in mystery and ambiguity. It seems fitting that we never find out what was in Falkland's trunk, which, like the black veil in Radcliffe, haunts the text as a symbol for all secrets, locked and guarded. Caleb's desire to know what was in 'the fatal trunk' is then identified as the source of all evil: 'from which all my misfortunes originated' (*Caleb Williams*, p. 315). Characteristically, Caleb is convinced that the trunk holds the true authorised version, 'a faithful narrative' (p. 315), of the story of Falkland. The trunk if opened, would reveal the story that *Caleb Williams*, however, claims to become at its end. While opening the trunk therefore becomes a metaphor for revelation and – as some critics have thought – revolution, or at least Godwin's revolutionary act of writing, it never occurs: instead of its contents, we get the narrative of *Caleb Williams*.

While *Caleb Williams* is an extension of the exploration of the critique on society's destruction of the individual begun in *Political Justice*, it also, appropriately considering the Godwinian imperative of self-scrutiny, analyses its own impulses and motives. The revolutionary seeker of truth who tries to change society through writing becomes the gothic villain, the alienated outcast, an Ancient Mariner doomed to repeat his own story. Throughout his works, Godwin created versions of himself in his heroes – Caleb, Fleetwood, St Leon – well-intentioned figures who are torn between the desire for knowledge and for relations with others, two desires which Caleb misguidedly conflates. In Godwin's world, as in Burke's, the quest for knowledge is punished by the loss of human relations. The philosophical author thus seems to justify his own enterprise and makes himself the one lone author in control of his own intention by scapegoating other authors, as gothic doubles from whom he ultimately detaches himself by showing their quest for knowledge and authority become a gothic one. So, while Caleb fails to become a proper author, in the text *Caleb Williams* Godwin himself tries to implement his theory of using reading to change society, creating relations with others through his text. It certainly was an influential work. But it didn't change the world, and soon the changes in British sentiment towards radical ideas, as well as shifts in taste, affected readings of it. The writer with revolutionary aims ultimately provoked a widespread reaction, in which his disinterest and scientific objectivity was suspected of concealing rampant selfishness. The reaction against Godwin's thinking manifested itself in a number of parodies which drew, too, on the tradition, encouraged by Burke in the *Reflections*, that the Revolution was the unnatural creation of a conspiracy of radicals and philosophers, an artificial monster fabricated out of the evil dreams in their heated brains.[41] In these parodies, the Godwinian philosopher was represented at best as an incompetent theorist, whose need to act benevolently, calculating the abstract benefit of the whole, prevented all practical action. At worst, however, the metaphysician was portrayed as a gothic villain: a cold, calculating, ruthless individual who used his philosophy for his own self-interest, and whose denial of passion was a cover for a life of unrestrained lust. The philosophy of enlightenment was seen suspiciously as a duplicitous veil hiding satanic forces of darkness, and philosophy itself as a gothic enterprise.[42] Perhaps *poetical* justice triumphed when the author was himself turned into a character (*St Godwin* in one parody), in other writers' gothic plots – including that of his daughter.

2 The Reveries of a Solitary Woman

In *Caleb Williams* Godwin attempted to expose the ways in which public forms of oppression have infiltrated and contaminated the private relations between men, by giving 'a general review of the modes of domestic and unrecorded despotism, by which man becomes the destroyer of man'.[1] For Mary Wollstonecraft, however, such a review evades a related but separate issue: how 'things as they are' pervert the domestic relation between the sexes so that man becomes the destroyer of *woman*. Like Godwin's work, her final novel *Maria, or The Wrongs of Woman*, uses a double title to suggest the identification of an individual person and the social situation that has shaped that person. Her aim is to expose the mystification of the true power relations between the sexes, by 'exhibiting the misery and oppression, peculiar to women, that arise out of the partial laws and customs of society'.[2] Wollstonecraft's goal as a reformer is to help release women from an entrapment in false systems of representation which, perpetuated by custom and prejudice, impede their individuality. Writing is a revolutionary and revelationary act in which she rends the veils that have confined and oppressed women, keeping them, like gothic heroines, 'immured in their families, groping in the dark'.[3]

Like Godwin, Wollstonecraft sees how political models influence and invade our private worlds. The bourgeois ideal of the separate spheres separates the domestic from the political, as a female realm of love and harmony which is opposed to a male commercial jungle of strife and conflict. Like the middle ages, then, the private sphere is idealised as a refuge from the modern public world of atomistic individualism, a place in which older organic relations still survive. For Wollstonecraft, therefore, it becomes a world of feudal oppression, which further reproduces the very power relations it appears to repudiate in more intense, as intimate, forms. For women, especially, the home idealised as a paradise of harmonious relations is more likely to be a gothic prison. The home is a torture chamber of horrors, a feudal castle in which, freed from the restraints of society, the man may exercise his will and so rule with absolute despotism.

In *A Vindication of the Rights of Woman*, Wollstonecraft attacks ways in which female nature has been artificially constructed in such a way so that women are trapped in illusions of ideology which prevent them from recognising the gothic reality of their lot. Like Godwin, she sees female acquiescence as the product of pernicious social influences which distort an essential human nature that she identifies with reason. Ignorant of their true nature, women are defined by men in terms that are in fact artificial: 'females have been insulated, as it were; and, while they have been stripped of the virtues that should clothe humanity, they have been decked with artificial graces that enable them to exercise a short-lived tyranny' (*Vindication*, p. 37).

Like *Political Justice*, *A Vindication* follows the model of Rousseau, to attempt to strip away artificial ideas of human nature to reveal a hidden truth. The identification of women with feeling and sensibility is exposed as an artificial construct passing itself off as human nature. Like slaves, women are taught to despise freedom and to see their servitude as a higher form of existence. Through the idealisation of the domestic private world, imprisonment is represented as freedom, so that women themselves are reluctant to be liberated. In turn, representations of the true nature of women help condition them in ways that then serve to justify their continued relegation to this sphere. Used to submitting blindly to external authority, women never develop the ability to reason and think for themselves, as: 'obliged to submit to authority blindly, their faculties are weakened' (ibid., p. 155). They are kept in a state of untried innocence, Miltonic 'excremental whiteness'. Kept at home with children, they remain children; they are not innocent but ignorant, as 'in order to preserve their innocence, as ignorance is courteously termed, truth is hidden from them' (p. 44) – as we will see in the case of Lewis's Antonia. Governed by others, and taught to seek power over men indirectly, they never learn to govern themselves. Like the aristocracy, to which she frequently compares them, they therefore have nothing to labour for, no trials or contests to develop through. While men can strive, women are kept static; as Wollstonecraft complains in the preface to *Maria*:

> In many works of this species, the hero is allowed to be mortal, and to become wise and virtuous as well as happy, by a train of events and circumstances. The heroines, on the contrary, are to be born immaculate; and to act like goddesses of wisdom, just come forth highly finished Minervas from the head of Jove.
>
> (*Maria*, p. 73)

For Wollstonecraft, such stasis is unnatural, as life on earth is a process of constant work and trial in which we move forward to a final goal in heaven: 'life is a labor of patience – a conflict'; and 'our finding things unsatisfactory here, should force us to think of the better country to which we are going'.[4] Like Godwin, her radicalism reflects her early Protestant upbringing, and her continuing belief in the value of hard work. Women are not allowed to develop or advance through experience and trial; confined to a timeless never-never land of nuptial bliss, there is no place for them to advance to. The plot of their lives must necessarily be a stunted anti-teleological one, which hides a male plot to keep them in a state of suspended animation and arrested development. Absorbed in particulars, they never develop the ability to abstract, or to perceive the logical order between things:

> To do every thing in an orderly manner, is a most important precept, which women, who, generally speaking, receive only a disorderly kind of education, seldom attend to with that degree of exactness that men, who from their infancy are broken into method, observe. This negligent kind of guess-work . . . prevents their generalizing matters of fact – so they do to-day, what they did yesterday, merely because they did it yesterday. . . . They dwell on effects, and modifications, without tracing them back to causes.
>
> (*Vindication*, pp. 22–3)

Unable to reason, they cannot scrutinise or interpret even their own actions, and so are caught in a chain of habit which binds them in mechanically repetitive behaviour. Things as they are thus deprive women of the essential attribute of human nature, which is reason, the one authority the individual should obey, as the only source of true freedom: 'it is the right use of reason alone which makes us independent of every thing – excepting the unclouded Reason – "Whose service is perfect freedom"' (ibid., p. 121).[5] They become slaves then, too, of their own feelings, 'the prey of their senses, delicately termed sensibility, and are blown about by every momentary gust of feeling' (p. 60).

Confined to the private domestic sphere, women thus are ironically allowed both too much and too little freedom. Repressed through domestic imprisonment, denied the true limits and inward authority of reason, they are encouraged to indulge their feelings and sensibility. The result of such conditioning is shown in many gothic novels, including, as we will see, Radcliffe, in which female sensibility is enflamed by domestic repression until it becomes murderous. The separation of women, seen as necessary for bourgeois society, is thus revealed to be socially destructive. For Wollstonecraft, the identification of men with reason and women with feeling turns the sexes into enemies with nothing in common. As Radcliffe will also suggest, it further makes friendship within the sexes impossible, as women relate to each other as rivals for male attention. Sexual segregation thus divides society, turning it into a gothic world of victors and victims caught in 'this insidious state of warfare, that undermines morality, and divides mankind!' (ibid., p. 97). Social reformation therefore depends upon the healing of the rupture between the sexes, which requires the education of women: 'till women are more rationally educated, the progress of human virtue and improvement in knowledge must receive continual checks' (p. 40). A reformation of female manners is a means of reforming the world: 'It is time to effect a revolution in female manners – time to restore to them their lost dignity – and make them, as a part of the human species, labour by reforming themselves to reform the world' (p. 45). Just as Burke and Godwin presented their authorial voices as proof of their arguments, Wollstonecraft offers herself as evidence of woman's essentially rational nature that would be revealed through such a reformation.[6]

Like Godwin, Wollstonecraft's first enemy was Burke, whom she attacked earlier in *Vindication of the Rights of Men* (1790), the first published response to his *Reflections on the Revolution in France*.[7] For Wollstonecraft, Burke is also the champion of gothic political and aesthetic orders that oppress women even as they claim to protect them.[8] The present plight of women is thus implicitly traced to a feudal and gothic aesthetic which masks tyranny under the cover of chivalric protection. However, in Wollstonecraft's later works, the position of women is traced to a modern source, which conceals oppression under the rhetorical cloak of complementarity:

> The social relations of the sexes are indeed truly admirable: from their union there results a moral person, of which the woman may be termed the eyes, and the man the hand, with this dependence on each other, that it is from the man that the woman is to learn what she is to see, and it is of the woman that the man is to learn what he ought to do. If woman could recur to the first principles of things as well as man, and man was capacitated to enter into their *minutiae* as well as woman, always independent of each other, they would live in perpetual discord, and their union could not subsist. But in the present harmony which naturally subsists between them, their different faculties tend to one common end; it is difficult to say which of them conduces the most to it: each follows the impulse of the other; each is obedient, and both are masters.
>
> (*Vindication*, pp. 86–7)

Ironically the enlightened revolutionary Rousseau, whom Wollstonecraft is here quoting, is seen as the source of a new and more insidious myth about the difference between the sexes. The man who claimed to strip himself and society naked, to reveal essential human nature, has his own method turned against him to show how, in so doing, he has stripped women of rights and invested them with wrongs.

Wollstonecraft's relation to Rousseau is a complex one.[9] While she attacks his image of the couple, she attempts to appropriate his image of the artist as exiled wanderer to represent her own fate as a woman. Her female solitary is a combination of Rousseau and Milton's Satan, punished for rebelling against an unjust patriarchal order. Such alienation can give women a sense of their own autonomy and therefore power, like Mary who at times in her solitude feels 'herself independent' (*Mary*, p. 45). In *The Letters Written During a Short Residence in Sweden, Norway and Denmark*, Wollstonecraft presents herself as a female solitary, whose journey into the northland is also a symbolic quest for self-knowledge.[10] At the same time, however, these letters were written (and the journey itself undertaken) as an attempt to regain the love of Imlay; furthermore, according to Godwin, their effect was to instill love in the reader: 'If ever there was a book calculated to make a man in love with its author, this appears to me the book.'[11] If the female solitary is seeking self-knowledge, a self-consciousness that is the basis for autonomy and independence, she is also questing for relations with others. Her quest for love is thwarted, however, as it takes place in a world which formulates the relation between the sexes in a way that makes true love impossible. In *A Vindication of the Rights of Woman*, Wollstonecraft claims that Milton's representation of Adam and Eve drives her in disgust to identify with Satan: 'Similar feelings has Milton's pleasing picture of paradisial happiness ever raised in my mind; yet, instead of envying the lovely pair, I have, with conscious dignity, or Satanic pride, turned to hell for sublimer objects' (p. 25, n. 3).[12] Similarly, the inadequacy and perniciousness of Rousseau's concept of the couple sentences the female to a life of loneliness. The female as alienated Rousseauian wanderer is thus the creation of Rousseau's representation of the relations between the sexes. However, the female outside of society lacks the grandeur of the devil, philosopher, or even the gothic villain – at worst, as in the case of Jemima, she is the fallen woman as monster.

For Wollstonecraft, however, like Godwin too, a solution to things as they are is suggested by the act of publication itself, imagined as a form of apocalyptic revelation that will reform the system, and strip away false notions of female capabilities. The important symbolic potential of reading and writing as symbols of freedom and self-determination takes on a new significance for women in the eighteenth century. Both offered women ways of escaping the private sphere and forming relations with the world outside of the home. Like the gothic itself, however, literary production and consumption seem inherently ambiguous occupations, a subversion of the separation of the spheres that is at the same time both radical and reactionary, rebellious and submissive.[13] Books provided a means of remaining in the home, and so conforming to the dominant image of the perfect female, and yet communicating, in an albeit mediated fashion, with the world outside. Thus books could be used as a conservative tool to confirm women's status in the home (and certainly many of the texts served to validate the new ideal of womanhood). In *A Vindication of the Rights of Woman*, Wollstonecraft condemns works, especially novels, which undermine female capacity for reason by encouraging unrestrained sensibility and imagination. However, her own use of the novel form suggests also the radical possibility literature offered to women, in which, while appearing to conform to the status quo, it could critique it and attempt to extend its limits. Like Godwin, she tries to effect a revolution in which she turns her enemies' weapons back upon themselves, using fictional conventions to expose the societal conventions that keep women bound. In her last novel in particular the fictionalised representation of 'things as they are' is presented as the means of changing them.

Like *Caleb Williams, Maria or The Wrongs of Woman* focuses on the political potential of reading and writing. In both texts, as Tilottama Rajan argues, reading is represented as an apocalyptic and revolutionary act which reveals a hidden truth: 'that which brings the truth to light'; 'the unearthing of truth and the correction of past (mis)representations.'[14] Power and authority are thus the property not of the author, but of the reader. This is obviously a gratifying message for *Maria*'s readers, who are encouraged to feel that they are the heroic liberating forces at work, who will effect 'a divinatory reading that will liberate the true significance of the text from the prison of things as they are'.[15]

Wollstonecraft's novel appears to adopt a Godwinian as well as gothic plot, translating the oedipal antagonism between Falkland and Caleb into the conflict between Maria and George. Husband and wife become hunter and hunted, in which the male pursuer confines his victim, though not insane as Caleb was in Godwin's first ending, to a madhouse. Like *Caleb Williams*, too, the text appears to be a realistic novel of reform, embodying its author's philosophic precepts in a narrative form which centres on a character who is, here also nominally, closely identified with its author.[16] The novel shows relentlessly how society and its conventions confine women, using the demonic private space of the madhouse as the central metaphor for female experience. A society which denies women reason, while encouraging them to feel and indulge their imaginations, makes them mad.

The novel begins with an invocation and then exorcism of conventions, suggesting that it will show things as they are, beyond the mediation of distorting forms of representation. It seems to be an extension of Wollstonecraft's desire in *A Vindication of the Rights of Woman* to strip the false images of women to reveal their essential nature. In the opening, those false images are associated with the gothic form itself:

Abodes of horror have frequently been described, and castles,

filled with spectres and chimeras, conjured up by the magic
spell of genius to harrow the soul, and absorb the wondering
mind. But, formed of such stuff as dreams are made of, what
were they to the mansion of despair, in one corner of which
Maria sat, endeavouring to recal her scattered thoughts!

(*Maria*, p. 75)

Gothic trappings are suddenly conjured up in the first sentence,
only to be as abruptly stripped away in the second, in which we are
told that reality exceeds imaginary gothic horror.[17] Conventions
are to be banished, in this exposé of reality. But the nature of that
reality is deferred at the onset. The opening is extremely obscure,
as at the end of the first paragraph we still don't know where the
narrative is taking place, only where it's *not*. The reader is both
located and disoriented by the opening. Wollstonecraft creates a
suspense that draws us into the narrative and identifies us with the
heroine, Maria who, we learn gradually, has been kidnapped, to
find herself in a madhouse. With the discovery of her situation we
realise that reality is worse than fiction or, rather, that for women
reality *is* gothic. The conventions of the gothic, which the opening
appears to call up only to exorcise, haunt the text: they serve as a
spectre underlying the reality which supposedly lay beneath the
gothic appearance of the opening.

To keep herself from going mad, Maria occupies herself with
reading and writing to her daughter. Like *Frankenstein*, the text
posits its own creation as a possible alternative to evil forces. As in
another famous gothic work, *Dracula*, reading and writing the story
are antidotes to evil, which in *Dracula* (which partially takes place
in an asylum) is identified not only with vampirism but also, as in
Maria, with madness. Reading and writing are idealised as the basis
for the formation of a community, as it is through stories that the
characters come to know each other and combat the evil forces
that threaten them. Books are the medium that allow the characters in the madhouse to escape their isolation, as Darnford sends
his books to Maria, and ultimately they meet in order to share the
narratives of their own lives. The novel itself is formed out of a
series of narratives describing individual experiences and patterns
of development that are intertwined and yet disconnected. The
text is both synonymous with the identity of the central character,
Maria, whose story holds the work together, and composed of a
collection of stories. It therefore suggests that individual identity

can itself be created through the combination of different sources and influences.

As Rajan has noted also, the novel is concerned with the different forms characters use to shape their own stories, and the conventions they adopt when they order their experiences.[18] Each character narrates his or her own childhood and development, shaping it according to the genre that suits his or her taste. Darnford represents himself as a typical romantic satanic or Byronic hero whose fall, however, appears not to be irrevocable. Spoiled as a child (like Godwin's Tyrrel, who also did not learn to internalise external forms of authority), his idealism has been misplaced. Erring on the side of sensibility, he seems a perfect complement to Maria, the fallen hero waiting to be redeemed by the love of a good woman. Fortunately for him, this is exactly what he finds in the madhouse to which he, too, has been unjustly confined.

Jemima's story is quite a different genre altogether; an unsentimental and realistic narrative of lower-class life. Jemima, as the model for the child repudiated by its family, considered an alien from birth, 'a creature of another species' (*Maria*, p. 107), is, as we will see later, one prototype for the monster in *Frankenstein*. Treated as an outcast even by her own family, there is no place she can enter into society, except by taking the role of either victim or – very occasionally, when she finds a female weaker than herself – victor. The abused cannot revolt against those above her, but becomes an abuser in her own turn. The system turns women against each other, as Maria discovers when, after fleeing her marriage and seeking help from other abused wives, all betray her, either through sympathy with the oppressor or fear of their own husbands. Jemima's story describes a vicious circle of domination, which, from a female perspective, reworks most closely the major concerns with class oppression and the lot of the servant from *Caleb Williams*. Doomed by both her class and sex, Jemima's only hope is to become the guardian at the madhouse, the servant of the very order that tyrannises over her.

However, the act of telling the story seems to undo the message it conveys of female helplessness, implying that representation is itself a form of change. The narration of this shocking life to Maria and Darnford seems to hold out the possibility of a break from the confining forms, both narrative and societal, which Jemima is trapped in. The story influences Maria by opening her mind:

Active as love was in the heart of Maria, the story she had just heard made her thoughts take a wider range. .... Thinking of Jemima's peculiar fate and her own, she was led to consider the oppressed state of women, and to lament that she had given birth to a daughter.

(ibid., p. 120)

Like Caleb, she begins to see her own particular situation as part of a universal condition: 'Was not the world a vast prison, and women born slaves?' (p. 79). Women are oppressed so that they become monsters like Jemima, whose 'nature' is used as the justification for further oppression: 'By allowing women but one way of rising in the world, the fostering the libertinism of men, society makes monsters of them, and then their ignoble vices are brought forward as a proof of inferiority of intellect' (p. 137). The means of changing that condition, however, begins with the establishment of community through reciprocal sympathy.

Different as they may be in kind or genre, the stories in *Maria*, like those in *Caleb Williams*, are obsessive repetitions of a single one: variations on the Rousseauian pattern in which, because of the corruption of the social system, people develop into, not Locke's rational autonomous persons, but social outcasts. While the stories depict the isolation of individual identity, their narration has the effect of bridging that isolation as, through story telling, the characters influence each other, and ultimately the reader. Hearing Darnford's story, Maria identifies with him and pities his suffering. If Jemima's story influences Maria, the growing love between Maria and Darnford has its effect on her; touched by their love, she is able to open herself up to them and 'voluntarily began an account of herself' (ibid., p. 101). The intertwining of the discrete stories provides a model for the formation within the madhouse of an alternative society made up of the outcasts who are joined by sentiment. The love between Maria and Darnford begins with reading, and is consummated by the exchanging of their stories. Confinement becomes in fact a positive factor that enables male and female to meet outside of societal prejudices as essential equals, who are both victims of unjust oppression. Isolated by imprisonment, Darnford is as powerless as the female, a fact that may increase his capacity to sympathise with Maria's suffering. The incarcerated male seems the perfect counterpart to our heroine. The prison itself is what ironically seems to hold out the possibility for a true relationship between male and female based not on domination but equality, a shared exploitation and unjust punishment. In turn, love appears to transform the prison:

> So much of heaven did they enjoy, that paradise bloomed around them; or they, by a powerful spell, had been transported into Armida's garden. Love, the grand enchanter, 'lapt them in Elysium,' and every sense was harmonized to joy and social extacy. So animated, indeed, were their accents of tenderness, in discussing what, in other circumstances, would have been commonplace subjects, that Jemima felt, with surprise, a tear of pleasure trickling down her rugged cheeks. . . . She seemed indeed to breathe more freely; the cloud of suspicion cleared away from her brow; she felt herself, for once in her life, treated like a fellow-creature.
>
> (ibid., p. 101)

Love appears an apocalyptic force, able to explode the most narrow enclosure and transform it into a place of freedom, and capable of opening up the narrowest, most self-interested character. For Rousseau and Godwin, the prison is associated with a stoic triumph of the individual mind over matter, in which the independent self frees itself from all external restraints and needs.[19] In *Maria*, however, the heart of the prison is not the independent self, but the couple. Wollstonecraft seems to anticipate the Romantics for whom love, not Godwinian reason, is the liberating force that will overcome limits and transform society.

Prison therefore becomes a place of freedom, where love and the imagination can both be exercised beyond the restraints of conventions. Yet the link between desire and the imagination, both of which enable us to go out of our isolated selves and identify with others, is a dangerous one, especially for women. When Maria first reads Darnford's text, she begins to create fantasies about him: 'She read them over and over again; and fancy, treacherous fancy, began to sketch a character, congenial with her own, from these shadowy outlines' (ibid., p. 86). The text she reads provides her with a model for her reality, as she sees the as yet only half-glimpsed owner of the texts in the image of St Preux, fashioning her dream man into a sympathetic hero based on the rather suspect source of Rousseau. After hearing his story, she indulges herself further:

Having had to struggle incessantly with the vices of mankind, Maria's imagination found repose in pourtraying the possible virtues the world might contain. Pygmalion formed an ivory maid, and longed for an informing soul. She, on the contrary, combined all the qualities of a hero's mind, and fate presented a statue in which she might enshrine them.

(ibid., p. 99)

The story of Pygmalion was used by Rousseau as an allegory of the artist's ability to revolutionise the world, through godlike powers of realisation, which enable him to satisfy his desires and turn art into reality.[20] We will see other gothic versions of the Pygmalion myth, in which art becomes life, which suggest not the imagination's power to change the world, but its ability to create an illusory substitute for it. For Wollstonecraft, women's imagination and sensibility are fed by the poverty of their experiences; Maria is described as having romantic tendencies: 'she frequently appeared, like a large proportion of her sex, only born to feel' (ibid., p. 98). Denied satisfaction in reality, the imagination creates its own substitute. Repression causes an imaginary rebellion: it is when shut up that Maria's suffocated imagination and passion rebel and run riot. Moreover, the female imagination, freed only when cut off from any outside public life, may create a world that is an alternative to reality but can never transform it. It therefore can never be truly liberating but only create more palatable and so dangerous fictions, that in fact serve to make imprisonment even more attractive, just as both romances and gothic novels can represent female disempowerment in a way that idealises it and encourages women to confuse not only art with life, but weakness with power.

In *Maria* the Pygmalionesque creation is only an illusion that takes place, after all, in a madhouse. Its symbolic transformation into Armida's garden indicates further the limitations of both love and the imagination as liberating forces, and the dangers of sentiment, especially for women. In Tasso's *Gerusalemme Liberata*, Armida's garden is an illusory and artificial paradise that lures the heroes away from the reality of their quests (the delivery of Jerusalem) with promises of delusory pleasure. Love and duty, senses and spirit, female pleasure and male labour, art and reality, private and public, are opposed, and the former reduced to a fiction, wrought by a seductive enchantress.[21] For Godwin, Tasso's bower further becomes a symbol for the loss of individual identity through an excess sympathy with others which degrades us from our true selves.[22] Like Armida's bower, the madhouse is in danger of becoming a private world of pleasure, an end in itself, an aesthetic palace of art detached from reality. While reading is a cure for madness, a way of keeping sane, it leads right back to it, to entrapment in the bower of the imagination which, by offering illusory satisfactions, impedes the progress and trial in the real world necessary for human growth and development. The love of Maria and Darnford, begun through fictions, could be simply a self-contained fiction, possible only in the private world of the madhouse, where the imagination, cut off from reality, constructs fantasies that can have no reference to or place in the world outside, and which, if indulged too long, would lead to real madness.

Maria's own story, narrated last in the sequence of tales, suggests how women, taught to be unnatural, cannot distinguish art from life, the creations of their own imaginations from the 'real world' around them. Her narrative gives us both an explanatory cause of her incarceration, and also shows how the prison is a repetition of her life so far. Her past and present are thus linked by both causality and analogy, suggesting how female development is trapped in a vicious circle. Her highly sentimental story is an example of how women are culturally conditioned in such a way that love for them is always a romantic fiction. Her parents' 'love marriage' disguises the fact that her father – 'a captain of a man of war' (p. 125) who marries late and imports a military model for relations into his home – sees his union as an act of great condescension which places his wife in eternal debt to him. She in turn internalises the misogyny that underlies this attitude, neglecting her daughters and spoiling her son who, like James Harlowe, becomes a selfish, self-indulged, petty tyrant. The daughters' fates are of no familial concern; Maria herself will try to help her sisters, but their stories become examples of the common fate of talented but impoverished women for whom there is no public position. Condemned to the degrading fate of governess (which Wollstonecraft had herself experienced and briefly but cuttingly denounces), the youngest declines and dies. Her story is an example of wasted female potential that corresponds to the story of the prisoner Bridewell Caleb meets in prison who, unjustly incarcerated, languishes and dies just before he is finally to be brought to trial.[23]

Maria marries to escape this unbearable situation, hoping to find in union with George Venables an alternative to the microcosmic society represented too accurately by her family. In retrospect, therefore, her idealisation of Darnford can be seen as a repetition of her earlier, more inexperienced idealisation of George, whom her naive fancy painted as a sentimental hero. Flight from her family leads only to the prison of marriage in which she is 'caught in a trap, and caged for life', 'bastilled' (ibid., pp. 144, 155). Marriage is, however, also a revelation, in which the sentimental veneer is stripped from George, leaving a sordid reality. From potential hero and liberator from familial tyranny, he quickly sinks into a caricature of Lovelacian masculinity (with a dash of Solmes tossed in to make him doubly repulsive): a gross, dishevelled, mercenary rake, totally ruled by self-interest. The couple immediately degenerates into a parody of complementarity. Maria is a stereotypical female, motivated by altruism (which ultimately is fulfilled in maternity); George a selfish, egocentric male. He plays on these stereotypes, accusing her of romantic and sentimental notions. He himself is therefore a version of the gothic rational villain, who masquerades as the enlightened philosopher and spokesman of a free open marriage, when, for his own financial interests, he encourages her to take a lover. As always, disinterest conceals more insidious self-interest; the possessive individual is also a feudal lord who locks up his wife when she defies him.

Maria's narrative then shows how attempts to find freedom from conventions lead back to imprisonment within them. The madhouse is revealed as the true essence of female life in the private sphere. Her story is written as a mother's warning to the daughter she fears she may die before seeing. In Maria's own life, the sins of the parents seem perpetuated in the child. However, telling her life is seen as a potential means of breaking the vicious cycle of female inheritance. It opens with advice drawn from her own experience: 'From my narrative, my dear girl, you may gather the instruction, the counsel, which is meant rather to exercise than influence your mind' (ibid., p. 124). The story is a message through which the mother hopes to communicate with her child, so that the past may reach out to and benevolently influence the future. But this act of union is designed to create discontinuity between past and future, to ensure that, 'warned by my example' (p. 124) the daughter's life will be different from that of the mother.

However, Maria's story for her daughter is read only after the child has been discovered to be dead. The attempt at setting up a system of communication between past and future that will create change is aborted by the elimination of the future. Instead of going forward and out into the world, the narrative comes backward to be read in the prison in which it was written, and by Maria's dream lover, Darnford. The message comes full circle, to the man who, perhaps in other ways, becomes the substitute for Maria's child. He is the polar opposite of George, an example of the new 'man of feeling' and idealised sentimental hero increasingly popular in the fiction of the time as the heroine's dream partner.[24] As the model for the ideal reader in the fiction, however, Darnford reveals the problems of the system of communication that is being set up in the prison. The society of readers is one possible only in a world cut off from real life, a self-contained, self-referential, autonomous private system that cannot refer to the real world and is therefore powerless to change it. The tale reaches out for sympathy that it only gets when it returns to its point of origin. It can only be read by others who share Maria's situation, and are thus equally trapped and powerless, unable to reach and transform others outside of the idealised couple who are produced within the restraints of the prison.

Moreover, Maria and Darnford meet as equals only within the prison; as soon as they leave it, Wollstonecraft has problems representing any relation between them at all. In the real public world the differences between male and female and their social statuses return and prevent reconciliation. But, in general, the relations between the lovers and the parts of the narrative are rather obscure, as the plot's inability to create secure connections between its different parts suggests Wollstonecraft's inability to imagine a coherent narrative that will bring male and female together in a realistic way. While Wollstonecraft is quite comfortable describing Maria's encounters with Darnford's *texts*, the description of their first actual meeting as *persons* is the first gap in the narrative, in which the hitherto straightforward line of plot breaks down (ibid., p. 93), and jumps forward to later visits. From what we have, it appears that Wollstonecraft was trying to fit Darnford into Maria's earlier story, by imagining for him the almost embarrassingly clichéd role of her heroic rescuer. That they have met before is hinted several times. In the unfinished scene where George comes to retrieve his escaped wife (modelled on the Hampstead scene in

89

Clarissa),[25] a gentleman appears to rescue Maria; his actual part in her delivery is unclear, as the scene is fragmented, and his identity is also undetermined. As editor, Godwin helps us make the connections, explaining that his wife had decided as an afterthought to make Darnford Maria's deliverer, but had not had time to work out the details (ibid., p. 175). Darnford's sketchiness in the plot reveals, however, that he is never more than a plastic dream man, a statue which Wollstonecraft tries positioning in different places without complete success, and who never really comes to life.

The end of the first, most finished, section of the text comes with the conclusion of Maria's narrative, which brings us full circle back to the madhouse. With Maria's discovery that she is 'buried alive', the manuscript ends suddenly: 'Some lines were here crossed out, and the memoirs broke off abruptly with the names of Jemima and Darnford' (ibid., p. 185). Darnford's name is the last word both of the manuscript and of the line of narrative proper; it marks where Wollstonecraft's difficulty in developing her story increases. She can get Maria back to where she started, so that the character becomes the author, but only through a circular plot line that is ultimately a reproduction of the enclosure of the madhouse.

The last of the remaining unfinished few pages are a series of fragments, isolated parts not shaped into a single whole, in which Wollstonecraft was trying to imagine what might happen to the lovers after leaving the prison. The connections between these fragments, like the relations of the lovers with each other and with society, is unclear. It seems somewhat severe to criticise an author for not completing a manuscript when a more final closure was imposed by the absolute authority of death. Moreover, the unfinished state of the text fixes it forever in the act of composition, enabling us to see the writer at work trying to pull the strands of the plot together. According to Godwin, Wollstonecraft in general had a great deal of uncharacteristic difficulty in writing her last work.[26] Left as it is, we can see the places in which she had particular trouble. While she is able to imagine three separate and effective individual narratives, she seems unable to imagine these coming together into a single, unified coherent story, or to imagine a satisfactory way for bringing the characters themselves together to a satisfactory resolution. What we have left is a series of fragments, in which making connections and creating a whole – both a community and a narrative – out of the characters and parts of the narrative is itself the problem.

Like Godwin, Wollstonecraft imagined antithetical endings for her story: several tragic ones and one that is comic, or rather romantic. In all versions, Maria escapes from the madhouse with the help of, not Darnford (who plays some part in her leaving but the real connection hasn't been thought out), but Jemima. As a typical sentimental hero, Darnford is too passive to accomplish anything so active and energetic as a rescue; moreover, Jemima's role here is a redemption of the figure of the servant, in which the slave of the system becomes a loyal retainer devoted to her mistress who gains the power to free Maria. This act anticipates, too, the establishment of the all-female world in the final ending. Freedom, however, first turns out only to be another version of the madhouse, when Maria comes up against the law. In response to her eloquent and rational plea for female freedom and self-determination, the judge responds with a caricature of Burkean prejudice and fear of change:

> For his part, he had always determined to oppose all innovation, and the new-fangled notions which incroached on the good old rules of conduct. We did not want French principles in public or private life – and, if women were allowed to plead their feelings, as an excuse or palliation of infidelity, it was opening a flood-gate for immorality.
>
> (ibid., pp. 198–9)

As in *Caleb Williams*, the individual is defeated by society, which crushes individuality as an enemy to its order. Those who truly think for themselves must be shut up, as social freedom is gained through blind obedience to authority.

The climactic trial scene is followed by several fragments. The relationship between Maria and Darnford has come to an end, foreseen after Maria's release from the madhouse, when his tender and sympathising nature begins to reveal signs of disguised selfishness. In the first series of the endings, which Godwin includes as a series of disconnected fragments, he betrays her; in one she commits suicide. Only one ending, which Godwin cannily positioned last, was more extensively sketched out. Wollstonecraft's final scene of fiction drew upon her own life, echoing her earlier suicide attempt after her rejection by Imlay. Art and life coincide as, like her creator, Maria swallows laudanum to escape from 'this hell of disappointment' (ibid., p. 202). Dying, her memories turn to her dead child, and to the hopes that in heaven she herself will find a supportive father; she gains a sense of herself as simultaneously a mother and a child in an ambiguous collapsing of familial roles and female identities. But just as she loses consciousness, memory becomes reality as, in the nick of time, Jemima rushes in, bearing the child who was not dead after all but hidden by Maria's husband and brother. Mother and child become two separate characters once more, who therefore can be reunited, as Maria quickly vomits up the poison, crying 'The conflict is over! I will live for my child!' (ibid., p. 203).

Like Godwin's second and published ending, Wollstonecraft's involves a reconciliation between a parental figure and a child. Godwin's text had shown a typical gothic dynamic of male oedipal relations in which the son ambiguously rebelled against the father, desiring both to overthrow him and to become him. As has been noted, Wollstonecraft draws upon the conventions of the female gothic, which replaces father–son relations with mother–daughter ones, relations which are obviously not oedipal but have their own complicated dynamics of identification and rivalry. As we will see further with Radcliffe and Lewis, the typical gothic plot suggests that the hero or heroine's development requires a coming to terms with his or her parental past. While for the male the recovery of familial relations is usually associated with oedipal antagonism which makes his goal of autonomy impossible, for Radcliffe and her followers the heroine's discovery of the identity of her true mother enables her to fulfil her proper female role in the private sphere. If the goal of male development is symbolically to become one's own father through the attainment of independence, the goal of proper female development is equally to become one's own mother, in marriage. Or, as Oscar Wilde later put it ironically: 'Every woman becomes like her mother. That is her tragedy.'

In Wollstonecraft's works in general the figure of the mother plays a significant role. Women's ability to be mothers is the one mark of sexual difference she admits in her egalitarian system. Moreover, motherhood gives her an image for female authority, as it requires the exercise of reason and the ability to take responsibility for dependents. In the present state of things, however, women's conditioning often makes them inadequate mothers. Many of Wollstonecraft's characters have either weak or neglectful mothers: those of Mary, Henry, Maria, Darnford, and Wollstonecraft herself are victims of the system who themselves perpetuate it. In the earlier sentimental and semi-autobiographical romance, *Mary*,

Mary's story opens with that of her mother, suggesting how the mother's tale determines the daughter's life. But to be motherless is equally undesirable; Jemima, who in this again resembles both Frankenstein's monster and author, had 'the misfortune of having been thrown into the world without the grand support of life – a mother's affection', to which lack she attributes the 'greater part of my misery' (ibid., p. 106). She still inherits from her mother a dubious legacy, however, as others constantly tell her 'that I was born a strumpet; it ran in my blood' (p. 108). In Wollstonecraft's version of the gothic family curse, 'the weakness of the mother will be visited on the children' (*Vindication*, p. 177).

Maria is an attempt to break this vicious cycle of female inheritance in which the daughter simply becomes the mother. The representation of the past is seen as in itself a means of breaking free from it. Certainly in the depiction of the heroine as herself a mother Wollstonecraft has made a revolutionary break from earlier literary conventions. Maria's story begins where most stories of female development end; the goal of the typical female sentimental quest is made the beginning of the revolutionary work. As I have already noted, *Maria* begins with a gothic flourish that disorients the reader and so makes us identify with the experience of the heroine. But there is a sudden shift, when the image of Maria's daughter restores her to herself, and to an identity that she associates with 'a mother's tenderness, a mother's self-denial' (*Maria*, p. 75). For both her and us to know who she is is to discover that she is a mother, who lives for others, and whose detachment from her child is seen as totally unnatural:

> Her infant's image was continually floating on Maria's sight, and the first smile of intelligence remembered, as none but a mother, an unhappy mother, can conceive. She heard her speaking half cooing, and felt the little twinkling fingers on her burning bosom – a bosom bursting with the nutriment for which this cherished child might now be pining in vain.
>
> (ibid., p. 75)

As many critics have noted, Wollstonecraft in general expresses a strong, deeply Puritan, distaste for the body, and for female sexuality in particular.[27] Female passion, rooted in the body but enflamed by an imagination too easily allied with appetite, leads to madness. Such bodily experience, however, is bound and redeemed in the act of mothering, as breast-feeding provides Wollstonecraft with an image for physical contact sublimated into a safely non-sexual and socially serviceable form.[28] Mothering is thus analogous to writing, a way of taking a cause of female degradation, female desire, and turning it into a cure. The two are further causally linked in the text, as it is because she is a mother that Maria writes her story. Mothering and writing are thus both parallel and sequential acts of creation which demonstrate how disorderly, regressive passions can be channelled and made progressive.

The text comes full circle when, at the end, Maria recovers her identity as a mother. This final reunion of mother and daughter stands in the place of the conventional union between the sexes, and as an alternative to the father–son rivalry common to the gothic and evident in *Caleb Williams*. However, this shift means that the novel retreats suddenly from the central problem of the relation between the sexes, into a world, like that of *Caleb Williams*, in which sexual difference has been eliminated with the establishment of an all-female community. To do so it in fact draws upon, while reversing, the pattern of the female gothic – already established by Radcliffe in *A Sicilian Romance* – in which the daughter's story ends when she discovers her mother is not dead after all but imprisoned by the evil father. The child helps liberate her parent, thus freeing herself also for her own marriage which will not repeat the errors of her parents. In *Maria*, however, it is the mother who herself has the power and authority to liberate her daughter and break the chain of tragic female inheritance. The reunion of mother and child, past and present, becomes a symbol of the hope of freeing the present from the past.

This ending, however, reproduces Maria's own constant repetition of imaginative error. It involves a generic regression in which the text that began with the gothic, then quickly moved into the realistic novel, finds a conclusion only through retreat into the benign, misty, wish-fulfilment world of the romance, symbolised by the baby at the mother's breast, in which, too, families are always reunited. It thus suggests the author's version of the error of the character with whom she over-identifies, and her inability to disentangle herself from the conventions she denounces.[29] Her own writing leads her back, not to madness, but to romantic fantasy. While exposing the fictitious plot, constructed by George and Maria's brother, the narrative itself falls prey to another, as it ends by gratifying the need for sentimental fictions it had previously attacked. Wollstonecraft strips away one fiction to reveal another,

94

as she swerves from an exposé of things as they are into a sentimental fantasy of the recovery of original bliss, a reunion in which
the dead are suddenly recalled to life. The mother herself is
suddenly given a divinatory power to raise the dead, in a sentimental
ending which suggests death and loss are merely patriarchal plots
which will disappear when exposed. Ironically and unintention-
ally, Wollstonecraft, like Rousseau, ends up by recovering the very
fictions she meant to uncover.

3   The Chymicall Wedding and the Bourgeois Marriage

This idea of conjoining the separated opposites in matter is
often described as the 'Chymicall Wedding' and depicted in
alchemical emblems as a coitus, often between a naked king
and queen. It is a marriage 'betwixt the agent and the patient
. . . male and female, Mercury and Sulphure vive'. In this
coitus is 'the sperme conceived', the seed of new form,
eventually to be born as the 'Philosophers' Child' or 'filius
macrocosmi', i.e. the Stone.

Charles Nicholl, *The Chemical Theatre*[1]

Wollstonecraft's death in childbirth which imposed premature
closure on her novel was allegorised by her enemies as a moral
cautionary tale of poetical justice. To conservatives, such as
Richard Polwhele, who attacked her in his poem *The Unsex'd Females*,
the radical woman was a gothic villainess, whose unnatural behaviour was finally punished by nature. The publication of *Maria*
was also a gothic event, in which life eerily echoed art. In the text
the mother sent a message to her daughter in case of her death;
for Mary Shelley, the text became a maternal voice speaking to her
daughter from beyond the grave. Moreover, in his assumption of
the role of editor of his late wife's last work, Godwin played Caleb
to her Falkland, as he too presented her work so that 'the world
may at least not hear and repeat a half-told and mangled tale'.[2]
Respecting his wife's last words, he kept editorial interference to a
minimum, publishing the text as it was left, full of gaps and loose
ends, and resisting the impulse to come between the author and
the reader by shaping the material. His own personal relation to
the author is never mentioned, as he takes a self-effacing role of

deferential subservience in appropriately Godwinian reverence for his wife's individuality and authority.[3]

However, Godwin's choice to publish the novel as part of Wollstonecraft's *Posthumous Works*, along with his own *Memoirs* of his wife, greatly affected audience reactions, and encouraged the tendency to read Wollstonecraft's writing autobiographically. Attempting to represent his wife with Godwinian objectivity, Godwin managed to offend both friends and foes with his calm revelation of her love affairs. Enemies denounced him for celebrating lust masquerading as enlightened behaviour, while Southey was disgusted by what he described as a cold unnatural act of dissection: Godwin showed 'a want of all feeling in stripping his dead wife naked'.[4] Ironically, however, Godwin's representation of their relationship drew on the language of perfect complementarity attacked by Wollstonecraft. He claimed that her passion balanced his reason, her typically female feeling his masculine thinking.[5] The two radicals are the perfect bourgeois couple, as the writer who had once denounced marriage as feudal tyranny came to idealise it after its loss as: 'the grand holiday of our human nature . . . the white spot, the little gleam of pure sunshine, which compensates for a thousand other hardships and calamities.'[6]

Shortly after Wollstonecraft's death also, Godwin began another gothic novel, which united and extended some of his concerns in *Caleb Williams* and hers in *Maria*, and which included portraits both of his wife and of marriage as an ideal. In the preface to *Travels of St Leon*, he explained how his ideas on marriage had changed since the *Enquiry Concerning Political Justice*: 'I apprehend domestic and private affections inseparable from the nature of man, and from what may be styled the culture of the heart, and am fully persuaded that they are not incompatible with a profound and active sense of justice in the mind of him that cherishes them. True wisdom will recommend to us individual attachments.'[7] From his own marriage, Godwin had learned Burke's belief that charity begins at home. The domestic sphere is not simply a microcosm reproducing social tyranny; inversely, it can be a true alternative, a place where loving relations are practised and from which they can extend out to redeem the public sphere, as: 'by kindling his sensibility, and harmonising his soul, they may be expected, if he is endowed with a liberal and manly spirit, to render him more prompt in the service of strangers and the public' (*St Leon*, p. x). The idealised family suggests a potential solution for bridging the gap between private and public, and particularly for showing how individuals can affect the social order rather than be mere effects of it.

In *St Leon*, marriage is paradise on earth,[8] as love between the sexes satisfies most completely the most essential of human needs:

> To feel that we are loved by one whose love we have deserved, to be employed in the mutual interchange of the marks of this love, habitually to study the happiness of one by whom our happiness is studied in return, this is the most desirable, as it is the genuine and unadulterated condition of human nature. I must have someone to sympathise with; I cannot bear to be cut off from all relations: I desire to experience a confidence, a concord, an attachment, that cannot rise between common acquaintance. In every state we long for some fond bosom on which to rest our weary head; some speaking eye with which to exchange the glances of intelligence and affection. Then the soul warms and expands itself; then it shuns the observation of every other beholder; then it melts with feelings that are inexpressible, but that the heart understands without the aid of words; then the eyes swim with rapture; then the frame languishes with enjoyment; then the soul burns with fire; then the two persons thus blest are no longer two; distance vanishes, one thought animates, one mind informs them. Thus love acts; thus it is ripened to perfection; never does man feel himself so much alive, so truly etherial, as when, bursting the bonds of diffidence, uncertainty and reserve, he pours himself entire into the bosom of the woman he adores.
>
> (ibid., pp. 39–40)

In this representation Godwin is echoing, with the enthusiasm of the convert, the emerging bourgeois conventions Wollstonecraft had attacked in her *Vindication*. Moreover, he extends by further idealising Rousseau's celebration of sexual difference, turning marriage into a sublimating force that refines human nature, a neoplatonic reconciliation of opposites, in which the two sexes become one. In the process, the bourgeois ideal merges with an earlier aristocratic one found in courtly love, in which human love is an image for spiritual desire.[9] Love becomes a reconciling force that heals all dualisms: self and other, material and ideal, male and female, even aristocratic past and bourgeois present.

In *St Leon*, however, it is not sufficient to heal the dualisms within the central figure. St Leon is a typical Godwinian hero, indebted to Rousseau,[10] who is torn between a need for autonomy and a deep desire for relations. In the text, these poles take the extreme form of a choice between marriage and gothic alienation. St Leon is divided between a sense of himself as 'formed to love' (ibid., p. 267), and yet born to be isolated: 'I was not a creature qualified for such dear and tender connections. I was destined by nature to wander a solitary outcast on the face of the earth' (p. 80). The internal conflict is embodied in two incompatible images of the ideal goals of human development, each of which seems to offer perfect happiness and harmony: marriage and the philosopher's stone. However, both are equally illusory images for union, especially imagined as the union between man and woman, which in fact create further polarisation and division.

Both of St Leon's impulses have obvious gender associations, as a traditionally female need for relationships is set against a stereotypical male need for independence. On the surface, the first seems to be associated also with a life of domestic happiness that is clearly middle class, and the second with heroic ideals of grandeur that appear feudal. The connection, often noted, between St Leon and Burke, seems therefore appropriate.[11] The text appears to set up an opposition between a desire for a life of private bourgeois content (female) and one for a life of public and feudal glory (male). St Leon's dying mother instills in him a sense that feudal honour, based on 'singleness and self-dependence', is the highest good. She reminds him: 'Remember your ancestors, knights of the Holy Cross. Remember your father. Follow your king' (ibid., p. 9). The Wandering Jew tells him further that the values exemplified by feudal male heroism are incompatible with domestic life, associated with women:

Was ever gallant action achieved by him who was incapable of separating himself from a woman? Was ever a great discovery prosecuted, or an important benefit conferred upon the human race, by him who was incapable of standing, and thinking, and feeling, alone? Under the usurping and dishonoured name of virtue, you have sunk into a slavery baser than that of the enchantress Alcina. In vain might honour, worth, and immortal renown proffer their favours to him who has made himself the basest of all sublunary things – the puppet of a woman, the plaything of her pleasure, wasting an inglorious life in the gratification of her wishes and the performances of her commands!

(ibid., p. 126)

After several pages of agonised internal conflict, St Leon agrees that by spending too much time with his family he has been 'uxurious and effeminate' (p. 137):

> To other men the domestic scene is the relaxation of their cares; when they enter it, they dismiss the business of the day, and call another cause. I only have concentrated in it the whole of my existence. By this means I have extinguished in myself the true energy of the human character. A man can never be respectable in the eyes of the world or in his own, except so far as he stands by himself and is truly independent. He may have friends; he may have domestic connections; but he must not in these connections lose his individuality.
>
> (p. 138)

He denounces himself for his ignominious retreat from the public sphere into the private world of the family.

St Leon thus introduces a common gothic theme, in which the tension between duty and desire, social order and the individual will, is embodied in a choice between marriage and service to a higher purpose or 'calling'. The Godwinian *Wieland*, *Frankenstein*, and *Jane Eyre*, for example, show individuals who must choose between private pleasure and public service. Superficially, these novels seem to suggest a valorisation of the bourgeois ideal of marriage, as the quest for a higher purpose is shown to be destructive. In *Wieland*, where the quest reveals its religious origins, as the hero feels that he has been called directly by God to destroy his family, it is clearly revealed as murderous. However, the texts also show that the conflict is itself produced by a separation of public and private that is bourgeois, and Protestant, in origins. For Burke, the feudal world was in fact based on an, albeit paternalistic, service of women, as heroic action was derived from not opposed to the love of women.[12] The modern world reveals, however, a fear of women and the home it creates as an ideal separate from the public sphere. As part of its reaction against Catholicism, Protestantism stressed the importance of active daily life in the public sphere as opposed to a contemplative life isolated from it.

Increasingly separated from the working world, the private world came to be seen as both a refuge from commercial enterprises and a potential distraction from one's higher calling. The Commonwealth argument that influenced the radicals of the 1790s maintained that: 'the release of civic virtue and patriotism required a turning away from private preoccupations to politics'.[13] Commonwealthmen 'urged men to move from the preoccupations of private life "to the higher engagements of public life"'.[14] Private life purged of public contamination has its own threat, in that it impedes action in the world, offering a seductively satisfying realm of pleasure and art that might prove hostile to social duties and struggle in the world. Domestic life is regressive rather than progressive. The home is potentially another false bower of bliss, invoked above by Godwin in the form of Ariosto's Alcina, impeding the true quest of bourgeois heroism that takes place in the marketplace and requires the independence that women threaten.

St Leon's character is thus a conflicting mixture of male and female, aristocratic and bourgeois, desires and values. As in all of Godwin's novels, character is determined by early circumstances. St Leon is crucially influenced by his early attendance at the heroic Field of the Cloth of Gold, which to him epitomises 'the age of chivalry' (ibid., p. 7), and the feudal values – honour, reputation – that he upholds. But it also marks the end of that age, and the beginning of a new commercial world which he denounces: the later defeat of Francis I gives 'a deadly wound to the reign of chivalry, and a secure foundation to that of craft, dissimulation, corruption, and commerce' (p. 26). Like Burke again, St Leon deplores the death of feudalism, and the degradation of human relations to economic bonds, representing it as a fall from glory into an age of base self-interest. Godwin himself, however, shared this concern with the effect of commerce upon human relations, as did Wollstonecraft, who complained that: 'The interests of nations are bartered by speculating merchants', and 'The sword has been merciful, compared with the depredations made on human life by contractors, and by the swarm of locusts who have battened on the pestilence they spread abroad.'[15] But while St Leon laments this fall, he significantly internalises it as he switches his attention from symbolic gold, representing the past chivalric world, to the literal gold he can win through gambling. His sudden obsession seems strange, especially as such a low occupation seems antithetical to his high origins. He, however, sees them as essentially and causally related: 'The whole tendency of my education had been to inspire me with a proud and restless desire of distinction' (p. 27). Mercantile greed is not opposed to aristocratic nobility but its direct descendant. St Leon therefore naturally develops a passion for gold that becomes his 'malignant genius' (p. 53), 'a demon that poisoned all my joys, that . . . drove me forth . . . a solitary wanderer on the face of the earth' (p. 68). Like Caleb, his own habit possesses him, becoming a force over which he has no control: 'There are habits of the mind and modes of occupying the attention, in which, when once we have engaged, there seems a sort of physical impossibility of ever withdrawing ourselves' (p. 258). Habit is 'sunk into my heart . . . twisted with all the fibres of my bosom' (p. 258); character becomes fate, as St Leon seems a typical Godwinian hero, a passive figure, driven by external events which call forth internal forces over which he has no control.

If the Field of the Cloth of Gold introduces gold into the novel as a symbolic substance, signifying nobility and worth, through gambling it comes to represent a more material substance. In turn, however, St Leon's gambling leads – if indirectly – to his knowledge of the philosopher's stone, which has as one of its properties the power to change base substances into gold. His turn to alchemy seems a return from low self-interest to a recovery of his higher heritage, especially as he plans to use his new transformational powers to help mankind. Yet alchemy is an ambivalent enterprise throughout the text, as it would have been for a rational philosopher who wanted to debunk all systems of superstition. From the seventeenth century on, alchemy was seen as the ancestor of modern enlightened science, 'a murky medieval half-light, out of which modern chemistry gradually began to emerge',[16] and therefore its opposite, as the embodiment of a primitive and superstitious time in which '"science" and "magic" were one and the same enterprise'.[17] Alchemy was a sign of the medieval belief in the intimate relation between spirit and flesh, human and nature. The alchemist's work depended upon the identification underlying apparent oppositions, as it aimed to turn matter into spirit. It did so by a process of 'dissolving and disintegrating, breaking down the physique of substance to free the "divine breath" or quintessential spirit within it'.[18] The alchemist saw himself as involved in 'a work of redemption: he was healing the corruption and chaos of matter'.[19] His art perfected nature, uniting body and spirit, death and rebirth, and, through the image of the 'chymicall wedding' for the philosopher's stone, the male and female principles.[20] Alchemy was a gothic enterprise of death and resurrection, based on a 'rhythm of breakdown and reconstruction, severing and synthesis'[21] which brought opposites together. Its symbolic potential was perceived by Christianity, which appropriated the stone as a type for Christ, and later by romantic poets, who saw in the process of sublimation a metaphor for the idealising powers of the imagination, which also 'turns/Bodies to spirit by sublimation strange',[22] as 'its secret alchemy turns to potable gold the poisonous waters which flow from death through life'.[23]

While modern science grew out of alchemy, it did so by finally repudiating it. Its original source was turned into its opposite, which was demonised and discredited as superstition. The alchemist's view of a nature embued with spirit and essentially related to human beings was replaced by the modern mechanistic view of nature as a machine from which humans are naturally detached. Baconian science, which dismissed mystery from the universe as a mere idol, replaced the alchemical relational stance with an oppositional one; as Charles Nicholl argues, Bacon 'typified that process of separation central to the scientific development of the seventeenth century – a disentangling of physical properties from metaphysical speculation; of empirical experiment from preconceived cosmological patterns; of, in Bacon's own words, "laborious and sober enquirie" from "high and vapourous imaginations". In this separation originates our own distinctions, that implicit frontier between science and magic.'[24] Such a model itself provides the means by which science can free itself from its murky, gothic origins, as it neatly and absolutely divides the pure, empirical and rational present from a contaminated, mystified or idolatrous past. This opposition was upheld by the increase in the seventeenth century of satirical attacks on the alchemist as a base deceiver and con artist,[25] attacks which were later revived during the French Revolution when illuminati, free masons, and secret societies were attacked as conspiracies established to destroy civilisation for their own base interests.

As Nicholl and others have noted, the separation of modern science from its own dark past was less absolute than it appeared; which at least partially explains the anxiety behind the need to create absolute differences.[26] As the rational present creates itself by defining itself against an irrational gothic past, any sign of similarity between the two threatens the identity of the present.

The past has to be something completely different. But like many of the radicals, Godwin's own political hopes, his dreams of prolonging life, drew on older hopes of gaining immortality through magical means.[27] Science was seen as being able to realise the dreams of the alchemist, as we will see with Victor Frankenstein, whose early reading of Paracelsus and Albertus Magnus influences his scientific projects.

Within *St Leon*, moreover, alchemy is an ambivalent enterprise, divided between the opposites of high and low, male and female, it claimed to reconcile. St Leon and his mysterious instructor conceive of it as noble and glorious. St Leon imagines himself, as his descendent Victor Frankenstein will later, as the source of immense good in the world, who will use base means to effect high purposes. The power to create gold is a means not an end, as St Leon realises that in the modern commercial world the wealthy man 'possesses the attribute which we are accustomed to ascribe to the Creator of the universe: he may say to a man, "Be rich," and he is rich. . . . He holds the fate of nations and of the world in his hand' (ibid., p. 162). Being all powerful he will be all good, as, like Godwin, he believes that 'Weakness and want are the parents of vice' (p. 163). Alchemy is no fraud here, it is a scientific power, in which base matter is turned into gold, which is then turned to high purposes. Moreover, it also bestows immortality on St Leon, fulfilling Godwin's utopian hope at the end of *Political Justice* of transcending nature, as 'for me the laws of nature are suspended; the eternal wheels of the universe roll backward; and I am destined to be triumphant over fate and time' (p. 163). However, while to St Leon the man with the philosopher's stone is a Godlike transformer of the world, to Marguerite he is a low, grasping, mercenary being: 'a projector and a chemist, a cold-blooded mortal, raking in the ashes of a crucible for a selfish and solitary advantage . . . all your dealings are secrecy and darkness' (*St Leon*, p. 210). From the female point of view, the male quest for glory is a base materialistic enterprise, opposed to the interests of the family.

In her attack Marguerite suggests a common ground between Godwin's enlightened rational belief that secrecy is a sign of deceit and oppression, and the conservative Burke's suspicion that idealistic projects of self-professed illuminati conceal the covert materialism of sheer self-interest. In their critique of individualism as disruptive of social order, gothic novels often establish a connection between privacy and duplicitous secrecy. Privacy is the necessary right of the individual, who must be free to exercise his will in his own home. The 1790s use of spies was thus an invasion of the right of privacy. But it is a telling one that suggests, too, a suspicion frequently expressed by Godwin (himself a rather furtively private person), that privacy is proof of guilt. Falkland's secrecy is a result of his crime; St Leon's is a sign of his guilty secret, and his son Charles expresses Godwin's own opinion concerning the need for openness and sincerity between men: 'A just and a brave man acts fearlessly and with explicitness; he does not shun, but courts, the scrutiny of mankind; he lives in the face of day, and the whole world confesses the clearness of his spirit and the rectitude of his conduct' (ibid., p. 189). St Leon's innocent young daughter also tells him, 'I think none but bad people lock and bolt themselves up so. It puts mind of the giants with their drawbridges and their pitfalls' (p. 132). Isolation permits the recreation of the torture chamber in the privacy of one's own home. St Leon himself defends the government intervention in private lives which Godwin had attacked, claiming that: 'the prime source of individual security in human affairs, [is] that whatever any man does, may be subjected to examination, and whatever does not admit of being satisfactorily accounted for, exposes him whom it concerns to the most injurious suspicions' (p. 199).[28] Secret societies especially are therefore suspected of being up to no good, as both Burke and countless gothic novels illustrate. As the translator of *Horrid Mysteries* claims, secret associations which originate in a desire to fight systems of oppression became themselves new forms of tyranny for the very reason that they are private, and cannot be monitored; 'benevolence needs no mysterious veil', and mystery protects only deception. He therefore warns his readers against listening to 'the seducing voice of secret, corresponding, and other societies of a similar nature, that pretend to reform the defects of government, while selfish views are concealed under the imposing outside of philosophy and patriotism'.[29]

For St Leon, secrecy and privacy finally make all human relations impossible. Where the aim of science was to dispel mystery, alchemy requires it. St Leon becomes omnipotent, an unmoved mover of ideal Godwinian objectivity: 'I was like a God, who dispenses his bounties profusely through twenty climates, but who at the same time sits, separate, elevated, and alone, in the highest heaven' (ibid., p. 377). But the pursuit of knowledge that sets him above nature isolates him from others, who see him as an unnatural subhuman creature of a different species, like Jemima and Frankenstein's monster: 'a monster that did not deserve to exist' (p. 363). Alchemy and marriage are especially incompatible; his power depends upon concealment, and the most intimate and ideal form of relations, while it requires reverence, cannot be built on secrecy. Marguerite tells him: 'It sets too great a distance between the parties. It destroys the communion of spirit which is the soul of the marriage-tie' (p. 209). As St Leon later realises, 'Mystery was the great and unconquerable bane of my situation ... the poisonous influence of mystery' (pp. 393–4). Knowledge creates a form of privacy that is the opposite of the private world of the family as it obscures relations and so keeps human beings apart. Knowledge destroys the connubial paradise:

> In my domestic scene I beheld the golden age renewed, the simplicity of pastoral life without its grossness, a situation remote from cities and courts, from traffic and hypocrisy, yet not unadorned with taste, imagination, and knowledge. Never was a family more united in sentiments and affection. Now all this beauteous scene was defaced! All was silence, suspicion, and reserve. ... Though corporally, we might sit in the same apartment, in mind a gulf, wide, impassable, and tremendous, gaped between us.
>
> (pp. 199–200)

His inability to share his knowledge with his wife creates an unbridgeable gap between them, and she finally pines away. His relations with his children are similarly destroyed. He loses his family and further, like Caleb, his reputation, as he is suspected of all sorts of crimes. His only relation is to the reader, to whom alone he can express the feelings that elsewhere he must hide. But his relationship with the reader is one of absolute distance and difference rather than identification, for he tells his story as a moral cautionary tale to prevent others from following on his quest: 'Let no man, after me, pant for the acquisition of the philosopher's stone!' (p. 466).

St Leon's situation is doubled however in the figure of the equally alienated Bethlem Gabor. Gabor is a version of the robber who has turned to crime because of the injustice of society – in this case the murder of his family. His story seems a variation on that of St Leon, who is therefore drawn to him, as someone with whom he can sympathise and identify: 'There was a similarity in our fortunes that secretly endeared him to me. We had each by the malice of a hostile destiny, though in a very different manner, been deprived of our families; we were each of us alone. Fated each to be hereafter for ever alone; we blended ourselves the one with the other as perfectly as we could' (p. 398). In his desperate need for friendship, he finds a degree of likeness in this taciturn 'creature of another nature' (p. 397).

This apparent identity hides a deep enmity. What St Leon sees as similarity, Gabor, however, perceives as absolute difference. He hates St Leon because:

> Instead of, like me, seeking occasions of glorious mischief and vengeance, you took upon yourself to be the benefactor and parent of mankind. . . . With the spirit of a slave who, the more he is beaten, becomes the more servile and submissive, you remunerated injuries with benefits. . . . Chicken-hearted wretch! poor, soulless poltroon! . . . I hate the man in whom kindness produces no responsive affection, and injustice no swell, no glow of resentment. I hated you the more, because, having suffered what I had suffered, your feelings and conduct on the occasion have been the reverse of mine. Your character, I thank God! is of all beings the most opposite to that of Bethlem Gabor.
>
> (p. 416)

Gabor is the satanic gothic villain, caught in a circle of revenge, in which injustice perpetuates itself. St Leon resists this cycle; while Gabor's hatred provokes in him 'resistance' and rouses him to 'opposition' (p. 423), it is never answered with hatred. After Gabor's death, he pays a tribute to him as 'a great and admirable man. He had within him all the ingredients of sublimity' (p. 427). Like Caleb, and later the monster of Frankenstein, he speaks justly of his dead tormentor. But St Leon's attempts to break out of the cycle of revenge, as Caleb did, by repaying hatred with love and objective admiration, constantly prove as disastrous as the most destructive machinations of his enemy. His good intentions ruin all those he cares for, as his dreams come true as nightmares: 'the curse of the *opus magnum* attend[ed] upon my projects, and render[ed] all my exertions abortive . . . still, still my evil genius pursued me, and blasted every concern in which I presumed to interfere' (p. 466). Cause and effect are again opposed, as good motives have, alas, disastrous consequences, especially as his benevolence is misinterpreted by an ungrateful society as devious self-interest. While St Leon blames his fate and evil genius, in a pre-emptive self-defense, Godwin seems intent on blaming also an ignorant and superstitious society who suspiciously sees a benevolent enlightened man as a malicious power of darkness. The alchemist becomes a version of the alienated individual, persecuted by a society that is suspicious of all powers it cannot understand, and therefore of all non-conformity; he is both Burke (the upholder of the feudal mystique) and Godwin himself, denounced after 1798 by an ungrateful public.[30]

With good intentions, St Leon chooses alchemy as a means of helping humanity, only to find that his knowledge alienates him from it. He becomes a solitary wanderer whose story is potentially endless, as death cannot offer closure. The text ends, however, through a peculiar reunion between an alienated parent and child when, in a suitably dramatic and epic action, St Leon's son accidentally frees him from Gabor's prison. The son's heroic rescue of the father suggests a revision of the parental relations at the end of both *Caleb Williams* and *Maria*. While in the latter, the parent had rescued the child, here the son rescues the parent. Moreover, the ending reverses that of *Caleb Williams* in which the son's tale suddenly turned into that of the father, as St Leon's own story is concluded with that of his son. His story ends as he asserts his identity as a father, 'I was the hero's father', and so consoles himself that 'this busy and anxious world of ours yet contains something in its stores that is worth living for' (*St Leon*, p. 478). The work concludes with a sense of genealogical succession, in which the end of the father's narrative becomes the beginning of that of the son.

While the narrative thus creates a sense of inheritance, it does so by depending upon a fiction of disinheritance, and a radical break with the past. St Leon must finally be left behind, as he represents a static force that cannot progress – arrested development on a large scale, as 'for me the laws of nature are suspended; the eternal wheels of the universe roll backward' (p. 21). Father and son, related essentially through sequence, are therefore set up as mirror images of each other, of regress and progress. Like St Leon, Charles is eager for friendship because of his own isolation. The father's text ends with the son's version of the same family romance which shows his own development into the isolated hero who was able to rescue his own father. In leaving St Leon, Charles had announced: 'I must henceforth stand by myself, as if a man could be author of his own existence' (p. 193). He became a totally isolated and autonomous being, as he describes himself: 'I am alone in the world. I have no father, no mother, and no brethren. I am an exile from my country, and cut off for ever from those of my own lineage and blood' (p. 438). The disastrous quest of the father gives the son a legitimate reason for breaking from his family; the father's guilt frees the son from any potential separation guilt of his own. In leaving his family, he is able to become the ideal bourgeois self-made man, independent and 'the author of his own existence'. Freed from all normal relations, he can create himself anew, without the burden of the past, like an ideal gothic orphan whose detachment from the past is potentially liberating for self-creation.

Furthermore, the son's story breaks with his father's by reversing it. In desiring a power that reconciles opposites, St Leon sought what he already had in the form of marriage. By seeking a unifying power he creates division. His story is the Frankensteinian one in which an idealistic male quest for knowledge and power destroys the female world of love and the family. He becomes a romantic wanderer, like the Ancient Mariner, trapped in a never-ending story. Charles's story, however, proceeds from isolation to relation, as he regains the paradise that his father had foolishly lost. Forced to leave relationships, to become totally self-sufficient, the son is ultimately rewarded with a marriage of his own. After a few more trials and misunderstandings, caused again by St Leon's backfiring benevolence, Charles marries the woman who is the perfect complement for him: soft and delicate where he is strong and rugged. He is restored to the paradise of marriage lost by his father. In this new Eden, there is no place for St Leon, whom Charles, ignorant of his father's real identity, knows only through his public reputation as an evil sorcerer. The model oedipal son, tidily disentangled from oedipal guilt, he breaks completely with his past to create new ideal relations for the future. As the text ends abruptly, the discontinuity between the generations is shown. In contrast to *Caleb Williams'* relentlessly unified form, the general structure of *St Leon* is wandering, baggy, and thus more typically gothic. Moreover, as it follows St Leon's life, the story is potentially endless. Closure is brought about through a disruption in the line of succession and narrative as the book suddenly and arbitrarily stops.

As in *The Castle of Otranto*, the present must detach itself completely from the contamination of a corrupt past. Forced to break with the past, to leave his family, Charles is freed to develop into a middle class ideal of autonomy and self-determination. Like science detaching itself from its murky alchemical roots, he creates his new identity by freeing himself from his past. But if the end breaks succession, it also creates it, as the father's endless wandering, his circular life, mirrored in the repetitive structure of the text, is both erased and fulfilled by his son's teleological narrative of development. Together the narratives of father and son form an alchemical process of a 'circular . . . going-out and coming-back',[31] as the text presents a domestic version of falling and rising, a paradise lost and regained. Paradise, in the form of marriage, is restored when the present frees itself from the past, whose guilt justifies this separation. But free to become whatever it wants, the present returns to, repeats and revises, the past. Feudal life is recovered on a bourgeois principle, as right by birth is replaced by right by merit; the disinheritance from the past allows the son to earn for himself what the father had been born with and lost: domestic bliss *and* a life of heroic soldiering. The son thus puts together what the father took apart, becoming a place where polarised values, including those encapsulated in marriage and alchemy, meet. Whereas *Caleb Williams* and *Maria* experimented with antithetical conclusions of alienation and reunion, in *St Leon* both possibilities converge. The ending brings together the tragedy of the eternally alienated individual, the father, and the romance of the son, who represents an idealised reconciliation of its central conflicts. Through him, the repudiation of the past becomes the means of recovering it in its 'true' and 'pure' form – which is to say the form that ratifies the needs and values of the present.

Part III

Part III

1 From Here to Here:
Radcliffe's Plot of Female Development

ぐ鲞ン

In their uses of gothic conventions, both Godwin and Wollstonecraft are reacting to the works of Ann Radcliffe, traditionally seen as the originator of the conservative female gothic. For Scott she was 'the first poetess of romantic fiction', who is also among the few who can be truly called: 'the founders of a class, or school. She led the way in a peculiar style of composition, affecting powerfully the mind of the reader . . . appealing to those powerful and general sources of interest, latent sense and supernatural awe, and curiosity concerning whatever is hidden and mysterious.' She is the mistress of suspense, who put Burke's theories of the sublime into action, and: 'Made use of obscurity and suspense, the most fertile source, perhaps, of sublime emotion; for there are few dangers that do not become familiar to the firm mind, if they are presented to consideration as certainties, and in all their open and declared character; whilst, on the other hand, the bravest have shrunk from the dark and doubtful.' Her art was one of conceal-ment, of 'throwing the narrative into mystery, affording half inti-mations of veiled and secret horrors'.[1] Her use of secrecy extended to her private life, which she – unlike Rousseau or Godwin and Wollstonecraft – jealously protected. A shy and retiring member of a well-off middle-class family, she was rather embarrassed about her public career as an author: as the Edinburgh Review noted after her death, she 'never appeared in public, nor mingled in private society, but kept herself apart, like the sweet bird that sings its solitary notes, shrouded and unseen'.[2] Radcliffe here anticipates Shelley's description of the ideal artist as a romantic nightingale, who influences society by being outside of it.[3] However, for her as for Falkland and St Leon, the guarding of privacy made her in fact more open to public speculations; the mystery of her own life stimulated the public's imagination to construct a suitable fiction around it, and it was rumoured that she had been driven mad by her own stories. While the artist demand-ed a total separation of her art and life, her audience, educated by reading gothic novels, insisted that the two were the same.

The bifurcation of Radcliffe's life, divided between an eventless life and sensational literature, is in many ways a subject of her work, especially her most famous creation, *The Mysteries of Udolpho,*

113

which explores the relation between female madness, passion, and the dangers of the indulged imagination. As Wollstonecraft feared, the paucity of women's lives causes them to indulge their overactive imaginations, filling lacks with their fantasies which, unrestrained by reason, can lead to madness. Emily's story is in fact a limited one in which, despite her endless to and froing from place to place, little actually happens to her. For David Durant therefore, *The Mysteries of Udolpho* is a novel of anti-education, or *Unbildung*, in which Emily remains unchanged by her experiences, learning nothing from the events she passively endures.[4] However, this surface stasis is a result of Radcliffe's disinterest in character, and character development, in favour of plot development. Change occurs not through natural internal processes in Emily but through sometimes embarrassingly artificial external fictions. Plot, not character, is the agent of action in Radcliffe's world, and the hero is the author who alone has the power to make things happen and instigate change. *The Mysteries of Udolpho* is Radcliffe's attempt to work within while expanding the conventional restrictions on women denounced by Wollstonecraft, which force them in life to be static, unchanging beings who can never mature, and in literature demands equally that heroines be born pure, and, in order to remain so, be denied any experiences at all.

The opening setting draws attention to the timelessness and suspense of Emily's childhood idyll. She lives in harmony with nature and her loving parents in a never-never world, a truly happy valley called, appropriately if unimaginatively, 'La Vallée'. La Vallée is a sheltered and highly sentimental world, a version of a Rousseauian ideal community, presided over by the wise and benevolent St Aubert.[5] As has often been noted, Radcliffe's characters are not individuals in any meaningful sense, for Radcliffe attacks the whole concept of individualism, which she, like Burke, sees as threatening to community. Her characters, like her settings, tend to be generic. St Aubert is a stock figure of the wise father who, like all of Radcliffe's types, is found in her other novels as well. In its most pure form, this type appears in the figure of La Luc in the *Romance of the Forest*, where he is clearly derived from Rousseau's Savoyard vicar. Wollstonecraft's oddly twinned enemies, the reactionary Burke and the revolutionary Rousseau, are united by Radcliffe, as benign influences on her work who, as we will see later (pp. 137–8), merge finally with the authorial guardian spirit of Milton. Strikingly, considering his infamous abandonment of his children, Rousseau appears in Radcliffe's image of the good and responsible father, exemplified in St Aubert, who:

> endeavoured, therefore, to strengthen her mind; to enure her to habits of self-command; to teach her to reject the first impulse of her feelings, and to look, with cool examination, upon the disappointments he sometimes threw in her way.[6]

Radcliffe rather flagrantly redeems Rousseau through revision; he is magically transformed from a transgressive individual and notoriously irresponsible father into the paternal setter of limits. He becomes a figure for the good father who doesn't indulge his children (Radcliffe will show later the disastrous consequences of that) but accustoms them to the frustrations of their will that social life will require. Even in isolation, Emily is being prepared for life in society, which means accepting that one cannot have one's own way. Emily's education, both with her father and after his death, involves further learning to find a middle course of balanced self-government, in which sentiment is not repressed into a cold, unfeeling stoicism but controlled by the higher faculty of reason, as: 'happiness arises in a state of peace, not of tumult. It is of a temperate and uniform nature, and can no more exist in a heart, that is continually alive to minute circumstances, than in one that is dead to feeling' (*Udolpho*, p. 80).

If St Aubert is a version of Rousseau, Emily is a feminised 'Emile', whose course is a gothic variation on his progress from isolation to social integration. Rousseau counsels that the child be raised in isolation, away from the corruption of society, to become secure in himself, so that when he enters the public sphere he will be able to withstand its evil influences. La Vallée is for Emily such a world of isolation, her version of the Crusoesque island idealised by Rousseau. It is an Edenic world of innocence, and harmony between parents and child, humans and nature. The opening scenes of La Vallée suggest a muted natural world, that obligingly corresponds to human feeling, echoing sensitively St Aubert's 'pensive melancholy' (ibid., p. 2). It is a world of shade, in which it seems to be always St Aubert's favourite time of day – the threshold time of evening, which hovers between day and night, light and darkness. The deaths of St Aubert's two sons have introduced a gentle sense of loss into this garden, and the disappearance of Emily's portrait a sense of mystery. Yet this is clearly a world of gentle obscurity rather than the sublime, a world modeled on the mood of 'Il Penseroso', and Milton's description of Paradise. While in this world, St Aubert and Emily can speculate fancifully about the presence of supernatural forces, and safely indulge their imaginations as they are restrained by the gentle force of reason.[7] Nature and art meet in the image of the peasant's dance: 'The peasants of this gay climate were often seen on an evening, when the day's labour was done, dancing in groups on the margins of the river' (ibid., p. 3). This liminal geographical and temporal location is suggestive. La Vallée is a threshold world, built on a river, near beautiful pastoral fields, but cut off from the outside world by mountains that shelter and protect it:

> To the south, the view was bounded by the majestic Pyrenees, whose summits, veiled in clouds, or exhibiting awful forms, seen, and lost again, as the partial vapours rolled along, were sometimes barren, and gleamed through the blue tinge of air, and sometimes frowned with forests of gloomy pine, that swept downward to their base. These tremendous precipices were contrasted by the soft green of the pastures and woods that hung upon their skirts; among whose flocks, and herds, and simple cottages, the eye, after having scaled the cliffs above, delighted to repose.
>
> (ibid., p. 1)

The opening setting thus brings together into a picturesque whole the two types of landscape which will become polarised later in the text, when Emily's travels take her to places which exemplify either the awful sublime of mountains or the soft beautiful of a pastoral rural world. As in Burke, the two aesthetic principles have clear gender associations, the sublime with the male and the beautiful with the female.[8] La Vallée itself unites male and female elements, which also outside its harmonious boundaries will become opposed.

The idealisation of La Vallée as a place where opposites are harmoniously intertwined is itself, however, part of a pattern of oppositions within the text. One of the most common of these is a contrast which itself draws on the antithetical sources of Rousseau and Burke, again joined together by Radcliffe. This is the opposition between the natural, simple, happy, and loving country, a private realm of the family governed by sentiment and sympathy, and the artificial, cruel, mercenary, and hypocritical city (especially Paris, seen as the centre of decadence), inhabited by isolated individuals who are ruled by self-interest. We are told that St

Aubert brought his family to this place to escape from a corrupt and corrupting society. La Vallée is thus the epitome of the idealised private world of selflessness and benign relations which is set in opposition to the public realm of self-interest, male conflict, and aggression, represented most literally in the Italian civil war that lurks in the background of the story. Yet the two antithetical worlds also define each other, as a necessary and natural relation exists between them. Each of Emily's parents has a sibling who is part of that outside world and yet can enter into La Vallée; more importantly, it is ultimately only through entrance into this wider world that Emily will be able to develop.

Emily's movement from an isolated world into the social one, from a situation of detachment from social relations to an involvement in them, is a gothic version of the process of education Rousseau imagines in *Emile*. However, whereas Emile can naturally enter into society, it is only by means of circumstances beyond her control which leave her purity and passivity as a heroine unquestioned that Emily is ejected from her happy valley, as Radcliffe resorts to the extreme but time-honoured authorial device of parental elimination. Left to her own devices, Emily clearly would never have gone anywhere at all, and it is only through external intervention that she is irritated into action from her state of original pleasing inertia. From being a member of a close-knit family, Emily finds herself suddenly the archetypal gothic heroine: an unprotected orphan, alone, helpless, and without the power of self-determination, in a foreign land.

Emily's initial development is thus set up not as a natural transition but as an abrupt fall from a state of community into one of isolation: a historical and personal shift from childhood and a feudal kinship system into a bourgeois marketplace of adult individuality. Her responses to her experiences will suggest the dangers of solipsism as an extreme form of modern individuality. Generically, moreover, she is suddenly thrust from a sentimental past into a gothic present. The two worlds, and stages of Emily's life, seem totally opposed. However, the new world she enters is also clearly a nightmare version of her own perfect past, in which many of the elements of La Vallée are exaggerated and replayed in a gothic form. Outside the gentle world of La Vallée, in which mountains sheltered the family, Emily is suddenly surrounded by dangerously sublime landscapes of 'the higher regions of the air, where immense glaciers exhibited their frozen horrors, and eternal snow whitened the summits of the mountains' (ibid., p. 42), ones which also show '"beauty sleeping in the lap of horror"' (p. 55), and in which Emily constantly expects to find lurking banditti.

Similarly, Emily's parents are replaced by a series of gothic parental substitutes. The original parents, married for love, are replaced by Mme Cheron and Montoni, married through reciprocal swindling, a couple who are in fact deadly enemies. Moreover, this typical reduction of male and female to opposite principles has consequences for the relations *within* the sexes as well as *between* them. Like Mary Wollstonecraft, Radcliffe is concerned with the way in which female rivalry, rather than bonding, is the product of the separation of the sexes.[9] Mme Cheron's only means of power is tormenting those women who are weaker than herself. Isolated in the domestic world, confined in the various spaces of the novel, women fight amongst themselves for male attention. Similarly, left to themselves, men become caught up in oedipal conflict, present in the text in foreign civil wars and quarrels between the villains (who ultimately manage to neatly bump each other off). These take place largely outside of Emily's vision, being part of the social forces that determine her fate but of which she as a female cannot know. The division of the sexes not only turns them against each other, but creates civil war within the separate spheres.

Emily's own marriage to Valancourt is established early as a means of recreating the happiness of the parents. Valancourt is Emily's Adam, a young version of St Aubert, the perfect sentimental feminised hero: sensitive and cultured (he reads Petrarch, appreciates nature, and his favourite time of day is the evening), a sheep in wolf's clothing.[10] Their marriage, based on complementarity and love, is interrupted and replaced (literally, as the preparations for the first are used for the second) by that of Mme Cheron and Montoni. As a parody not only of the parents but also of the sentimental union between Emily and Valancourt, the gothic marriage between Montoni and Mme Cheron becomes the central barrier to the sentimental ideal.

A figure, therefore, for both the gothic father and bridegroom (who in later gothic fictions become increasingly identified), Montoni especially represents division in the text. His name makes his generic plot function clear: he is to play the role of the forbidding father who keeps the lovers apart, just as the Alps do in

Emily's imagination. However, mountains play an ambiguous part in the text: at the opening, they offer protection and shelter; during Emily and her father's journey they come to represent the sublime; afterwards, through association, they represent for Emily both her father and Valancourt, with whom she first encountered them.[11] For the lovers, however, they become a symbol of separation and for the complete, demonically sublime and gothically paternal, power Montoni has over Emily. Mountains thus suggest a male power which, originally protective and unifying, associated with her father and her fatherlike lover, becomes divisive and threatening as Emily develops.

Udolpho is a gothic version of La Vallée. Like La Vallée it is detached from society, but its isolation is a sign of the total power of its ruler who, far from social restraints, is able to exercise his own will. It is a private space where the freedom of uncontrolled individualism is destructive, as also in the case of Laurentini whose abandonment to her own passions within these walls – we learn later – had murderous consequences. La Vallée was isolated to keep *out* exactly the forces, passions, and conflict, that Udolpho, like the castle in Poe's 'Masque of the Red Death', will wall *in*. The first description of the ruined, and therefore sublime, building, emphasises its power. As has often been noticed, Radcliffe's characters are measured by their responsiveness to nature, suggesting the interdependence of virtue and taste;[12] furthermore, a building or city's relationship to its natural surroundings is telling of its true nature. La Vallée was in harmony with the natural world; Venice, through which Emily passes on her way to Montoni's castle, parodies La Vallée as an image for a false sublimation of nature into art; Udolpho, however, totally dominates the natural world: 'Silent, lonely and sublime, it seemed to stand the sovereign of the scene, and to frown defiance on all, who dared to invade its solitary reign' (ibid., p. 227).

The castle's sublime rule over the natural world mirrors Montoni's total authority over Emily within it. Montoni is the human version of the sublimity of the mountains, whose impenetrability reveals to Emily her lack of power over her own fate and keeps her in the dark; she complains: 'Oh could I know . . . what passes in that mind; could I know the thoughts, that are known there, I should no longer be condemned to this torturing suspense' (p. 243). Udolpho is a private domestic sphere of feudal power, based on the absolute authority of the despotic lord. At the same time, however, as being a feudal tyrant, Montoni is equally an example of the modern possessive individual, motivated only by his own avaricious will. Emily suspects Montoni to be the leader of banditti; while this proves incorrect, he is out to steal her property and, as a leader of mercenary forces, he – like St Leon – combines feudal activities with modern commercial values. He is the isolated individual who rejects society's restraints in order to gratify his will in privacy. His main vice is not lust but avarice (like St Leon again he is a gambler), reinforcing the central conflict between relations based on love and those based on greed. He is a version of the rational schemer who, like most gothic villains, disdains superstition. In this he becomes a gothic St Aubert, who also advises Emily to control herself, and endure patiently what she cannot change. Several times Montoni scolds her for succumbing to romantic feelings, and chides her for being a baby. But if he urges Emily to be a self-controlled adult, it is only so that he can indulge his own uncontrolled will. His vision of female maturity is that of total acquiescence to male authority; in his terms, self-control means complete abdication of female control and will to male sublime power. The rational self-government advocated by St Aubert is perverted by Montoni into stoic submission, seen as the only possible fate for a woman in a world controlled by men.

Although Udolpho is an embodiment of Montoni's gothic and sublime authority, the figure of the castle is an ambiguous one. From Walpole on, it is a stock gothic property, one frequently with a livelier and more active role than that of any character, which has been read as a symbol of both patriarchal power and the maternal body.[13] As in *Otranto*, the question of the ownership of the castle is central to the mystery of the narrative it dominates. Udolpho is Montoni's property, but like the other spaces Emily will spend time in, it is also associated with a woman – in this case, the original and rightful owner whose place Montoni has perhaps wrongfully assumed. Behind ('underneath' is a better spatial metaphor, especially considering Radcliffe's earlier *Sicilian Romance*, or Lewis's later *Castle Spectre*) the present male owner of the castle is a female possessor. From Walpole Radcliffe inherits a concern with inheritance itself, and the question of the rightful ownership of property. She, too, draws upon the authority of Shakespeare; echoes from *Hamlet*, especially (the scenes with the superstitious sentinels, numerous references to Montoni's Claudius-like carousing, direct quotations and allusions during the scenes with Sister Agnes), use allusion as a textual background to suggest that below the surface narrative lurks a story of usurpation. What is unusual, too, is that the suggested dispossession and perhaps murder is of a female by a male. Is this a subversive myth of the usurpation of female property and power by a patriarchal order?[14] Does the fortress, then, like Wollstonecraft's madhouse, represent the confines that men impose upon women to deprive them of their rightful powers?

Like *Maria's* madhouse, Udolpho is a place of confinement in which the repressed female imagination is able to escape and run riot. Readers have often been quite critical of Emily's behaviour at Udolpho, claiming she indulges her imagination in a way which will require ultimate authorial correction.[15] She becomes obsessed with a series of mysteries: her father's odd behaviour, the disappearance of Laurentini, the strange music heard at La Vallée, near the Convent St Clair, and also at Udolpho. Most significant and horrifying of all is something Emily sees in a room at Udolpho. Her servant Annette tells her that behind a black veil in the room is a picture of the vanished woman, Laurentini; but when the curious Emily finally succumbs to the impulse to lift the veil, we are only told that what is revealed was 'no picture' (ibid., p. 249). We, like Austen's Catherine Morland, are left to infer that if it's not a representation of Laurentini it must be the real thing – her body, the signified itself rather than a mere sign. For us, as for both Emily and Catherine, the black veil becomes a symbol for all mysteries, which serves to link them together, suggesting a common origin. However, this fixation on the veil itself reveals that Emily's connection of the various occurrences has a dubious basis. Her interpretive method is associative and analogic rather than rational, as she groups together the various mysteries she encounters. In this her mind mirrors the apparent structure of the text itself, which is based on association, the faculty denounced by Locke as subversive of rational order, and by Wollstonecraft as particularly insidious for women.[16]

What Emily's imagination links together through association, Radcliffe will pull apart with reason. Emily, hearing the same mysterious music at Udolpho she heard earlier at La Vallée, posits a single source for the two, and identifies that source as Valancourt. The truth revealed defies such neat and tidy plotting, as the ghostly musician turns out to be an unidentified flying Frenchman named Du Pont, imprisoned by Montoni, in love with Emily, who rather abruptly, unexpectedly and, indeed, accidentally, helps rescue our heroine. Such an abrupt and messy introduction of a new character seems intensely irritating and a flagrant violation of the codes of authorial integrity, which undermines our faith in Radcliffe's competence not to mention control. Yet it turns out that Du Pont has been in the text all along, as his existence clears up some of the mysteries from the beginning of the novel. In general, in the last half of the book, elements submerged in the first part – of which neither Emily nor the reader could possibly have had previous knowledge – are brought to light in order to provide rational explanations for the earlier mysteries. Again, this seems to violate our expectations concerning novelistic and aesthetic coherence: you just *don't* suddenly introduce new characters to solve old mysteries and to do so seems a sign of sheer sloppiness. As we will see in a moment, Radcliffe will do this frequently, and provide solutions that seem in different ways to be cheats. Through this process of gradual enlightenment and clumsily artificial revelation, Emily's past and present, as well as the beginning and end of the novel, are brought together.

Such a bringing together, however, depends upon a process of detachment and separation, an undoing of Emily's associations and, at times, of the narrative structure itself. As readers have often complained, the episodes at Udolpho form in fact only a small part of the book. The relation between the gothic and the sentimental parts of the text seems at times as tenuous as that between the gothic and realistic parts of Austen's spoof on Radcliffe, *Northanger Abbey*. Similarly, the different places which Emily visits – La Vallée, Toulouse, Venice, Udolpho, the rural retreat to which Emily is taken briefly from Udolpho, Chateau-le-Blanc, the convent of St Clair – at first seem totally unrelated except through contrived narrative accidents.

The text spends considerable time in these different spaces. Yet what is also foregrounded is the lengthy journey that links the various parts and places of the novel together. As Emily and St Aubert first set out from La Vallée we are told that 'instead of taking the more direct road' that would get them quickly to their destination they choose one that, 'winding over the heights, afforded more extensive views and greater variety of romantic scenery' (ibid., p. 27). We are certainly going to be subjected to lots of views and scenery in *Udolpho*, as the narrative takes its winding way to get to its goal. The unfolding of the story is impeded by deferral and repetition that keeps it from quickly reaching its obvious destination of wedded bliss. The real barrier in the text is the proliferation of plot, the multiplication of episodes that Radcliffe, more despotic than any aunt, seems arbitrarily and artificially to construct. Various things interrupt the narrative flow and serve to arrest time and development: the subplot; Emily's poetic effusions and moments of intense lyric feeling; the repeated descriptive passages which freeze the action; the fragmentation of the stories told by other characters – which are usually told in bits and pieces, begun at one time, then interrupted, and deferred till a later time, preferably after midnight in a cell equipped with the requisite 'human scull and bones, lying beside an hour-glass' (p. 577). Radcliffe also often uses Walpole's figure of the loquacious servant who cannot get to a point, and whose speeches become a comic version of her own construction of suspense and narrative through indirection and deferral.

Narrative progression is arrested or at least suspended through these various devices. Although the story moves from the stasis of La Vallée into a world of action and movement, the plot seems to deliberately delay its own development towards closure.[17] If, as some readers have felt, Emily's fixation on mystery prevents her from 'growing up', the plot's obsession with suspense equally retards it. The sense that Radcliffe's plot is one of non-development seems increased by the fact that, as noted earlier, the novel consists of a series of intense static moments of feeling between which, critics have complained, there is no necessary connection nor sense of progression.[18] The text dwells on a series of portraits of women – of Emily, the Marchioness, Laurentini – which further emphasises the stasis of female identity.

However, to hold these isolated moments together and create a sense of plausible development, Radcliffe draws attention to the powers of time. Time is the natural source of revelation that will explain the relation between these apparently unconnected elements, as Dorothée counsels patience: 'Time . . . may explain this mysterious affair; meanwhile let us watch the event in silence' (p. 537). It is also a sublimating force that will gradually transform Emily's grief for her losses into a pleasing melancholy, until 'time had softened her grief for the loss of St Aubert, though it could not annihilate it, and she felt a soothing sadness in indulging the recollections, which this scene recalled' (p. 493). During the last part of the book there is an almost ritualistic emphasis on time, as Emily returns to the place where her father died, exactly a year later, just in time for the peasant festival they had observed before. The anniversary may seem surprising: it is in fact a short time since St Aubert has died, it is only the narrative length that has made it seem interminably long.

The narrative thus both creates a sense of time and delays time. By so doing it creates the illusion that change occurs organically, as part of the natural seasonal rhythm of change. At the beginning of the text, La Vallée was a kind of twilight zone of apparent timelessness; at the end it becomes a 'penseroso' world still positioned within the Miltonic tradition,[19] but now also within the seasons. Emily returns at autumn, her father's favourite season, to which she writes a poem, in which it becomes an 'Emblem of Life' (p. 592). The time associated with fall becomes absorbed into the final scene of return, as an image for a natural temporal process of loss and recovery.

Returning to the places she has inhabited, Emily finds them also changed, both by loss (as La Vallée seemed to her emptied by the absence of her parents) and by additions – when previously she had been in the area, the Chateau-le-Blanc had been uninhabited; on her return she finds it brought to life by the death of the old owner and arrival of the new. The introduction of the second plot of the De Villefort family fragments the line of the narrative. Their story is twice related to Emily's, both by analogy, as the clear doubling between herself and Blanche suggests, and also by sequence, as the two stories link up. Moreover, the Chateau repeats and combines elements of La Vallée and Udolpho. It is associated both with a gothic past and with a modern owner and his family. Blanche, the daughter of the family, is a new, younger version of Emily, fresh out of the convent, who is about to enter the world of society. Having had a literally cloistered childhood, she has romantic ideas about life (encouraged by the fact that the convent library contained nothing but medieval romances). For her, the Chateau is a fairy tale world of liberation from a past confinement.

Blanche's appreciation of her new home is contrasted with the attitude of the evil stepmother of the family, whose wickedness, however, is confined to superficiality, love of Paris, and the reading of sentimental novels and radical philosophical works – one of which, Tompkins suggests, is Godwin's *Enquiry Concerning Political Justice*.[20] The key to her character lies in her failure to appreciate the Chateau. She sees it only as 'a dismal place', 'this barbarous spot' (p. 469), and dismisses its works of art as 'savage art' (p. 471). The castle that offers Blanche freedom, especially a liberty to explore both inside and outside, is for the older woman a place of imprisonment. Again, character is revealed by the response to external surroundings, architectural space as well as the natural world (which Blanche admires and the Countess loathes). The Count is the Burkean defender of tradition, who venerates the chateau, chiding his wife's rudeness by reminding her that 'This barbarous spot was inhabited by my ancestors' (p. 460), and 'This place, madam, was the work of my ancestors' (p. 471).

The veneration of the Count, however, is not the blind ancestor-worship associated by Godwin and Wollstonecraft with Burke. He loves the past, but warns Emily of the dangers of dwelling in it too much. On his arrival he immediately orders repairs to make the place comfortable for a modern family.[21] In his desire to restore and reanimate his property De Villefort stands between Emily's two uncles: Montoni and M. Quesnel. The *nouveau-riche* M. Quesnel buys the impoverished St Aubert's ancestral home and, with no respect for the land or building, begins tearing things down to create a more fashionable dwelling. To St Aubert's horror, he renovates and modernises the old estate, and has plans to cut down the ancient chestnut trees of St Aubert's youth to replace them with more fashionable – as foreign, significantly Italian – poplars. Like Mme Cheron and the Countess De Villefort, M. Quesnel is a vulgar moderniser, a chaser after novelty (as Burke had called Rousseau) who wants to institute artificial change based on foreign fashions, with no concern for the organic native tradition. Montoni, on the other hand, is reluctant to make any repairs at all to Udolpho, and only does those which will consolidate its power as a feudal fortress. Between change that would eradicate the past completely and the denial of change, the Count stands as an emblem of moderation, of Burkean organic change, based on the nourishment of indigenous traditions in which, as Burke said, 'in what we improve we are never wholly new; in what we retain we are never wholly obsolete'.[22]

Emily's relation to the Chateau seems purely accidental: escaping from Udolpho she is shipwrecked and rescued by the Count. Coincidence turns out to hide a deeper connection between this place and not only Udolpho but La Vallée. It is the missing link in Emily's journey home, a half-way house in her recovery of her property, and also in her quest for her past.

It also turns out to be connected to the convent St Clair, where her father died and was buried. The convent is the most frightening private space of all because of its enticing appearance as a haven from strife, an all female bower of harmonious sisterly relations that could protect Emily from the male oedipal world of trouble and desire. The all-girl world of the convent seems to offer a benign version of the family, made up of 'sisters' and a maternal abbess. The introduction of Blanche, previously cloistered by her jealous stepmother, allows Radcliffe to expose the duplicity of convents; as Blanche tells Emily, they are places where nature and religion are kept out rather than in. What Emily will also discover – and this is part of Radcliffe's gothic anti-Catholic sentiment, which Lewis will take even further – is that, inversely, convents don't wall *passion* out, but rather wall it in. Here repressed desire takes the extreme form of a mad nun, Sister Agnes, who is haunted by her own passions and some crime she committed about twenty years ago.

Udolpho, the Chateau, and the convent, are thus all connected by containing stories of a mysterious female. Emily assumes that these stories are all the same one, which she further sees as connected to her own. All mysteries seem to go back to the time of Emily's birth, beginning when she began, and making her question her own origins. In the same way that all mysteries link up in Emily's imagination through association, and that all men remind her of her father and Valancourt (himself a younger version of her father), all women seem to be for her potentially reducible to a single figure – that of her mother.

Through Emily's obsessive association of all women's stories with her own life, the text seems to work towards a total identification of all its female characters, as if, in Radcliffe's world of stereotypical characters, there is only one female type. Blanche is a version of her narrative precursor Emily, but Emily seems a version of everyone else whose story has come before hers. Hearing the tale of Laurentini's disappearance, she identifies it with her own: 'A strange kind of presentiment frequently, on this day, occurred to her; – it seemed as if her fate rested here, and was by some invisible means connected with this castle' (p. 250). Mme Cheron also seems a repetition of Laurentini, when Annette notes that 'it is plain, therefore, she is gone the way of the first lady of the castle' (p. 333). At the very beginning (p. 5), Radcliffe states directly that, 'In person, Emily resembled her mother; having the same elegant symmetry of form, the same delicacy of features, and the same blue eyes, full of tender sweetness' (a subtle clue which might stop us, if not Emily, from doubting her origins); yet through the text she will be told she resembles many of the women she meets or whose story she hears. Dorothée will see an uncanny likeness between Emily and the late Marchioness; Sister Agnes will see her similarity to both the Marchioness and to herself: 'We are sisters, then, indeed' (p. 574). In her attack on individualism, Radcliffe seems to deny women any discrete identity, so that they are all simply a version of the same story, a story that is furthermore irritatingly recycled with minimal variation throughout her different novels.

However, although the narrative seems to work towards a total identification of all women, Radcliffe ultimately is concerned with distinguishing them, and splitting them into separate, if stock, types of female identity. In Emily's confusion about her own identity, she begins to suspect that Sister Agnes is the Marchioness, and that she is also her true mother. It turns out the nun is *not* the Marchioness but Laurentini, who in fact murdered the Marchioness. The relation between these two women is not one of identification but antagonism. Emily's discovery divides the figure of the mother, which had confused two separate women, into the antithetical stereotypes of the passionate, dangerous, and sexual female and the passive, obedient, and spiritual one, who turn out to be related to each other as victor and victim. The types are revealed in two contrasting portraits. The Marchioness, as the first glimpse of her miniature shows, is the sensitive but overly passive female who becomes the victim, first of a father who forces her to marry against her will, and then of a jealous husband and his mistress who poison her. The portrait of Laurentini reveals her, in contrast, to be the woman of unrestrained passion who becomes the victor over the woman who represses feeling from filial obedience. The two, however, are polar victims of equally inadequate upbringings. Whereas the Marchioness's father determined her will, Laurentini, whose story is very similar to Emily's (offering obviously a moral cautionary tale about the dangers of spoiling children), is an only child whose parents also died when she was young. As they hadn't taught her self-control, she is left free to indulge her passions. As Burke could have told her, such freedom is slavery to her own tyrannical passions, and leads ultimately to the convent cell, as well as murder and madness. The two extreme images of female behaviour are equally untenable, as the overly socialised woman of filial obedience and duty is the victim of the unsocialised woman of unlicensed will and passion. Women are not identified, but opposed, gothic doubles of each other, bound in a sadomasochistic chain. The secret at the centre of the convent is not sisterly love but once more female rivalry, taken to its murderous extreme.[23] What links the convent, Udolpho, and the Chateau together is that they are all private spheres associated with women turning against each other.

The question is, then, now that their identities and their relations to each other have been determined, what is their relation to Emily and the world of La Vallée? Which is her mother? Neither would be very desirable if the goal of female development is to become one's mother. The obvious answer is that she's the child of neither. She is connected to them both – Laurentini has made her her heir, and the Marchioness turns out to be another but previously unsuspected aunt. But Emily is related to these two opposites as a tertium quid or golden mean between them, a true-born British Trimmer, who exemplifies middle-class moderation as, taught by her father and experience, she balances sensibility and reason, activity and passivity. After 700 pages of suspicion and suspense, Emily turns out to be exactly who she thought she was at the beginning.

Radcliffe's bathetic, non-oedipal revelation of identity was a daring one. Readers had recently complained of Charlotte Smith's *Old Manor House*, published in 1793, the year before *Udolpho*, for a similar deflation of romantic expectations concerning the heroine's identity.[24] To modern readers, moreover, this end seems completely regressive: the heroine's development simply confirms her original identity and returns her to La Vallée and a state of childhood, in which Valancourt now substitutes for St Aubert.[25] All the terrors and evil turn out to be non-existent – Montoni himself is suddenly swept offstage, reduced to a pasteboard bogey man and neatly dispatched in a page. The barriers between the lovers were all simply illusions which vanish following the final explanations and revelations. All oppositions removed, the novel retreats into an idealised world of romance, 'a pastoral world where female virtues and patriarchal authority are not in conflict'.[26]

If recent readers object especially to the conclusion's apparent confirmation of a conservative ideology of powerless and stagnant femininity, early readers' outrage centred on the bathetic revelation of the mystery behind the black veil. Having been teased for *hundreds* of pages with the notion that something really nasty – something substantial, a real body, not a spook or cheap substitute of any kind – lurks behind the veil, readers were irritated to find that what it in fact covers is simply the wax effigy of a dead body, constructed as a *momento mori* by one of the earlier owners of Udolpho as a means of disciplining his own unruly passions. It's not real, only another form of representation (though a pretty grotesque one at that). To compound the offence, the act of revelation, the stripping of the veil itself, is presented not as a climactic moment in the narrative, but a peripheral aside of an author attempting (somewhat feebly) to tidy up some loose ends. The moment of revelation is not climactic and terrifying but crude and rather silly. Coleridge expressed the general sense of frustration:

> Curiosity is raised oftener than it is gratified; or rather, it is raised so high that no adequate gratification can be given it; the interest is completely dissolved when once the adventure is finished, and the reader, when he is got to the end of work, looks about in vain for the spell which had bound him so strongly to it.[27]

Even Scott had to admit that readers felt cheated by Radcliffe's explanations of the sources of her various mysteries, which offer 'some inadequate cause': 'the reader feels tricked, and as in the case of a child who has once seen the scenes of a theatre too nearly, the idea of pasteboard, cords, and pullies destroys for ever the illusion with which they were first seen from the proper point of view. . . . Mrs. Radcliffe, a mistress of the art of exciting curiosity, has not been uniformly fortunate in the mode of gratifying it.'[28] With characteristic chivalric gallantry, however, he came to her defence, blaming her readers for the unfortunate conclusion. In an age of reason, he argued, no author was allowed to leave any mystery unexplained or unidentified as having a natural cause; modern readers, 'like children, demand that each particular circumstance and incident of the narrative shall be fully accounted for'.[29] The ending is marred by the discrepancy between the author's romantic imagination and the reader's enlightened conventions which are not mutually satisfied by Radcliffe's signature 'explained supernatural'. Her resolution produces more problems than it solves as the explanations seem inadequate; attempting to tidy things up, to bring boy and girl, aesthetics and moral, together, to satisfy reason as well as the imagination, she instead exposes the abyss between effects and causes.

I will return in a moment to another function of this kind of disjunction in Radcliffe's text. It is clear, however, that the gap between drawn-out suspense and perfunctory revelation itself reveals that the author's real interest is not in revelation but suspense, not what's behind the black veil, but the figure of the veil itself.[30] In medieval sign theory, the veil is associated with the letter of the text, the veil of allegory, which when lifted through the process of interpretation reveals its hidden truth, as reading becomes a form of biblical revelation.[31] For Burke, as we saw, human revelation attempts to realise an apocalypse now, producing catastrophic recoveries of not paradise but chaos.[32] As Jane Austen indicated in *Northanger Abbey*, the black veil became synonymous with Radcliffe's art, which satisfactorily conceals and frustratingly reveals, forcing us to focus on the veil itself rather than a hidden apocalyptic meaning.[33] Like Burke, Radcliffe is concerned with the role that cloaks and coverings play in defining human identity: how art shapes nature. It is significant that behind her veil is not the naked truth, nor a dead body, nor even nothing, but a wax figure – another form of representation. What the coverings of art hide is more art. As has often been noted, there is no nature in Radcliffe's world, despite the endlessly tedious descriptions of landscape. All of these came from travel journals and pictures, as Radcliffe, like Milton before her, saw nature through books – including of course, Milton's.[34] In Radcliffe nature always appears in the process of being shaped by the human mind. We see the artificial landscape, already shaped by previous authors or painters whose works Radcliffe is drawing upon, then we see Emily's response to it. What this response generally demonstrates is an appropriation of the natural world for the human, either through moralisation in which the human mind, detached from what it sees, reads meaning into the landscape, or through poetic creation in which the mind goes to work to shape the natural landscape into a work of art, or through memory in which the natural world becomes associated with the human (usually St Aubert and Valancourt, whom Emily is constantly projecting into what she sees). Nature is never fully detached from the human mind, which is itself a veil covering it. The reality Radcliffe represents has already been mediated, shaped and veiled by conventions, both literary and social, which cannot be simply cast off. For her, like

Burke, it is not what is underneath the coverings but the coverings themselves that are significant as they constitute our human 'nature'.

The black veil is thus an appropriate image for Radcliffe's artistry and its cloaking of the world. The image reappears in different forms throughout *Udolpho*. Emily wears a black veil to her father's funeral, and throws a veil over her face for protection; on a metaphorical level, the veil is also associated with the muted shades of twilight and dawn. On a religious level, nature is the veil of God, according to the biblical and allegorical tradition invoked by both Burke and Radcliffe in order to reaffirm a sense of connection between the natural and the supernatural. But the veil is also associated with loss, often of a world in which such connections were assumed. Both old castles are full of tapestries, usually depicting the past, and evoking a sense of nostalgia for a lost glory; Blanche finds a 'faded tapestry' showing scenes of the Trojan War and almost weeps, 'recollecting, that the hands, which had wove it, were, like the poet, whose thoughts of fire they had attempted to express, long since mouldered into dust' (p. 474). Most significantly of all, however, in the room of the Marchioness, Dorothée finds a black veil which she abruptly throws over Emily's head to show how strong the resemblance between the two women is. The veil is thus the medium for bringing the lost past back to life, although Dorothée hopes the future will be happier than the past: 'I thought . . . how like you would look to my dear mistress in that veil; – may your life, ma'amselle, be a happier one than hers!' (p. 534). In this room too, the black pall covers the deathbed of the Marchioness, which suddenly moves, as if the dead had really returned. These different coverings and veils fill a range of functions: they create an atmosphere of soothing melancholy, and also one of more sublime mystery; they serve as protection of women, but suggest too the oppression of women (an ambiguity revealed by the identification of the veil with both the convent and marriage); they create continuity between past and present, but in so doing may suggest too rigidly determining an identification of the two.

However, while veils suggest the carrying over of the past into the present through time, they also enable discontinuity. Despite the superficial resemblance, underneath the veil, Emily is *not* the same as the Marchioness, and the black pall does not cover a ghost but – at long last! – Emily's dreaded banditti. The gap between covering and covered, mystery and revelation, sign and signified, effect and cause, is the source of both our as well as Emily's disappointment and, ultimately, liberation.

While the text moves towards the identification of all women and the repetition of the past in the present, it also creates constant instances of disjunction. The narrative is full of scenes such as the one in Emily's father's study, when she goes to carry through his dying command. The power of her overactive imagination is so great that it seems to call him back to life – she sees him before her very eyes – something in the room moves – it is – the dog!! Typically suspense is built up through interruptions and deferrals of narrative only to be undercut by such bathetic endings, in which large effects are revealed to have minimal causes. We might read these as rehearsals, designed to prepare us for the final disappointment. But they have a further function as well, as they demonstrate the saving grace of a discontinuity between imagination and reality. Emily is constantly having premonitions of disaster: leaving La Vallée she feels sure she will never return; parting from Valancourt, she is certain she will never see him again. Seeing the flame on the sentinel's lance at Udolpho, 'She thought it was an omen of her own fate' (p. 408), a thought increased for the reader by the scene's ominous echoes of *Hamlet*. Returned home at last, the melancholy fall atmosphere, 'foretelling the death of the year . . . in her fancy, seemed to announce the death of Valancourt' (p. 619). Occasionally feminine intuition proves correct; sometimes it is fulfilled in strange ways. At Udolpho Emily fears her aunt has been murdered; it turns out that Mme Cheron hasn't been, but later Emily will suddenly discover that she has *another* aunt who was – though not at Udolpho but at the Chateau-le-Blanc. Wherever she goes she is obsessively, ludicrously, worried about banditti, whom she constantly fears threaten her; it is Blanche instead who encounters robbers dressed, like Valancourt (several times mistaken for a banditti), as hunters.[35] Things written about in Emily and Blanche's awful poems – shipwrecks, murders by banditti, crossings of perilous passes – are later experienced in real life, suggesting a continuity between art and life. But more often than not premonition provides a dubious tool by which to predict narrative turns. The discontinuity between premonition and fulfilment is a relief, freeing Emily from an overly determined conclusion. The sentinel's lance is not a supernatural omen, but, like the fireflies at La Vallée they recall, a natural phenomenon that can be rationally explained and which has no specific relevance to Emily's situation.

Udolpho shows a world in which the author's task is to control the imagination's imperious and dangerous demands for realisation. The past strives to become present through various forms of haunting. The fake resurrections of Ludovico and Valancourt (who are both believed dead and turn up again), as well as Ludovico's Provençal ghost story, play on the notion of the return of the dead. As noted before, in Radcliffe's earlier *Sicilian Romance*, the heroine's mother, presumed dead, turns out to have been hidden by her evil husband. This pseudo-resurrection quickly became a convention in other gothic novels, one which Radcliffe herself avoided repeating; in the *Romance of the Forest*, Adeline recovers only her father's manuscript which testifies to his horrid murder, and the dead do not come back to life. *Udolpho*, however, flirts with the possibility that death is not final. At various times, characters debate the existence of ghosts. The possibility that the dead can return to earth to watch over the living can be a source of comfort and defence against complete loss. So St Aubert, just before his death, muses: 'I hope we shall be permitted to look down on those we have left on the earth' (p. 67). But the return of the dead can be a source of terror, as the superstitious servants indicate when they fear the ghosts of the various chateaux. Emily herself is not immune to such fears, nor to being scared by even a friendly ghost. Fulfilling her father's last request, she thinks she sees her dead father in his study, and the effect is not consoling:

> her eyes glancing a second time on the arm-chair, which stood in an obscure part of the closet, the countenance of her dead father appeared there . . . on looking up, there appeared to her alarmed fancy the same countenance in the chair. The illusion, another instance of the unhappy effect which solitude and grief had gradually produced upon her mind, subdued her spirits; she rushed forward into the chamber, and sunk almost senseless into a chair.
>
> (pp. 102–3)

As the narrator's rational voice assures us, however, there are no spooks here. The episode is an example of the dangers of sensibility, and the overindulged imagination.

But it is also an example of the power of the human mind – both imagination and memory – to resurrect the dead, as part of the necromantic function of art, which offers immortality.[36] Memories of the past are necessary for Emily as a principle of continuity:

memory enables her to join together two parts of a life and story which often seem to have no relation to each other. At Udolpho especially, however, Emily broods on the violent contrast between her idyllic past and her demonic present:

> The gentleness and goodness of her parents, together with the scenes of her early happiness, often stole on her mind, like the visions of a higher world; while the characters and circumstances, now passing beneath her eye, excited both terror and surprise. . . . Her present life appeared like the dream of a distempered imagination, or like one of those frightful fictions, in which the wild genius of the poets some- times delighted.
>
> (p. 296)

Both past and present seem equally unreal antitheses: the past too good, the present too awful. Emily's development involves a radi- cal disjunction between an apparently unrelated sentimental past and gothic present. This discrepancy makes her doubt the reality of both, as well as her own sanity:

> So romantic and improbable, indeed, did her present situation appear to Emily herself, particularly when she compared it with the repose and beauty of her early days, that there were moments, when she could almost have believed herself the victim of frightful visions, glaring upon a disordered fancy.
>
> (p. 407)

Moreover, the extremity of the change in her life provokes in her a nostalgia that at times seems a death drive, a will to end all uncertainty and suspense through death, imagined as a reunion with her parents:

> The scenes of La Vallée, in the early morn of her life, when she was protected and beloved by parents equally loved, appeared in Emily's memory tenderly beautiful . . . she wept again over her forlorn and perilous situation, a review of which entirely overcame the small remains of her fortitude, and, reducing her to temporary despondence, she wished to be released from the heavy load of life, that had so long oppressed her, and prayed to Heaven to take her, in its mercy, to her parents.
>
> (p. 417)

Emily's typical defence against an unpleasant present is to remember an ideal past, to want to retreat into a cloistered private world of the family. Immediately after St Aubert's death she thinks of entering the convent in which he is buried, as a way of staying close to him and of recreating in the convent the sheltered domestic life to which she is accustomed.

Memory serves as a necessary link between Emily's past and present, especially during times when they seem most disconnected. Chapter X of the last volume begins with a quotation from the 'Pleasures of Memory' which describes how 'Our thoughts are link'd by many a hidden chain' (p. 580). Like Locke's consciousness, memory holds Emily together as a unified person, identical through time and through drastic changes in circumstances and place. But while at first the problem in the text seems that the different parts of Emily's life, represented by the various places she visits, have no relation to one another, by the end it seems that they are too closely connected. The danger of memory is that it works to deny loss by eradicating difference, collapsing past and present, and turning the present into a repetition of the past.[37] In the Marchioness's room, preserved exactly as it was when she died, time seems to have stood still to the ancient Dorothée, whose casting the black veil over Emily seems an attempt to assert the identification of the past with the present. For the mad Laurentini, too, the difference between the dead Marchioness and the living Emily disappears. Memory, too, can be a reactionary force against abrupt change. In Emily's case, it is literally a reaction to the sudden and complete loss of her parents and her home, and the apparent loss of Valancourt. The complete discrepancy between the stages of her life, her sense that she has lost everything, causes her to retreat into nostalgic memories of a romantic past as protection from and compensation for a gothic present. Emily's fear that all partings are fatal is a product of her parents' radical separation from her by death. Other losses which she assumes to be final also turn out to be only temporary, so that some of what was once lost is ultimately recovered, in a romance ending that both recalls and is different from Wollstonecraft's second conclusion.[38]

Detachment and division, thus, are necessary limits imposed by the author. The separation of the lovers is itself a necessary part of a final rhythm of taking apart and putting back together. Radcliffe dwells lugubriously on several parting scenes between Emily and Valancourt. Significantly, in these scenes Emily is better able to let go than he is, partially because as a woman she knows that they cannot simply run off and get married outside of society. Valancourt, however, in parting becomes suddenly and dangerously a spokesman for the primacy of individual desire, who coaxes Emily: 'Why should we confide the happiness of our lives to the will of people who have no right to interrupt, and, except in giving you to me, have no power to promote it? O Emily! venture to trust your own heart, venture to be mine for ever' (p. 154). For Valancourt, social duty and individual desires are antithetical; the first is merely an artificial restraint, the second the only true authority. For Radcliffe, however, the two must be reconciled; the individualist male, always close to the rational gothic villain, must be restrained by the socialised female. But in order to be reunited, the two characters and their stories are first divided.

In the story of Valancourt, Radcliffe provides a standard male *Bildungsroman*, reductively compressed and relegated to the margins of her text (a neat inversion of the more orthodox way of imagining the relation between centre and periphery), in which the innocent youth goes to the corrupt city and falls. His crime is that of St Leon, gambling, a vice also associated with Montoni, suggesting again the proximity between even the most sentimental hero and the mercenary self-interested individual. Ultimately, however, feelings win over money as the basis of relations, and he is redeemed through the love of the proverbial good woman. His redemption is achieved through a purgatorial time in prison. Confined, made helpless and passive, he – like Wollstonecraft's Darnford – has undergone an experience analogous to that of the typical female of the time.[39] While Emily, despite her incarceration, has been travelling, he has been inactive in prison. Because of the separation of the lovers, their experiences become parallel lines that in the end converge, bringing the separate spheres, normally totally isolated in terms of education and experience, together. Male and female, private and public, La Vallée and Paris, past and present, separate antithetical spheres that, cut off from each other seem sterile and self-destructive, unite in the final marriage.

Through the circular process of the text Emily recovers some, though not all, of what she has lost. The dead parents do not literally return (as the mother does in the *Sicilian Romance*), but are symbolically recovered as she discovers they are still her parents after all. While readings of the female gothic have often worked on uncovering a female subtext beneath a surface patriarchal narrative,[40] in *Udolpho* the surface focus on revealing the identity of her mother conceals another concern with the role of the father. While Emily's mother's identity is reaffirmed, her father's is subtly transformed. Throughout Emily's journeys the sense of her father's continuing presence comforts her. Typically, she thinks of him when looking out into the natural world; his image recalled becomes a link which leads her to meditate upon the supernatural world: the heavenly Father with whom, she assumes, St Aubert now resides. The dead father thus proves a medium between past and present, human and natural, natural and supernatural. In the final chapter, his continuing presence as a symbol of Burkean organic continuity is suggested. Following their marriage, the couple retreat to La Vallée, and specifically to St Aubert's favourite tree:

> Valancourt led her to the plane-tree on the terrace, where he had first ventured to declare his love, and where now the remembrance of the anxiety he had then suffered, and the retrospect of all the dangers and misfortunes they had each encountered, since last they sat together beneath its broad branches, exalted the sense of their present felicity, which, on this spot, sacred to the memory of St Aubert, they solemnly vowed to deserve, as far as possible, by endeavouring to imitate his benevolence, – by remembering, that superior attainments of every sort bring with them duties of superior exertion, – and by affording to their fellow-beings, together with that portion of ordinary comforts, which prosperity always owes to misfortune, the example of lives passed in happy thankfulness to GOD, and, therefore, in careful tenderness to his creatures.[41]

(p. 671)

The dead father is carried into the present when transformed into a kind of *genius loci* who sheds a good influence upon them. The human past becomes part of the natural landscape in which the future will begin; the human and the natural are shown again to be deeply connected and to point further to a genuine supernatural realm.

The recovery of the father marks his transformation further from a figure identified with Rousseau to one closer to Miltonic models of authority. As I suggested earlier, Radcliffe's Rousseau is not the figure of individualist sensibility found in radicals such as

137

Godwin and Wollstonecraft. She audaciously rehabilitates him from the solitary wanderer into an image for strong parental authority. At the end of the text, however, she turns from this foreign source to a figure for Protestant and native self-government – Milton.[42] The final chapter showing the return home has as its epigraph a quotation from Milton's *Comus*, in which Milton's Guardian Spirit returns home having finished his work on earth and describes his own boundaries:

> Now my task is smoothly done,
> I can fly, or I can run
> Quickly to the green earth's end,
> Where the bow'd welkin low doth bend,
> And, from thence, can soar as soon
> To the corners of the moon.[43]

(p. 670)

The plot of *Comus*, a poem echoed or quoted in a number of significant passages by Radcliffe,[44] provides one obvious model for her narrative. Like Milton's text, Radcliffe's tells of a young woman, separated from her family, who is threatened by sinister forces, but who is safely returned home.

There may be deeper links with *Comus* as well. The masque form in general, with its carnivalesque representation of a licensed subversion of norms followed by the reinvestment of authority, raises political questions similar to those currently asked of the female gothic. But Milton's masque in particular has one subversive element in its use of an aristocratic form to celebrate antithetical bourgeois values. Pamela Clemit has shown how radical writers, and Godwin in particular, drew on Milton's text to represent their own class conflicts.[45] In Radcliffe, class conflict is suggested and overcome, when an aristocratic world quietly gives way to bourgeois ideals. This transition is expressed in the new distribution of property. The Chateau-le-Blanc has already descended from Marquis De Ville*roi* to Count De Ville*fort*, suggesting the transition from rule based on birth to one on individual ability. Udolpho now passes to the impoverished Mme Bonnac so that it is restored to a female line, now a non-aristocratic one, and La Vallée becomes the home of the new nuclear family, the couple Emily and Valancourt. Moreover, Emily is able to sell Mme Cheron's estate in order to fulfil her father's dream of redeeming the ancestral home that financial disasters forced him to sell to the hideous M. Quesnel. Tradition is thus rescued by merit from crass modernisation, and restored to the proper heir. The bourgeois ideal of marriage revives the chivalric past, as Radcliffe reminds us indirectly through another version of her veil:

> The feasts were held in the great hall of the castle, which, on this occasion, was hung with superb new tapestry, representing the exploits of Charlemagne and his twelve peers; here, were seen the Saracens, with their horrible visors, advancing to battle; and there, were displayed the wild solemnities of incantation, and the necromantic feats, exhibited by the magician *Jarl* before the Emperor. The sumptuous banners of the family of Villeroi, which had long slept in dust, were once more unfurled, to wave over the gothic points of painted casements; and music echoed, in many a lingering close, through every winding gallery and colonnade of that vast edifice.
>
> (pp. 670–1)

Udolpho thus offers an idealised myth about the origins of the middle class, represented as emerging in continuity with as well as antagonism against an older aristocratic order which is repaired and restored, rather than eradicated. It shows a Reformation, in which a Catholic past produces a world of Protestant values, and parental government is succeeded by self-government. Despite, or rather because of, the surface focus on disjunction, change occurs without radical break, because it follows the natural, and cyclical, rhythm of the seasons. In its circular form, the novel might be read also as suggesting a pattern for female development and experience which feminist critics have claimed is an alternative to the traditional male teleological narrative. The discovery of female identity emerges in continuity with the mother rather than an oedipal rupture with the father.

Like Burke, too, Radcliffe creates a fiction of gradual, organic change. The agent of change, however, is not characters within the fiction, but plot, or rather the fabricator of the plot, the author. The ending draws attention to the creator behind the story, as the veil of fiction briefly lifts. The ending thus is a revolution from the beginning, in which the opening epigraph put the reader in the place of Emily about to enter Udolpho:

Fate sits on these dark battlements, and frowns,
And, as the portals open to receive me,
Her voice, in sullen echoes through the courts,
Tells of a nameless deed.

The text is Udolpho itself, which we enter and may, in the middle, fear we will never exit alive. At the end, however, we move suddenly to the author's point of view, modelled again on that of Milton's Guardian Spirit, who says farewell to his characters. Closure is achieved by a rather abrupt separation in which the writer suddenly stands *outside* her text, to pronounce a moral:

> O! useful may it be to have shewn, that, though the vicious can sometimes pour affliction upon the good, their power is transient and their punishment certain; and that innocence, though oppressed by injustice, shall, supported by patience, finally triumph over misfortune!
>
> And, if the weak hand, that has recorded this tale, has, by its scenes, beguiled the mourner of one hour of sorrow, or, by its moral, taught him to sustain it – the effort, however humble, has not been vain, nor is the writer unrewarded.
>
> (p. 672)

Like Milton's Guardian Spirit, Radcliffe has got her heroine home, and can now return to her own home – not the celestial sphere of the Spirit, but the domestic sphere in which Radcliffe contentedly cloistered herself as if it were paradise. The virtues she praises are those appropriate to the realm she, having finished the slightly dubious public act of writing, now retires to, and to which she consigns her heroine.

The flat moral is completely conventional, but so is the gesture: that of the artist saying farewell to her art. The fact that she does so with a moral may make it easy to miss how Radcliffe here is revealing her role as the Guardian Spirit, or Prospero-like magician, behind the plot. As Robert Miles has noted, the gothic father who secludes his daughter to protect her looks back to the Shakespearean model of Prospero.[46] But the end of the text shifts that authority from St Aubert to Radcliffe herself. The author is revealed as the model for the external power and controls that for both Burke and Radcliffe are necessary guarantees for individual freedom.[47] She is a force of artificial and necessary discontinuity, who brings an end to her story. Change is both natural and for humans artificial, as Radcliffe accepts the Burkean premise that change is antithetical to human, or at least English, nature; that we are held together as individuals by habits and prejudices which give us coherence and which we abandon reluctantly. The tendency of human beings is, like the plot of *Udolpho*, to repeat themselves with only slight variations, to become fixed in repetition compulsions which move towards reducing all action and persons to homogeneity. Left to her own devices, Emily would never have gone anywhere; she leaves home reluctantly, while Valancourt parts from her screaming and kicking, at which Radcliffe appeals to 'Those, who know, from experience, how much the heart becomes attached even to inanimate objects, to which it has been long accustomed, how unwillingly it resigns them' (p. 119). Humans are essentially passive and regressive, refusing to take responsibility for their own lives, loving the same, the familiar, refusing change and loss; human nature is gothic, driven by Freud's death drive in which we desire to hold onto the past, to cling to the dead. As Freud would later claim, progress requires repression, as development is dreaded as a fall from paradise. Art itself is a defence against change, as a form of memory, and a means of holding onto and immortalising the past. Naive Godwinian faith in self-government is misplaced as people need to be forced to change and to take responsibility for their own actions by external forces beyond their control.

Just as Godwin's apparent attack on the past ended with its hidden reconciliation with the present, Radcliffe's attack on the present ends by redefining its relation to the past. Emily's development looked like a fall from a sentimental gothic past into a vulgar and more truly gothic present. In the end, Emily's circular journey is a dialectic in which preliminary alienation and estrangement is a prelude to a final reunion at a higher level; history becomes a version of a *felix culpa* which makes the modern middle class the new improved version of and true heir to an aristocratic past. The author is herself the image for this meeting, as both feudal lord, the benevolent and Miltonic setter of limits, and model rational self-governing bourgeois individual, the artist who uses her art to reform the past. It is sadly appropriate, however, considering Radcliffe's view of human nature, that the revolutionary form she perfected became a new type of generic tyranny, which hasn't changed much in the last two hundred years.

2 Lewis's Gothic Revolution

In a letter written to his mother shortly after the publication of *Udolpho*, Matthew Lewis wrote enthusiastically that, apart from the tediously sentimental first section, it was 'one of the most interesting Books that ever have been published'. Lewis's interest was partially self-interest, as he noted a resemblance between Montoni and himself: 'I confess that it struck me, and as He is the Villain of the tale, I did not feel much flattered by the likeness.'[1] Within a year of the publication of *Udolpho* and his own narcissistic reading of it, Lewis recreated it, omitting the boring bits and focusing on a villain with whom he would become identified. Where Radcliffe is the consummate concealer, however, Lewis presents himself as the complete revealer, who takes all of the terrors that Radcliffe leaves submerged and exposes them, turning gothic potentials into reality. In revising her work, Lewis thus sets up an antithetical image of the author, and of the artist's relation to her work. In Radcliffe the artist is separate from her work, a secularised *deus ab extra*, who brings together and separates, reveals and conceals, as needed, because she acts as a principle of law, conventions, order, discretion, and restraint. For Lewis, the artist is a lawless force, a Rousseauian exhibitionist, who obeys no limits and cannot be restrained. However, lawlessness is not a sign of power and authority but ultimately passivity; the author is caught up in his own plot, which Lewis, like Walpole and Godwin before him, composed quickly – according to him, within ten weeks. As his immediate identification with Montoni and his later identification with his own fictitious Monk suggest, for Lewis the artist is not God, nor even the Satan with whom Milton was identified, but the gothic villain, whose demonic revelations result in a tragic catastrophe.

The Monk rewrites Radcliffe's plot as an oedipal narrative which describes a family romance gone wrong. Radcliffe's tale of female *Bildungsroman* is revised and expanded to include the stories of both male and female development. The central couple is reformed into the opposition of victor and victim, as Emily and Valancourt are recreated as Antonia and Ambrosio, whose relation is one of opposition that is bridged only through incest. Yet their narratives are also set up as parallel lines. The main plot of *The Monk* is divided between the two *Bildungsromanen*, which follow both the male and female entrance into the world, and development from innocence into experience, from a protected and enclosed

142

world into a wider one of social relations. In the case of both
Ambrosio and Antonia, however, the private and sheltered world
of innocence is associated not with safety, like La Vallée, but with
repression. The home has become a prison, a place detached from
society even while bound to it, which will not allow its inhabitants
to go beyond its confines.

Ambrosio is cut off from society as he is raised in a monastery, a
world, like that of La Vallée, set apart from the corruption of the
public realm. Early on in the text he tells the false initiate Rosario
that the monastery is, however, the perfect balance between
isolation and community, the space that mediates between the
individual and society. Ambrosio, who contains elements of the
parodic Godwinian philosopher, points out that man's highest
state is independence, but also 'Man was born for society'.[2] The
Abbey reconciles these two opposites, being an Asylum from the
evils of the world, which secludes its inhabitants from corruption,
yet keeps them 'in possession of the benefits of society' (*The Monk*,
p. 54). The religious enclosure thus plays the role of the family (as
its use of familial roles implies) in mediating between the individual and society, and, specifically in Ambrosio's case, socialising
the essential individual, the child.

In reality, however, both the monastery and Ambrosio himself
are *loci* where opposites are not reconciled but totally set apart. As
in *Udolpho*, the cloister is not a place where virtue and religion are
contained and where nature is sublimated into art, but one where
they are repressed. Cloistering becomes a metaphor for the repression of flesh, body, nature (all ultimately reduced to and
identified with sexuality), and the illusory idealisation of spirit,
mind, and art. The structure of the cloister is an image of that
repression whose tools are superstition and deception. It is a
seductive spectacle on the surface which, however, conceals a
labyrinth inhabited by the devil and, later, the grotesque Madonna
of Agnes and her rotting child. The passage between these two
places is blocked by a statue, appropriately of the more traditional
Madonna. Not only religion, but art too is used as a tool of
mystification: the nuns have been told this sacred statue cannot be
touched, as a means of keeping them from discovering the truth it
conceals. The world of the church is one in which art is associated
with oppression, superstition, and blind idolatry, and is used as a
means of keeping us from discovering the dark and decadent truth
that lurks below.

Repression thus creates absolute division. The structure of the church's world is also reproduced within its head, Ambrosio, who becomes split into an innocent surface and evil substance. However, his story also suggests an inverse opposition, as it draws upon the Rousseauian model, in which a naturally good individual has been corrupted, and alienated from his authentic self, by social hypocrisy. This story mirrors other gothic fictions which describe the various evils specifically of a superstitiously religious education. In Schiller's *Ghost-Seer* (the model for later figures including Hogg's justified sinner and Brockden Brown's Godwinian Wieland) the Prince is marked for life by his strict upbringing. Reaching adulthood he rebels against what he was taught, but can never escape his childhood influences: 'A servile and bigoted education was the source of this dread: this had impressed frightful images upon his tender brain, which, during the remainder of his life, he was never able to wholly obliterate. Religious melancholy was an hereditary disorder in his family.'[3] In the middle of *The Monk* we are suddenly told by the narrator that Ambrosio was in fact originally good, but ruined by an unnatural education. The monks twisted his true nature: 'The noble frankness of his temper was exchanged for servile humility; and in order to break his natural spirit, the Monks terrified his young mind, by placing before him all the horrors with which Superstition could furnish them' (p. 237). This upbringing creates an internal opposition between education and nature: 'the different sentiments, with which Education and Nature had inspired him, were combating in his bosom' (p. 238). Ambrosio's self-division seems therefore to be a product of social conditioning that demands a repression of nature. Education doesn't make men whole individuals, but creates an internal abyss between a natural private self, which is essentially good, and an artificial and superficial public self, which is not only evil but further perverts the former by invading and distorting its desires.

By placing this revelation of the cause of Ambrosio's self-alienation at the centre of the text, Lewis seems to suggest that it is a privileged insight into the true nature of things. As we will see further, however, authorial insight in *The Monk* is itself thematised as a dangerous form of revelation. Certainly this claim inverts the surface opposition of the beginning and end in the text, in which Ambrosio is divided between an appearance of innocence and integrity, and a reality of evil and doubleness. Distinguishing between truth and falsehood, essential and artificial self, therefore seems difficult. At the same time, however, such oppositions can be exploited as a means of power. By appearing whole and yet being capable of complete self-division, the individual gains power over others, manipulating the increasing gap between heavenly exterior and infernal interior. Initially, for Ambrosio as for later figures like Dorian Gray and Dr Jekyll, self-division is a means of gratifying private desires while still keeping up public appearances. Hypocrisy superficially reconciles the individual desires and social duties which Radcliffe had worked to bring together; it assumes an essential antagonism between them, which it then conceals by confusing the natural and the artificial.

Moreover, while Ambrosio, first as saint and later as Rousseauian hero turned gothic villain, seems to be an individual opposed to society, he is in reality its embodiment, who replicates its own hidden contradictions. Set off from the world beyond its walls, the monastery and its head are not an alternative to social order but an internalisation of it. The private thus is again a version of the public; the spiritual world only a more intense version of the commercial material one. Ironically, considering Lewis's own later dramatic writings, the society of the text is associated with theatrical illusion. Furthermore, the text opens with a quotation from *Measure for Measure* that suggests an identification between theatrical art and hypocrisy.[4] Fraud takes many different forms: from the vain hypocrisy of silly older women like Leonella and Jacintha, through the unnecessarily elaborate deceits of Theodore – who tells tall tales to the gullible nuns – to the more pernicious frauds of the Baroness and Prioress. The theatrical metaphors used through the text, from the opening scene in which the Church is set up as a spectacle and Ambrosio its star, suggest a world in which characters are actors playing roles that the public demands of them, but whose real, less socially acceptable, identities lurk under the surface appearances. The quotations from dramatic texts locate the text in a dramatic tradition, as they thematise that tradition. As we will see in a moment, the plot has a very staged quality, and deaths especially are staged (a Shakespearean ploy which twice replays *Romeo and Juliet* in gothic forms). Characters take on various disguises: Theodore, the romance page, is 'a very Proteus, changing his shape every day' (p. 283), playing different roles to help his master; Rosario turns out to be a woman in disguise (another obviously Shakespearean device); and Raymond, when he sets out to see the world, in a rather strange twist of logic that again suggests the difficulty of distinguishing essential and artificial identities, is advised to disguise himself so that he will be loved for his true self rather than his rank. The text dramatises a world in which everyone is playing a part, adopting a persona, which may or may not reveal the truth behind it.

Lewis's theatrical society depends upon a division between appearance and reality, which may be exploited for individual power. His world is further bifurcated by the division between the sexes, as the narrative is split between the antithetical but parallel stories of Antonia and Ambrosio. The separation of brother and sister through the dismemberment of the original family means that each grows up in a sexually segregated world. While opposites, they are also similar; as in both Wollstonecraft and Radcliffe, an experience of confinement potentially identifies the two sexes. At the beginning of the text, both appear in a state of 'excremental whiteness', innocence that is untried, that is the product of lack of experience. In both cases, too, the innocence is defined in purely sexual terms. Ambrosio, Leonella exults, is so innocent that 'He knows not in what consists the difference of Man and Woman'. While this makes a man a saint, it is, significantly, precisely what should make a woman a woman, and she tells her niece, 'You should not seem to remember, that there is such a thing as a Man in the world, and you ought to imagine every body to be of the same sex with yourself' (pp. 17–18).

Innocence is equated not only with the absence of sexuality, but more precisely with the repression of the fact that there are actually *two* sexes. The denial of sexual difference conceals an absolute difference. Though their origins may be identical, Ambrosio and Antonia become parallel lines, whose experiences are ultimately opposed; brother and sister become victor and victim, who meet only through an act of violent conjunction of opposites.

Like Wollstonecraft, Lewis focuses on the mother as a figure of authority crucial in a child's development.[5] He suggests that Ambrosio's perverted development, like that of Wollstonecraft's Jemima, is due to his lack of a mother. However, Antonia's downfall occurs through too much mothering. The two sisters, Elvira and Leonella, are set up as opposites, the latter a stereotype (and version of Mme Cheron, who is reincarnated in numerous forms in the text, which viciously attacks aunts of all kinds) of the garrulous and lustful old female, the former the rational and chaste widow. Whereas Leonella is all appearances and artifice, Elvira is seen as the enemy of hypocrisy and all forms of deception. Yet the one person she is not direct with and indeed deceives is her daughter. Like Wollstonecraft and Radcliffe, Lewis is interested in the relations between women, and how again the division between the sexes perverts the relations within them. Evil women see others as rivals whom they try to oppress, as both the Baroness and the Prioress bully Agnes. But well-meaning females are even worse, as in their attempts to help and protect other females they only end up keeping them in a state of extreme vulnerability. Unlike St Aubert, Elvira tries to shelter her daughter from the evils of the world, rather than preparing her for them gradually. Moreover, while Elvira's protection of her daughter is motivated by the anxiety that she not repeat the errors of her mother, Elvira's reading of those errors is overly reductive. Like Ambrosio who sees all sin in its simplest forms as sins of the flesh, Elvira can only see the one error she is aware that she herself has committed: marrying outside of her class. Fear of miscegenation produces its opposite: incest.

Concerned with monitoring her daughter's education, and controlling her transition from innocence to experience, Elvira not only keeps her at home but also censors Antonia's reading, though on a rather eccentric principle. Approving of romances (presumably even Gothic ballads such as that of Alonzo the Brave, the ghoulish tale of a demon lover's return to claim his faithless love, which Antonia later reads to comfort herself after her mother's death), Elvira finds the Bible improper reading for a young girl. To protect Antonia, the mother 'copied out with her own hand' the Bible, making sure that 'all improper passages [were] either altered or omitted' (p. 260).[6] God the Father's word is literally rewritten in the hand of the mother, and censored to suit her plots for her daughter, ironically rendering her unprepared to protect herself later against Ambrosio's male rhetoric.

The central image for the mother's protection of her daughter, however, is the veil she makes her wear out in public. Lewis obsessively draws upon the figure of the veil that he inherits and revises from Radcliffe. In his text, it has obvious associations both with marriage and the Church. While the veil is a means of protecting female chastity, with which it is symbolically identified, it is also a figure for hypocrisy, as the coverings of the Church are another form of deceit. A place of deceptive appearances, the Church is where women both take the veil and are unveiled; Don Christovel tells Lorenzo that it is the one place where the nuns can be seen with their veils removed. Religious worship is reduced to a sexual encounter, here a striptease.

In the first chapter, the image of the veil serves to heighten the voyeuristic aspect of a theatrical world in which everyone is gazing lasciviously at everyone else.[7] For Lewis, vision is desire, an equation which is significant as the gothic villain often has penetrating eyes. Yet because Antonia, unlike the nuns, is covered by her veil at church, she is first encountered by others, including Ambrosio, as a voice 'of unexampled sweetness' (p. 9). While vision reveals only surface appearances, voice is traditionally idealised as conveying the inner reality and essence of a person.[8] Significantly, both Antonia and Ambrosio are first represented as disembodied spiritual voices, whose souls speak to each other of a kinship the reader will only discover at the end. Antonia first encounters Ambrosio at church as a voice which (suggestively) 'seemed to penetrate into her very soul' (p. 18); later Ambrosio is in turn taken by 'that voice to which no Man ever listened without interest' (p. 240), as it is 'so sweet, so harmonious!' (p. 241). Voice suggests a deeper affinity, as Elvira and Antonia speak naively of the effect of Ambrosio's voice on them. Elvira notes: 'surely, Antonia, I have heard it before. It seemed perfectly familiar to my ear. . . . There were certain tones which touched my very heart'. To which Antonia replies: 'it produced the same effect upon me. . . . I know not why, but I feel more at my ease while conversing with him, than I usually do with people who are unknown to me' (p. 250). In his first attempt at seduction, Ambrosio will ask Antonia if she has ever met a man 'The sound of whose voice soothed you, pleased you, penetrated to your very soul?'. To which she, oblivious to his point, naively replies: 'The very moment that I beheld you, I felt so pleased, so interested! I waited so eagerly to catch the sound of your voice, and when I heard it, it seemed so sweet! It spoke to me a language till then so unknown! Methought, it told me a thousand things which I wished to hear!' (pp. 261–2).

While voice reflects the spirit, it enflames the senses; given this opening to distort her meaning, Ambrosio pounces on her with almost vampiristic ferocity: 'He fastened his lips greedily upon hers, sucked in her pure delicious breath, violated with his bold hand the treasures of her bosom, and wound around him her soft and yielding limbs' (p. 262). Voice is set up as the opposite of body in the text, suggesting spirituality, and spiritual love. Yet ironically what it reveals here is not a spiritual but a physical relation: one of blood, and also of awakening carnal desires. The polarisation of physical and spiritual desires through social repression forces them to come together. Extremes meet violently in the act of incest, in which also different kinds of love, that of a brother and of a lover, become confused.

Hearing Antonia speak, Lorenzo also wants to see behind her veil. In the first chapter, a Godwinian reader might be tempted to read the veil as a figure for mystification and oppression, associated with the superstition of Catholicism and the repression imposed by even well-meaning parental authority, and to interpret unveiling as an act of liberation. Such an unveiling would be the imagistic correlative of the narrative's immediate representation and thus revelation of social hypocrisy. Yet if veiling is a dubious act, unveiling is also an act of control, particularly of men over women. Antonia first appears veiled, and tells Lorenzo that she never removes her veil in public. It is a means of protecting her privacy, of carrying it over even into the public world. However, the female is not in control of her own person in the public sphere. Despite her protests, Lorenzo proceeds to first take off her veil, which then allows him to take in her charms. He takes in her body bit by bit, in a kind of spontaneous blazon of imperfect parts that yet add up to an 'adorable' whole (pp. 11–12). His eyes are able to linger over every bit, though hers are unable to look back; being the object of attention disconcerts her, and she looks down, showing that 'She knew not what She was about' (p. 12).

It is significant, however, that it is Lorenzo and not Ambrosio who is the unveiler here. Antonia's unveiling by Lorenzo would seem to point towards a future lawful unveiling and possession by her rightful husband. In the opening scene, the potential for one conclusion to the story seems presented, as Lorenzo's act is one of claiming her, of replacing the veil of chastity with the bridal veil, and he immediately declares he wants to marry her. But the obstacles to this marriage are in turn displayed to us, through rather obvious forms of foreshadowing which seem to provide the reader with all the information about the plot necessary to reach the conclusion. In fact, *all* the plot developments are set out for us to see as, following the meeting between the two lovers, Lorenzo has a dream in which his marriage to Antonia is interrupted by a huge allegorical figure who rushes between them. While the monster is then swallowed by an abyss, Antonia 'disengaged herself from his embrace' only to ascend to heaven, calling out to Lorenzo 'Friend! we shall meet above!' (p. 28). And, as if that's not enough for the most obtuse reader, ten pages later Antonia's future is told by a gypsy who tells her that she will meet a man who appears good but will deceive her, and so 'Soon your Soul must speed to heaven' (p. 38). The rational Lorenzo pays no attention to his dream; Antonia is strangely unaffected by her fortune, and forgets about it immediately. Her mother's attempt to make her resistant to influences has made her incapable of internalising useful knowledge as well as pernicious. Foreknowledge is, alas, useless to arrest the predicted future.

However, for the wiser reader the entire plot is also clearly revealed to us at the very beginning, through a daring striptease which raises the veil of narrative allowing us a brief and tantalising glimpse of the end. The opening takes us into the world of the text but keeps us, with the author, on the outside, detached, looking in and so through what we see. Where Radcliffe brings us into her story by making us identify with her heroines, Lewis keeps us outside, to make us marvel at his authorial powers. The Church's hypocrisy is covered by an extremely flimsy veil; the reader is allowed to see through it from the start, as Lewis sets up veils only to have them almost immediately penetrated by authorial omniscience helping the reader through the world of illusion. The author keeps on revealing the reality behind appearances through continuous stripteases which make sure we are never taken in by disguises. So the narrator informs us that religion is all theatre, and a cover for sexual encounters: 'The Women came to show themselves, the Men to see the Women' (p. 7), both sexes to see the idol of the stage, Ambrosio. This initial revelation of the hypocrisy of the Church foreshadows the more literal exposition at the end; in the final scene of the chapter, the fates of Ambrosio and Antonia, the one sentenced to hell the other to heaven, are set out plainly.

The opening of chapter two then takes us into Ambrosio's mind to see behind his veil of appearances. When we first see Ambrosio, it is on the stage of the church, giving a sermon that moves all hearers, especially Antonia and her aunt. We only see him indirectly, however, from the outside, and his words are not even represented through direct quotation, as Lewis focuses instead on the influence they have on others. The veil over his character which keeps us at a distance from him drops suddenly at the opening of chapter two, however, when the author takes us inside not only Ambrosio's private cell, but also his mind. This intimate moment does not identify us with the hero, but detaches us from him, as through this sudden and dramatic shift the reader is enabled to both see and see through Ambrosio, to see the vanity behind his assurance of his own integrity. Voices turn out to be false after all, a theatrical illusion that is exposed when we see the reality behind them.

As we will see further, this immediate revelation of meaning gives the reader a sense of control and power over the narrative. The instant recognition of fraud gives us the illusion of our own interpretive omnipotence, our ability to recognise and see through the artifices of the fictitious world. At the same time, however, this act of flagrant revelation is a kind of authorial challenge to the reader, which allows the child prodigy to show off his own cleverness at being able to build up suspense when the ending is known from the very beginning. Lewis rewrites Radcliffe's use of foreshadowing, restoring its linear and enclosing effect. What is predicted *will* happen; in this text, there will be no saving gap between sign and signified. What this means is that the textual world seems rigidly determined, and at the end it will appear that that has been the case. But what the plots will also explore is the relation between a known conclusion and the suspense that defers it. The text shows the delay of the inevitable, and its consequences. While in Radcliffe, if you put off a tragic discovery long enough it might just go away altogether, in Lewis delay is only a means of working up to an even nastier and more explosive conclusion.

The principle of delay operates in different forms throughout Lewis's text, which recreates Radcliffean principles of deferral. Events take a long time to unfold, and the plot is dismembered into different parts. Rosario's revelation of identity requires several elaborate stages, as Matilda is one female who is able to use her own unveiling as a means of control. Her true identity is revealed gradually: first through the fiction of Rosario's sister, and then through the elaborate apparatus by which she saves Ambrosio's life at the apparent cost of her own. Her gradual self-revelation, which is also a revelation of a true sexual identity that is opposed to appearances, includes a literal striptease in which Ambrosio is able to see juicy parts of the female body that excite him, as his imagination extrapolates from revealed part to concealed whole.[9] Matilda's control of her own unveiling contrasts with the stripping of Antonia, first by Lorenzo and then later by Ambrosio. While for Antonia, unveiling signifies her domination, her female helplessness, for Matilda it is a sign of her self-determination that gives her power over the male.[10] Whereas Antonia is the stereotypical female, Matilda, who starts off as a male, acquires masculine authority. As her identity changes, so does her relation to Ambrosio. When the two become lovers she takes the lead role, presenting herself as a rational demystifier, who sees her lover as still caught in the web of religious superstition, and tempts him with the hopes of moving beyond the veils of superstition to a state of enlightenment. Whereas Ambrosio seems still confined by his religious upbringing, Matilda presents herself as an enlightened figure, able to control subterranean forces, as her descents to the cloister and summoning of Lucifer manifest. Her unfeminine assurance and domination over Ambrosio in fact cause him some uneasiness, as they do not correspond to his ideal of feminine behaviour. However, the final veil drops from her identity at the end of the text, when Lucifer reveals his own control, and the fact that behind this female is in fact a devil. The distinction between the sexes disturbed by the discovery that Rosario is a woman is reaffirmed by the discovery that the woman who has autonomy, reason, and authority is in reality a demon.

Other events also require rather elaborate staging, and are drawn out in ways that build suspense. Ambrosio's seduction of Antonia takes several frustrated attempts. His early rhetorical seduction is first foiled by her total lack of comprehension, then interrupted by Elvira who, beginning to suspect that the Monk's surface is false, banishes him. In order then to continue his pursuit, he is required to accept Matilda's offers of supernatural aid. With her help, he gets a sneak preview of Antonia bathing. Naked, she is still veiled as 'Though unconscious of being observed, an in-bred sense of modesty induced her to veil her charms' (p. 271). This scene is an even more voyeuristic repetition of Lorenzo's first unveiling of Antonia, in which the female, innocently unaware that she is observed, is reduced further to an object of vision and desire. The tantalising sight of the exposed bits of her body proves too much for Ambrosio; seeing the delicious parts, he is committed to obtaining the whole by means of a more literal and complete stripping. To obtain his desire, he first has to descend into the labyrinth where, hearing cries (which we realise are those of Agnes, as the two plots momentarily collide), he is tempted to turn back, but continues, rationalising, as Matilda has assured him that 'He always should have time sufficient for repentance' (p. 273). The night before his fatal arrival is also drawn out further through Antonia's sudden fears on saying goodnight to her mother, as a 'secret presentiment assured her that never must they meet again' (p. 296). In Antonia's case feminine intuition is right; like other elements of foreshadowing in the text, her fears will come true. Foreknowledge never stops anything from happening; it merely intensifies suspense by creating an atmosphere of certain doom. To delay the inevitable further, Ambrosio's journey to the bedroom is drawn out, as, fearful of exposure, he stops *en route*, contemplating going back, and then resolves to continue. The rape is then interrupted by the appearance of Elvira, warned by a dream of her daughter's danger. The mother's attempt to protect her daughter, like her other attempts to veil her innocence, and her threat 'I will unmask you, Villain' (p. 301), only make things worse. Ambrosio kills her, and her later attempts to warn her daughter through her ghostly appearance only ironically send the girl, still too innocent for her own good, into the hands of the Monk. He finally attains his desire through the most blatantly theatrical device of all: the staging of Antonia's false death, a technique drawn straight from Shakespeare (which is replayed in the subplot in the Prioress's imprisonment of Agnes). Antonia 'dies', ironically parting with Ambrosio: 'we shall meet again, Ambrosio! We shall one day meet in heaven: There shall our friendship be renewed, and my Mother shall view it with pleasure!' (p. 341). Even this end is also not final, however, as, in a parody of the apocalyptic prediction that the dead shall be raised, Antonia is resurrected in the subterranean passages of the cloister to meet Ambrosio sooner than she had anticipated, a resurrection which gives Lewis the chance to linger lovingly over his own disgusting version of Radcliffe's beauty in the lap of horror.

While these delays are means of heightening suspense, they also introduce the possibility of a definitive interruption of the sequence of events. By separating events out into separate stages, Lewis creates the sense that at some point in the process the inevitable might have been stopped.[11] The frequent interruptions of the action suggest that at some point it might have been broken off, and gone in another direction: Ambrosio *might* have forgiven Agnes, he *might* have turned back in the vault, he *might* not have killed Elvira. Delay thus includes both predetermination and free will, as it introduces the possibility of freedom, discontinuity, in a narrative in which every event seems predicted. It makes us wonder at what point in Ambrosio's gradual descent into damnation salvation becomes irretrievable, and if it is possible to tell when it is too late to turn back and repent.

As in the story of Faust and later religious gothic the boundary between salvation and damnation, spiritual freedom and slavery, is not as clear as one might think. The rational Matilda tries to convince Ambrosio that he is already fallen and therefore shouldn't have qualms about falling further; moreover, he will always have time to repent and avail himself of God's grace. In her final appearance to him, however, she tells him that God's forgiveness is not all-inclusive; his damnation is inevitable and so the best he can hope for is to delay it. Ambrosio himself still hopes, like Faust, that it is not too late to repent, but finally, hearing what he thinks are his executioners coming to take him to the stake, he despairs and abandons all hope of salvation. Delay seems only to make things worse, as the interruption of a plotted series of events intensifies Ambrosio's determination: 'His natural lust was increased by the ardour of the difficulties which opposed his satisfying it' (p. 379). Moreover, at the very end, Ambrosio's procrastination in signing the pact with Lucifer (which accounts for the fact that he has to call him twice – a rather awkward narrative staging that again serves only to defer an irrevocable choice of action) in turn increases the devil's fury. The problem is that action is always both too late and yet premature; in the end, Ambrosio delays, but not quite long enough – one moment longer and he would have been saved by a reprieve. Delay itself, the building of suspense, becomes a narrative mode of repression which produces a destructive explosion of pent-up energy.

The other important structural principle of delay in the text is that of the multiple plots. Ambrosio's story connects with those of Antonia and Lorenzo, the doomed lovers, and Agnes and Raymond, the successful ones. Lorenzo is the pivotal figure between the two; like Ambrosio he is both lover and brother, but not (and this is obviously a crucial difference between them) to the same woman, as he is able to distinguish between fraternal and erotic desire. The plots themselves run as parallel lines, telling of two different but related and similar love affairs. The story of Raymond and Agnes repeats that of the central story, telling of a male entering into the public world through a grand tour, and his love for a woman who has had a cloistered life and who, because of parental superstition, is destined to remain in that cloister. The subplot further contains a number of sub-subplots – that of the Bleeding Nun, and the story of Theodore's mother – which repeat themes from the main plot, suggesting, as in Radcliffe's world, the identification of all stories. Many critics have complained about the superfluity of these plots, their lack of organic connection to the main narrative; in fact, like Ambrosio and Antonia, they are too connected, reflecting the text's exploration of overdetermined and indeed incestuous narrative as well as familial relations. Moreover, while the stories are parallel, and in places intersect sequentially, they also get in each other's way, as narrative doubling proves rather inconvenient. The proliferation of plot suggests that narrative itself is a disruptive force that cannot be controlled. The subplots interrupt the plot proper in a way that has tragic consequences for Antonia and Ambrosio.[12] Lorenzo's double identity prevents him from acting quickly enough to save Antonia; his concern for his sister makes him forget his beloved, and so while he 'was anxious to unmask one religious Hypocrite, He was unconscious of the sorrows prepared for him by Another' (pp. 295–6). The stories are rivals for his, as well as our, attentions, and they ultimately work both with and against each other.

The problem with narrative is that it can't be in two places at once, a fact of life which for Lewis's plots has tragic consequences. Characters are absent at crucial moments because of other concerns (usually connected with a rather remarkable rash of familial deaths); a series of misadventures distracts the attention of those who might have helped Antonia in her time of need. In Radcliffe the subplot is (as it traditionally is) a means of displacement that allows the author to work through metaphorically the problems of the heroine in another location; in Lewis it becomes literally another concern which prevents Lorenzo from protecting his beloved. The advantage of Radcliffe's characters' lack of rigid individuality is that it enables them to substitute for one another. In Lewis's text, individual identity is in that respect absolute, so that such interplay is impossible, and the relations between the stories has tragic consequences for the hero and heroine.

Lewis is therefore setting up an anti-Radcliffean series of relations for both characters and elements of plot. For Radcliffe, as we saw, narrative provides a means of representing a saving discontinuity between beginning and end, while still bringing the two together.

Delay keeps gothic nightmares from becoming real, as Emily's fears turn out to be unfounded, and the thing behind the veil turns out to be not the naked truth but a ridiculously grotesque fiction. Lewis will graphically realise all the potentials for terror Radcliffe leaves implicit. Rebelling against her strategy of concealment, denouncing indirection as fraud, he sets himself up to be an artist of revelation and revolution. Such art is not, however, liberating. For Lewis, narrative is the means of establishing complete continuity, of teasing us with the possibility of breaks in sequence, only to lead us to the inevitable. All of the prophetic signs set out at the beginning will be fulfilled, in a tight enclosure in which the end is the revelation of the meaning foretold in the beginning, its manifestation and ruthless realisation.

The fulfilment or realisation of signs is also explored in the text's representation of art that becomes real. I have already mentioned the gothic's concern with works of art that take on a frightening life of their own. Statues, pictures, that come alive are a staple of gothic literature. Schiller's *Ghost-Seer* includes a picture of a Madonna, clearly the model for Lewis's, which is realised in a living woman. In *Otranto*, Matilda is in love with the picture of Alphonso the Good, only to find it come alive in the character of Theodore (the rational explanation is, of course, that Theodore is Alphonso's heir). In the gothic world, art is hard to distinguish from life, a fact that has concerned its critics, worried lest its readers extend this confusion into their own lives. In *The Monk*, the boundary between the two is also fragile. Life is itself art – a theatrical spectacle. As in the figure of Ambrosio, the text makes it difficult to determine what is true nature and what is artificial.

To complicate matters, art is both fraud and yet what is real when works of art come to life. Ambrosio's downfall begins when the portrait of the Madonna he admires becomes real. The first time we see Ambrosio alone in his cell, he exults over his imperviousness to sins of the flesh. Glancing up at the picture that has been 'the Object of his increasing wonder and adoration' for two years, he speculates that he might be tempted 'Should I meet in that world which I am constrained to enter some lovely Female, lovely . . . as you Madona [*sic*]' (p. 40). But he dismisses this idea on the grounds that what is beautiful in art would be degraded in life: 'What charms me, when ideal and considered as a superior Being, would disgust me, become Woman and tainted with all the failings of Mortality. It is not the Woman's beauty that fills me with such enthusiasm; It is the Painter's skill that I admire, it is the Divinity that I adore!' (p. 41). To the idealist, art is beautiful because it is *not* real; it remains pure and untouched in the realm of the mind. But this ideal female will become real, in Lewis's version of the Pygmalion story. Here, however, as in Radcliffe, there appears to be a rational explanation: this is part of Matilda's plot, in which art is perversely used as a medium for sexual seduction. The spiritual ideal is thus both opposed to a fleshly reality, and directly leads to it. However, at the end, Matilda's story is revealed to have been another fiction, an elaborately constructed narrative that gains its seductive power by suggesting the ability of desire to realise the ideal.

As Ambrosio foresaw, however, the realisation of his fantasies does not lead to satisfaction but disgust. He is quickly revolted by the flesh and blood Madonna, whose bossiness does not correspond to his ideal of femininity; later even the divine Antonia, when reduced to a sex object, will provoke his loathing. In general, the realisation of the imagination has disastrous consequences in the text. The imagination demands realisation, but fantasies that might be safe when indulged in private take on a frightening autonomy when they are manifested and projected beyond the boundaries of dreams. Like Frankenstein's monster, they prove to be creations that get away from their creator, and Matilda certainly has a plot all her own.

The rational lovers Raymond and Agnes similarly conjure up a fictitious figure that takes on a life of its own, and suddenly find themselves caught up in a truly gothic plot. Plotting to run away, they plan to turn the parental superstition that is impeding their union to their advantage, using the cover of the Bleeding Nun who first appears as a ghastly cartoon Agnes has idly sketched. Of course, the real ghost turns up, and Raymond finds himself embracing not the artist but the subject of her ghoulish artwork. The fictitious (or pictorial) personnage becomes real, and from using her for *his* plot, Raymond suddenly finds himself as part of *her* plot, a character not an author. Moreover, what appeared a rather unfortunate and unpredictable coincidence turns out to have been long determined: the Nun is Raymond's great-aunt, a Laurentini figure who (along with, for good measure, the lecherous Baroness who dies of a surfeit of passion) represents the dangers of repressed sexuality, and who stands in the same relation to Agnes that Laurentini did to Emily. She is an example of how female desire, first unnaturally cloistered and then completely unrestrained, becomes murderous.

However, while a symbol of explosive female sexuality, the Nun also desires final restraint, and has been waiting for Raymond who it was preordained would bury her. While Raymond and Agnes have wandered into supernatural plots, they do so in order to help tidy them up, to give rest to the wanderings of the ghost. Dangerous female sexuality is aroused by Raymond and Agnes's love (for which it is clearly also a symbol), but only to be put to final rest through burial. Raymond is able to extricate himself from this narrative beyond his control when his story hooks up with one of the oldest stock figures of gothic literature, St Leon's friend the Wandering Jew. The archetypal wanderer and figure for endless desire and narrative becomes transformed into a means of closure through an abrupt break; having promised to tell Raymond his story, he simply disappears. By this judicious device, the one example of authorial restraint and Radcliffean discontinuity, *The Monk* is kept from turning into a *Melmoth*, a text in which one narrative leads to another in a principle of infinite regression. We get off track momentarily, through the realisation of art by which Raymond, and Lewis's, plot is finally subsumed by a larger mythic plot; but, through a saving disjunction at this point which keeps the narrative from going backwards to turn into the story of the Wandering Jew, Raymond is freed from following the other plot, and is able to get back to Agnes. Ironically, however, this progress leads back to entrapment, as their premature union results in Agnes's pregnancy which lands her in the hands of another worse female tyrant, the Prioress, whose burial of the living Agnes replays in reverse Raymond's burial of the dead Beatrice.

Raymond and Agnes's vulnerability in this episode lies in their rationality, a rationality that is even more evident in Lorenzo, who is presented as an enlightened antithesis to the Monk. Lorenzo is not shocked to find that his friend has seduced his sister, but sees himself, in contrast to the rest of his family, as acting as a rational civilised man: "Tis the superstition of my Relations which has occasioned these misfortunes, and they are more the Offenders than yourself and Agnes. What has past between you cannot be recalled, but may yet be repaired by uniting you to my Sister' (p. 192). The rational son disassociates himself from his superstitious ancestors. However, to be enlightened in this gothic world is to be as ignorant and blind as Antonia, as superstition and reason are both polarised and yet identified. Typically in the gothic novel, it is the villain, such as Radcliffe's Montoni, who mocks superstition. In Lewis's text it is not the villain but the hero. But the two figures are doubles for each other, whose identity is indicated by the fact that they are often connected in Antonia's imagination.[13] In the opening scenes of the text that I have already discussed the two men seem set up as complete opposites: Ambrosio, at the very centre of the hypocritical and superstitious church world which gazes at him, and Lorenzo, the rational outsider standing aloof and looking in on that world. Both villain and hero thus offer versions of the author himself. The reader, however, also seeing things from the outside and seeing through them, is thus implicitly identified at first not with Ambrosio but with Lorenzo.[14] Our unveiling of the hypocrisy of the Church with our critical acumen is mirrored in his unveiling of Antonia, and from the start he provides us with an image for ourselves and our own hermeneutic activity as a rational objective procedure.

Lorenzo becomes the demystifier who uncovers fraud, taking the narrative and us down to the bowels of the Church in the final scene, which serves as an antitype or literal realisation of the interpretive unveiling we as readers produce at the beginning of the text. As all delayed realisations in the work, however, it is a disaster. Lorenzo approaches the Church as a revolutionary, leading his people, 'to free them from their monkish fetters' (p. 345). His Godwinian plan is to liberate his people's minds from the idolatry that confines them, to 'rend the veil from Hypocrisy' (p. 350). But revelation and revolution only produce darkness, as the mob, whom Lorenzo is incapable of restraining, take the law into their own hands. Law turns into a reign of terror, as the Prioress is torn apart; her body reduced to 'a mass of flesh, unsightly, shapeless, and disgusting' (p. 356). Then the rioters turn on the convent itself, with undiscriminating anger, as they, 'confounding the innocent with the guilty, had resolved to sacrifice all the Nuns of that order to their rage' (p. 357). Lorenzo watches in horror as the revolution that he had originated takes on a life of its own, outside of his control, and turns the convent into an apocalyptic conflagration. The plot he had constructed turns into a more gothic narrative than he had anticipated. The enlightened Godwinian author is unable to restrain the forces he has created.

The similarity between this metamorphosis of an enlightened project into a reign of terror and the course of the French Revolution has frequently been noted.[15] In different ways, both Burke and Godwin had predicted that the enlightenment dream would become a nightmare; that the ideal realised would be its own parody. For both Ambrosio and Lorenzo, the damned monk and the rational hero, the realisation of desire creates terror. The attainment of sexual fantasies produces disgust, while the enlightened attempt to demystify only produces a deeper darkness. The conclusion of both plots is an infernal, perhaps because again rather premature, apocalypse, in which the dead are raised only to be killed again (in the case of Antonia – Agnes does survive). Lorenzo's preoccupation with the unveiling of the Prioress distracts his attention from Antonia and the Prioress's male counterpart, Ambrosio. At the end, the two plots connect by accident, when Lorenzo and a few of the nuns take refuge in the subterranean passages of the church (now become a refuge as well as a prison). But the reunion of the two stories is disastrous. Matilda comes to warn Ambrosio of Lorenzo's approach, and urges him to destroy the evidence of his crimes, by killing Antonia. This he vehemently refuses to do, until Lorenzo's sudden appearance produces an almost automatic reaction: 'Without allowing himself a moment's reflection, He raised it [the dagger that Matilda had thoughtfully given him], and plunged it twice in the bosom of Antonia!' (p. 391). Lorenzo arrives only in time to cause Antonia's death, and to comfort her as she expires beautifully. The convergence of the plots identifies further the two men, hero and villain, whose meeting is murderous.

Antonia's death is the fitting end of her story of development which comes full circle in a gruesome literalisation of Radcliffe's fiction of return. Beginning as an ideal spiritual and angelic woman, a disembodied voice, Ambrosio's desire turns her into her opposite, an object of physical desire. Like the painted Madonna, she begins as a worshipped ideal, and is transformed by his Pygmalionesque lust into a degraded and despised reality. Death restores her original innocence in an even more intense, as literal, form: she is now truly an angel, who will live as an idealised image in Lorenzo's memory. Her development is thus a revolution in which she passes from one extreme state to another and, in a final reaction, returns to her beginning. She fulfils her own earlier prayer that she will 'yield to God my Spirit back, / As pure as when it first was mine' (p. 255). She dies just at the moment her mother's ghost had predicted, crying 'Three o'clock! . . . Mother, I come!' (p. 393).

She leaps from the arms of the man she might have married to a reunion with her dead mother. Death is spiritualisation, a flight from flesh, but also a regression of the daughter back into her first relationship with the mother from whom she, unlike Emily, has not managed to detach herself.[16] Despite her rape, Antonia returns to a state of innocence; death rescues her from normal development, and the attainment of female sexuality which in the text has been associated with a fate worse than death: the undead state of Agnes and the Bleeding Nun. She leaves the world of experience and recovers an all-female world of innocence. In a dark version of the female gothic's reunion of mother and daughter, the daughter's story comes full circle back to her own source.

In Radcliffe, the heroine's circular journey is a transformative one, in which the end both recovers and revises the beginning. In Lewis, it is as much of a dead end as Ambrosio's male linear development. In one final flagrant act of authorial deferral, Ambrosio's end is elaborately delayed. The tragic conclusion to his story is placed at the end of the text, following the romantic resolution of the other plots. This position reinforces his role as the alienated individual, exiled from the restored social community. Moreover, his ending is again drawn out. Thrown into prison, the Monk enters into his lengthy negotiations with the devil, which only end when he is tricked into selling his soul at the very moment when hope is possible. Unfortunately, he carelessly forgets to bargain for a deferral of his sentence of damnation. No procrastinator, Lucifer immediately throws him off a precipice. Ambrosio's death is drawn out further, however, allowing nature to take its revenge upon the master of artifice. Where in her end Antonia becomes once more a disembodied spirit, Ambrosio is reduced to pure matter destroyed by the nature he had violated:

The Sun now rose above the horizon; Its scorching beams darted full upon the head of the expiring Sinner. Myriads of insects were called forth by the warmth; They drank the blood which trickled from Ambrosio's wounds; He had no power to drive them from him, and they fastened upon his sores, darted their stings into his body, covered him with their multitudes, and inflicted on him tortures the most exquisite and insupportable. The Eagles of the rock tore his flesh piecemeal, and dug out his eye-balls with their crooked

161

beaks. A burning thirst tormented him; He heard the river's murmur as it rolled beside him, but strove in vain to drag himself towards the sound. Blind, maimed, helpless, and despairing, venting his rage in blasphemy and curses, execrating his existence, yet dreading the arrival of death destined to yield him up to greater torments, six miserable days did the Villain languish. On the Seventh a violent storm arose: The winds in fury rent up rocks and forests: The sky was now black with clouds, now sheeted with fire: The rain fell in torrents; It swelled the stream; The waves overflowed their banks; They reached the spot where Ambrosio lay, and when they abated carried with them into the river the Corse of the despairing Monk.

(p. 442)

In the end, Ambrosio becomes a debunked Prometheus. His seven-day torment is also Satan's clever parody of the divine act of creation. The approaching end is feared as worse than the suspense that precedes it, and is heralded by a natural apocalypse, a flood that, in an inversion of the biblical sequence, follows the conflagration of the convent. The two poles of Christian history, creation and apocalypse, collapse as they are rewritten by the infernal author Satan into a narrative of destruction.

Antonia and Ambrosio's parallel yet antithetical lives are, then, united in the act of rape, identified further by death, but separated by the act of dying. Lorenzo's dream, a Richardsonian fantasy of poetic justice in which the bad go to hell, the good to heaven, is fulfilled. While for Antonia death is a reunion with her mother, for Ambrosio it appears to involve total isolation from all human relations. Yet, at the end, the individual discovers that he was not as isolated as he had imagined. Ambrosio's death is preceded by the discovery of his true identity, which also involves re-establishing relations with his family. Before Ambrosio's final dismemberment, in an ironic replay of Christ's temptation by Satan, Lucifer (who obviously likes revising biblical scenes as much as Lewis enjoyed revising Radcliffe's) takes him up to the top of a precipice, to reveal his true identity: 'Hark, Ambrosio, while I unveil your crimes! . . . That Antonia whom you violated, was your Sister! That Elvira whom you murdered, gave you birth!' (p. 439). Like Oedipus, the hero only discovers his family after he has violated familial relations. The plot suggests how, for the individual

162

hero, whom we first encounter as a veritable orphan adopted into an all-male family, the discovery of relations, the realisation that his identity is defined not in isolation but through connections, is a catastrophe.

Moreover, the completely illusory nature of Ambrosio's individuality is exposed by the final revelation of the devil. Throughout the text Ambrosio has been torn by the classic conflict between individual will and social restraints, desire and duty, which he reconciled through hypocrisy. Earlier, Lewis has suggested that his inner desires, left to their own devices, would have been good. In the end, however, even Ambrosio's inner self is revealed to be the creation of another, as individual desire is reduced to an infernal myth. Like Caleb, he has been programmed, not only by the society he inhabits but also by a devil who exults:

> It was I who threw Matilda in your way; It was I who gave you entrance to Antonia's chamber; It was I who caused the dagger to be given you which pierced your Sister's bosom; and it was I who warned Elvira in dreams of your designs upon her Daughter, and thus, by preventing your profiting by her sleep, compelled you to add rape as well as incest to the catalogue of your crimes.
>
> (p. 440)

The individual discovers once more that he is not the author of his own narrative but only a character; the plotter has been part of a larger plot. He is the victim of social, natural, and finally supernatural agents, who in the end all conspire against him to expose his illusions about his own powers of self-determination.

In *The Monk*, then, male and female narratives of development are set up as opposites that meet when they both prove to be dead ends. The text's union of the two models offers a disastrous wedding of opposites, thematised also by the representation of a family whose reunion causes its destruction. Estranged from each other by circumstances, brother and sister meet as lover and beloved, and, finally, victor and victim. However, as in *Otranto*, the extermination of a cursed family line, which is here even more completely responsible for its own extermination, leaves a new order that survives. While the main plot is a dead end, in the subplot of Agnes and Raymond a real revival of the dead does occur. Lorenzo's raid of the convent has ambiguous consequences; while causing the death of his beloved, down in one subterranean vault, it enables him to discover and free his sister, who is reunited with and married to Raymond. Lorenzo's grief for Antonia is healed gradually, as he accepts the almost equally angelic Virginia, whom Lewis hastily manufactures at the end to replace Antonia. However, this marriage has been in fact long plotted and determined by Lorenzo's uncle. His desires thwarted by death, Lorenzo learns to channel his affections into a more appropriate object, a woman with a beautiful voice, caring (she nurses Agnes), beautiful, *and* of the right class. Individual desire and social duty, polarised in Ambrosio, are finally reconciled in Lorenzo. His acceptance of this substitute is more complete than that of Theodore at the end of *Otranto*: 'His esteem increased for her daily. Her unremitted endeavours to please him could not but succeed. His affection assumed stronger and warmer colours. Antonia's image was gradually effaced from his bosom; and Virginia became sole Mistress of that heart, which She well deserved to possess without a Partner' (pp. 419–20). The lost past, Agnes' dead child and Lorenzo's dead beloved, are relinquished gradually but thoroughly, without nostalgic regrets, by the surviving order.

While the main plot ends in polarisation, the subplot replays the romantic reconciliation of opposites we have seen in other works. The death of Antonia and Ambrosio and the marriages of the two couples mark the reestablishment of traditional social order in the text. The text thus appears as a process of social purification, in which the corruption and hypocrisy with which the narrative began has been exorcised through the scapegoats of Antonia and Ambrosio. The extreme poles of victor and victim meet by being annihilated, leaving a more moderate model for relations. Daniel Watkins has argued that in its exploration of the effect of forces beyond individual control the text indirectly exposes the power of social relations, and how they determine individual behaviour.[17] The original sin in the text is that of the mother, miscegenation, the crossing of social boundaries, an error reproduced in the stories of Marguerite, and potentially in that of Lorenzo. As in Walpole's text, the sins of the parents are visited on the children; the product of a transgression of class division, Ambrosio and Antonia are doomed. Furthermore, miscegenation, the unnatural mixing of opposites that should be kept apart, creates its opposite, incest, the equally unnatural mixing of the same. Both extremes are punished, leaving in the end a society reaffirmed by the consolidation of a middle path, the breeding of those who balance difference and likeness. The message of the story is thus, as Watkins argues, 'highly conservative and even reactionary'.[18]

The publication of *The Monk*, however, was seen as a literary revolution.[19] Fittingly, as it supports so many of his own theories, Sade hailed it as even preferable to the work of Radcliffe, whom he also admired. It was a symptom of the political Revolution, that brought real-life terrors surpassing those in literature, and so produced a need for more extreme and terrifying art to capture the experience of the time:

> There was not a man alive who had not experienced in the short span of four or five years more misfortunes than the most celebrated novelist could portray in a century. Thus, to compose works of interest, one had to call upon the aid of hell itself, and to find in the world of make-believe things wherewith one was fully familiar merely by delving into man's daily life in this age of iron![20]

While Sade hailed it as a just reflection of life in a turbulent time, many early English reviewers admired the work for its delineation of the 'stronger passions' and of 'artful temptation working on self-sufficient pride, superstition, and lasciviousness', for its skilful use of the German tradition, and its 'beautiful little ballads'.[21] Coleridge claimed it was 'the offspring of no uncommon genius'.[22] However, although the author showed signs of real talent, he was wasting it, as the text left Coleridge with 'the most painful impression . . . of great acquirements and splendid genius employed to furnish a *mormo* for children, a poison for youth, and a provocative for the debauchee'.[23] Like others, Coleridge attacked the work especially for its pernicious influence on its readers. He denounced it as a story 'which if a parent saw in the hands of a son or daughter, he might reasonably turn pale'.[24] Appropriately, considering his concern with parents controlling the reading of their children, Coleridge found Elvira's censorship of Antonia's Bible particularly blasphemous. *The Monk* became a part of the debates over the social role of literature. The outrage was intensified because the author was no private person but a member of parliament (suitably Lewis had inherited Beckford's position and was quickly claiming a similar notoriety). The author occupied an important position of social authority; as Coleridge cried in horror: 'Yes! the author of *The Monk* signs himself a Legislator! – We stare and tremble.'[25] A professed guardian of law and order seemed to be encouraging its total dissolution.

Lewis's response to the attainment of such infamy at the age of nineteen was ambivalent. Unlike Radcliffe, who kept herself in private, he sought fame and publicity; a member of the colonial *nouveau riche*, he tried to ally himself with those of aristocratic birth. He also allowed himself to become totally identified with both his titular character and the work itself, and was known for the rest of his life as 'Monk' Lewis. But that identification had discomforting aspects. Attacks on his work were also on his character, as the *Critical Review* indicated when it denounced the text as: 'a species of brutality, such as no observation of character can justify, because no good man would willingly suffer them to pass, how transiently, through his own mind'.[26] To have even imagined such crimes was a sign of deep depravity.

While nominally allowing himself to be identified with his work, Lewis attempted in other ways to detach himself from it, suggesting, as Robin Lyndenberg says, his 'fear of being identified and characterised by his novel: a fear of his reader's responses to the text and the assumptions about its creator'.[27] Some of his strategies are apparent in the text itself and its treatment of art and authority. Lewis ironises his own distance from the text.[28] For David Punter, the author is 'his own melodramatic villain' who keeps himself at a distance to maintain a sadistic power not only over his characters, but over his readers, whom he makes passive spectators, and 'the main object of Lewis's animosity, the vassal who is totally in the power of the narrator as lord'.[29] Violent swings in tone from tragedy to high farce, such as the juxtaposition of the death of Elvira with Jacintha's ludicrous revision of her death and resurrection, further enable the author to remain removed from his narrative.[30] As Lyndenberg argues, such measures suggest Lewis's 'deeper uncertainty about his role as a writer' which makes him 'affect a flippancy and indifference towards all literary activity'.[31]

Moreover, in the poetic preface, an imitation of Horace, Lewis expresses his ambivalence about the consequences of publication. Publication is here equated with death, as the work is sent out: 'Go then, and pass that dangerous bourn / Whence never Book can back return.' Its destination is the literary graveyard where unread texts rot:

In some dark dirty corner thrown,
Mouldy with damps, with cobwebs strown,
Your leaves shall be the Book-worm's prey.

If, however, the text is read it may expect an equally unpleasant
fate. Abusive critics will make the book wish 'for me, and home,
and quiet', to return to the privacy of its author. The traditional
literary *topos* of the invidious meanness of critics who prey on
creation is later taken up in the second chapter of volume 2, which
begins with a quotation from Pope, on the vanity of fame. The
romantic young Theodore, who is anxious to write poetry, is warned
by the more pragmatic and rational Raymond:

> you cannot employ your time worse than in making verses.
> An Author, whether good or bad, or between both, is an
> Animal whom every body is privileged to attack; For though
> All are not able to write books, all conceive themselves able
> to judge them . . . to enter the lists of literature is wilfully to
> expose yourself to the arrows of neglect, ridicule, envy, and
> disappointment. . . . But I am conscious, that all these sage
> observations are thrown away upon you. Authorship is a
> mania to conquer which no reasons are sufficiently strong;
> and you might as easily persuade me not to love, as I per-
> suade you not to write.
>
> (*The Monk*, pp. 198–9)

Writing, like erotic desire, is a form of possession, a compulsion, as
Lewis himself confessed that he was 'horribly bit by the rage of
writing'.[32] But it invariably leads to vicious attacks on the author's
identity, which it exposes through the act of publication.

The prefatorial description of the movement of the text from
the private sphere in which it was created to the public world in
which it will, no doubt, be destroyed, gives us a miniature
Bildungsroman, or *Kunstlerroman*, explaining the growth of the
author. Lewis's own development, thus, is set up as analogous to
the fates of Antonia and Ambrosio. In it he tries to reconcile his
desire for the security of privacy and his need for publicity. Fearful,
the author stays at home, only entering the world symbolically
through his text which, at the end of the preface, returns to its
creator. The return of the book causes the revelation of the author's
identity, given in a little self-portrait. The text's circular return to
its origins thus suggests an identification of public and private, text

167

and author, created and creator. As Lyndenberg notes, however, in revealing himself Lewis emphasises here his own emotional instability and unreliability.[33] He also draws attention to his age, an excuse he used also to appease the wrath of his father.[34] Given his youth and character, the author cannot be held responsible for what he has written. Moreover, he never imagined that his book would be taken as having any moral effect at all. As he explained to his father:

> [It] never struck me that the exhibition of vice, in her temporary triumph, might possibly do as much harm as her final exposure and punishment would do good. To do much good, indeed, was more than I expected of my book; having always believed that our conduct depends on our hearts and characters, not upon the books we read or the sentiments we hear. But though I did not expect much benefit to arise from the perusal of a trifling romance, written by a youth of twenty, I was in my own mind quite certain that no harm could be produced by a work whose subject was furnished by one of our best moralists.[35]

Lewis draws on *Areopagitica's* anti-censorship argument, that 'best books to a naughty mind are not inapplicable to occasions of evil'.[36] For Lewis, the author is, as Punter describes him, an aristocratic lord, but one with no particular moral authority, since responsibility lies with the reader. Authorial irresponsibility is justified, however, for, as Lyndenberg notes, the text makes the assertion of moral authority a worse crime, with graver consequences, than that of moral transgression.[37] The figure of Lorenzo becomes a scapegoat for the author, as the hero's acts 'may reveal in exaggerated form, Lewis's own fear of the responsibility of seizing moral authority in his narrative'.[38] The author is, further, a perpetual child, as he reveals that maturation, individual change, and development is a complete disaster. As the gothic so often dramatises in its villains, to take control and to assert one's own identity is to lose both. All direct attempts at taking authority and power, at effecting change through individuals, are disastrous. Art is at its best a mere fraud; at its worst it is the infernal arts not merely of Ambrosio, but of Lucifer, whose final revelation as author of the plots parodies Radcliffe's emergence at the end of her text as benign deity behind the action. The infernal author is thus the double of Lewis, who offers him a model for creation as parodic revision, especially in his rewriting of the story of creation as Ambrosio's end of apocalyptic destruction. While Lewis presents the artist as the innocent victim of critics who prey on literary creation, he simultaneously turns creation itself into a predatory act.[39] In a world in which art is associated with fraud and deceit, artistic creation is destructive. The only art that reveals any truth is the one that unveils its own falseness and gothic tendencies.

3 'A Way thus Dark and Circuitous':[1] The Revolution Comes Full Circle

Considering the view of artistic authority and creation expressed in *The Monk*, it seems fitting that most of Lewis's other works were either editions or translations, primarily from the German. For Scott, this was a case of arrested literary development, as Lewis's 'boyishness went through life with him. He was a child, and a spoiled child, but a child of high imagination; and so he wasted himself on ghost-stories and German romances.'[2] *The Monk* was his most 'original' work. But its reaction to Radcliffe did not go unnoticed by its original. Her last novel published before her retreat into seclusion is a response to him in which she recovers her usurped narrative.[3] Radcliffe reads Lewis's story of plots that get beyond their authors' control as a narrative of his own refusal to take responsible charge of the material he has appropriated. In retelling his story in *The Italian,* she reasserts narrative law and order, restoring the correct version he has corrupted, and re-establishes her authority, insisting on both the duty and the power of the author to control the plot she originated.

One of the easiest ways of seeing Radcliffe's correction of Lewis is by examining her reappropriation of her telltale image of the veil, which appears obsessively in this text. Its purpose is ambiguous, as it represents both reassuring protection and a sinister concealment of purpose. A veil protects by disguising Ellena in her escapes from her prisons; however, she is also threatened with being forced to take the veil, and is kidnapped when a veil is thrown over her face. In her confinement, veils provide her with a means of communicating safely, as guardedly, with other nuns and later Vivaldi; they are a medium for contact, but also an obstacle to union and freedom, as it is Ellena's novitiate veil that ostensibly prevents her immediate marriage with Vivaldi. When the lovers are parted, Vivaldi in the subterranean labyrinth of the Inquisition is bound by a black veil. Unable to see anything, he encounters his questioners as threateningly disembodied voices. To be veiled is to be at the mercy of a godlike power that sees without being seen, as the Inquisition's invisibility, like its mystery, is a source of its tyrannical and gothic potential to oppress and destroy others.

Even more directly, the opening scene of the first volume immediately establishes the relation between Radcliffe and Lewis's texts through the image of the veil. Like *The Monk*, we begin in a church, with a young man looking at a beautiful veiled woman, whose voice attracts his attention and makes him want to see behind the veil. Lewis's elaborately staged and delayed opening is greatly abbreviated here, however, with uncharacteristic directness on Radcliffe's part. We get right to the point in the first two sentences:

> It was in the church of San Lorenzo at Naples, in the year 1758, that Vincentio di Vivaldi first saw Ellena Rosalba. The sweetness and fine expression of her voice attracted his attention to her figure, which had a distinguished air of delicacy and grace; but her face was concealed in her veil.
>
> (*The Italian*, p. 5)

Like Antonia, this veiled female is accompanied by an older woman, here, as Radcliffe redeems the aunt Lewis slandered, Ellena's good aunt and maternal substitute, Bianchi. In general, the negative aspects of Lewis's opening scenes are reversed, as Radcliffe's church is purified of Lewis's theatricality and focus on religious hypocrisy. Moreover, while the unveiling promised in the first sentences is, as in Lewis's text, immediately fulfilled, it is not through Vivaldi's direct intervention. Nature, not masculine desire, removes the veil from Ellena's face, allowing him a brief vision as:

> the breeze from the water caught the veil, which Ellena had no longer a hand sufficiently disengaged to confine, and, wafting it partially aside, disclosed to him a countenance more touchingly beautiful than he had dared to image. Her features were of the Grecian outline, and, though they expressed the tranquillity of an elegant mind, her dark blue eyes sparkled with intelligence. She was assisting her companion so anxiously, that she did not immediately observe the admiration she had inspired; but the moment her eyes

met those of Vivaldi, she became conscious of their effect, and she hastily drew her veil.

(ibid., p. 6)

The relations between the women themselves and the onlooker is telling in its revision of Lewis's scene. Vivaldi comes to the aid of the women, but they are already assisting themselves; as we will learn in the next pages, they are financially independent. Moreover, Ellena is no passive and disembodied Antonia; she is too busy at first to see that she is exposed to masculine attention, but when she becomes conscious of Vivaldi's invasive gaze, she comes to her own defence, using the veil. Unlike Antonia, she is able to use weapons, even those often used against women, to protect herself.

When Vivaldi later rescues Ellena from the evil Abbess, who offers her a choice between two veils that will oppress her – the noviate and the marriage veil – this opening scene is replayed. Ellena lifts her veil so that Vivaldi may see her face and recognise her. Her union with Vivaldi becomes thematically associated with a form of revelation that will be liberation from mysterious systems of oppression. But as in Lewis also, the image of the lifted veil suggests a larger narrative strategy, in which the author is constantly revealing hidden things to free the reader from the tyranny of appearances.

As the text's obsession with tapestries and coverings implies, *Udolpho* stays on the surface; one rarely sees into the hearts of any characters aside from Emily, who herself is not much inclined to intense self-scrutiny. This is partially because for Radcliffe, like St Aubert, who trusts faces to reveal character (a belief for which he is mocked as naive by the truly superficial Mme Charon), surfaces are substance.[4] Although there are occasional pieces of information which we get and Emily doesn't (most significantly, we see behind the black veil in an authorial aside that Emily is not privy to), which elevate us above her, a figure like Montoni seems almost as inscrutable to us as he is to her. It is only at the end that the veil lifts, in an apocalyptic revelation of the meaning of the story, which suggests, too, as Montoni evaporates easily, that there never was anything behind his surface. But deferral of revelation has, as I have suggested, several consequences. In general, it tends to create a bathos in revelation, a risk run by the moral itself which may appear inadequate, or banal in comparison to the power of the mysteries of the story which cannot simply be explained by such a perfunctory message. The moral seems to stand in opposition to the aesthetic pleasure of the text, which may overpower it. Revelation seems an aesthetic disaster, as the sudden clarity at the end of the text is not as alluring as the dark mood of mystery throughout it. The attempt to unite the moral and the aesthetic at the end only emphasises their disjunction, an antithesis that Lewis will flagrantly exploit.

The Italian, however, tries to reconcile the moral and the aesthetic more fully than the earlier work, to draw together the two elements that, like other partners, including male and female, Lewis polarises. Reconciliation is achieved by a rhythm of continual veiling and unveiling. In *The Italian*, we get frequent glimpses into the hearts of the characters. So we see behind Schedoni's mask, and into his heart on frequent occasions (see, for example, pp. 34, 101, 110, 225–8); as in *The Monk*, hypocrisy is shown only to be immediately exposed. *Udolpho* works to identify us with the experience of the heroine in a way that may make us become dangerously passive and out of control, so that we need to be rescued at the end by paternalistic external authority. In *The Italian*, however, our detachment is established by the device of the opening frame, in which English travellers abroad witness a mysterious event. The text that follows is a confession they read to illuminate what they have seen. Like the fictitious reader in the frame, we are foreigners, in a strange land where people behave in ways unfamiliar to us. But our structural distancing from the action suggests Radcliffe's creation of a more detached interpretive perspective. While, as its opening epigram implied, *Udolpho* draws us into the text, in *The Italian*, we remain on the outside looking in, in a recreation of Lewis's voyeuristic position. Our detachment from the characters is paradoxically reinforced by the intimate moments which allow us to see into them. Seeing into the minds of others can be a means of separation as well as identification.

Unlike Lewis, however, Radcliffe does not allow us to fall into an easy sense of interpretive omnipotence through these revelations of the private worlds of characters that are veiled by their public actions. Despite the fact that the genres with which she is working (the sentimental novel as well as the gothic) are associated with the exploration of interiority, Radcliffe manifests a distrust of the revelation of private lives that is certainly at least partially responsible for the notorious flatness of her characters. Such flatness has often been traced to a conservative distrust of individualism, and Burkean fear of the consequences of an indulged subjectivity. But her disinterest in prying into the secret lives of her characters may also be a reflection of her own belief in the right to the same privacy that makes self-indulgence possible. Like Godwin, though for antithetical reasons, she shows how knowing others can become not a form of sympathetic identification and intimacy but an aggressive invasion of the right of privacy. She, too, attacks forms of interference and invasion, but associates them subtly with radical projects as well as tyrannical systems of authority. Even while he is a representative of the Catholic Church, Schedoni is in many ways a Godwinian philosopher, as well as a demonic author and reader like Caleb, who has a desire to know what lurks in the hearts of others. As in *The Monk*, vision is associated with a detached, apparently objective, way of knowing another, which in reality is allied with violent forms of objectification, especially murder. Schedoni's eyes, like those of so many Gothic villains – Manfred, Ambrosio, Vathek, Melmoth, Dracula – are weapons: 'so piercing that they seemed to penetrate, at a single glance, into the hearts of men, and to read their most secret thoughts; few persons could support their scrutiny, or even endure to meet them twice' (p. 35). Knowledge for him is power, as, seeing others' weaknesses he is able to control them: not only the Marchesa, whom he easily manipulates, but also Vivaldi, whose vulnerability to superstition he suspects, knowing the young man better than he does himself. Radcliffe reminds both herself and her reader that revealing others' secrets may be an act of oppression, rather than liberation.

Furthermore, Radcliffe suggests that revelation may have less dangerous but still ambiguous results. To illustrate this point, the text stages several significant unveilings twice: once in a flat bathetic version (which recalls Radcliffe's familiar pattern of overwrought expectation followed by banal disappointment), then afterwards in a true version in which expectations are fulfilled. As I mentioned, the unveiling of Ellena in the opening is replayed in the later rescue scene. But that scene itself relies on the central pattern of the text, in which a false unveiling occurs before the true can take place. So Vivaldi, searching a convent for Ellena, assumes, with the obsessive logic typical of a gothic character, that every veiled nun he sees is her. Watching the first female figure he happens to encounter unveil, he is proved wrong when 'a very lovely face appeared, but not Ellena's' (p. 119). As in *Udolpho*, there is a gap between expectation and satisfaction, a gap which, after the world of *The Monk* where expectation satisfied leads to disgust and destruction, seems to play an even more vital part. Yet deferral is here brief, much briefer than in *Udolpho*. Immediately after Vivaldi's disappointment, a second nun appears whom he, having learned little from the first interpretive error, also is certain is Ellena. This time, however, the unveiling proves him right. Similarly, going to meet Vivaldi shortly afterwards, Ellena assumes a masked man she meets is him; she lifts her veil as the arranged signal, only to be greeted by a total stranger. Shocked at her impropriety in thus exposing herself, she becomes cautious, only to meet Vivaldi who reveals himself to her. Finally, in the scenes in the Inquisition, Vivaldi is sure that one masked inquisitor is his mysterious visitor; the lifting of the cowl, however, proves him wrong, and it is only at his next interrogation that the true informant reveals himself by removing his cowl.

In *Udolpho*, there is frequently no predictable relation between presentiment and fulfilment, and a striking discrepancy as well as narrative distance between mystery and its revelation, effect and cause. In *The Monk*, however, the relation between presentiment and fulfilment is too strict, setting up a world in which analogy itself has been caught up in a rigidly governed and determined mechanistic system of cause and effect. *The Italian* strikes a balance between the two extremes, in a way that will reconcile the aesthetic pleasure in mystery and the moral imperative towards clarification. Moreover, this pattern of an erroneous unveiling that does not reveal truth followed by a true one that does, serves as an image for Radcliffe's relation to Lewis. It suggests a pattern for revision, in which Lewis's text is reduced to a false revelation, that is now followed by Radcliffe's correct as authorised version.

This model appears in the text's representation of other forms of repetition which set up a difference between a premature version of an event and its later completed version.[5] So Ellena and Vivaldi's wedding is interrupted, and deferred in order to be repeated and fulfilled only at the very end. At the end, too, Vivaldi's servant Paulo serves as a carnivalesque moralist, explaining the point of the entire story: 'we had to go through purgatory before we could reach paradise; but the second part is come at last' (p. 413). The Dantesque model here (recalled also in the scenes in the Inquisition, in which Dante's *Inferno* is frequently referred to) suggests a linear model for narrative, involving, too, a progression from darkness to light. Yet the linear model is accompanied by the circularity of the repetitive story.[6] The model itself is part of a repeated pattern, connected to Radcliffe's typical creation of chiaroscuro contrasts between light and dark, the beautiful and the sublime. Earlier in the story, Ellena and Schedoni, accompanied by a guide, leave the isolated seaside home of Spalatro where Schedoni has almost murdered Ellena. They pass through a gloomy landscape, spending the night in a haunted and sublime ruin where they fear they have been ambushed by the pursuing Spalatro. They suddenly emerge from this darkness into a carnival world of a fair, upon which the guide exclaims, 'to come, all of a sudden, to such a place as this, why it is like coming out of purgatory into paradise!' (p. 273). Vivaldi's entrance into Rome also involves a similar emergence from darkness into a carnival world of light, though one that has the inquisitorial inferno as its centre (see p. 195). These preliminary exits from dark to light are rehearsals for the end, when the couple have truly entered into a paradise described in images that recall and fulfil the earlier scenes of carnival festivity.

At the carnival Schedoni and Ellena see a performance of the story of Virginia, in which: 'The people above were acting what seemed to have been intended for a tragedy, but what their strange gestures, uncouth recitation, and incongruous countenances, had transformed into a comedy' (p. 274). In this carnival world, artistic intent and achievement are polarised, in what might be read as a dig at Lewis's transformation of the sublime into the ridiculous. But the story of Virginia has obvious relevance for Radcliffe's narrative, as Schedoni recognises. Watching the scenes in which the father kills his daughter, 'The feelings of Schedoni, at this instant, inflicted a punishment almost worthy of the crime he had meditated' (p. 275). Art realises and fulfils the action which he, fortunately, had not completed in life. In one respect though, *The Italian* itself is the production of Virginia that Schedoni and Ellena see, in which a tragic story is rewritten as a comedy. But whereas the play of the carnival defeats its actors' intentions, Radcliffe claims control over her own art, as she wrests it back from Lewis's usurpation. Where Lewis, in his attempt to turn her essentially comic plot into a tragedy, made it a ridiculous farce, she, in reappropriating it again, will correct it by repeating it and restoring it to its original form. Repetition is a means of recovering authorial control, and of turning tragedy into comedy, in which

175

Lewis's staging of a false tragic revelation is succeeded by its true form.

The central action of this process involves therefore the over-throw and exposure of false systems of authority, which keep the lovers apart, and their replacement with true authority, that brings them together. For Radcliffe, as for Lewis, the primary obstacle here is a monk, suggesting too an identification of false authority in the text with Lewis's work. Radcliffe's monk is not the seducer and brother of the heroine, but one whose relationship to his victim is even more perplexing: he begins as her would-be murderer, abruptly turns into her father, and in the end is exposed instead as her wicked uncle who murdered her real father. Schedoni is also a more complex character than Montoni, or appears that way for the reason that Radcliffe allows us to see into him. Perhaps this is poetically just for a character who sees so clearly and invasively into the privacies of others: in a Dantesque *contrapasso*, the exposer is himself gradually exposed. The character who both embodies the text's principle of concealment and suspense and yet also represents demonic forms of revelation recalls earlier villains. A version of the gothic philosopher later associated with Godwin, Schedoni more directly recalls the sophistry and diabolic rhetoric of Milton's Satan; he is a subtle arguer who 'cared not for truth, nor sought it by bold and broad argument, but loved to exert the wily cunning of his nature in hunting it through artificial perplexities' (p. 34). The false father is paired with a wicked mother, in this case Vivaldi's, so that both children seem potentially cursed with highly undesirable relations. As these two figures are locked, often closeted, in an unholy alliance, they appear to be a parodic set of parents whose ambiguous and un-natural coupling not only aims at murder rather than procreation but symbolically turns the relation between lovers into that of brother and sister.

Other images of false religious and parental authority are ex-posed and eliminated in the text. Vivaldi's father is a parody of Burkean conservatism, who denies the legitimacy of all individual desire, telling his son: 'you belong to your family, not your family to you; . . . you are only a guardian of its honour, and not at liberty to dispose of yourself' (p. 30). The Abbess is Radcliffe's version of Lewis's Prioress, a petty tyrant, who considers violations of class boundaries as worse than sacrilege. Her male counterpart is the Abate whose sin is ineffectuality:

thus, with a temper and disposition directly opposite to those of the severe and violent abbess, he was equally selfish, and almost equally culpable, since by permitting evil, he was nearly as injurious in his conduct as those who planned it. Indolence and timidity, a timidity the consequence of want of clear perception, deprived him of all energy of character; he was prudent rather than wise, and so fearful of being thought to do wrong that he seldom did right.

(p. 121)

Evil is a product of not only the abuse of power and authority, but the failure to exercise it.

The lovers themselves are revolutionary figures in their resistance to these false systems which unnaturally impede the fulfilment of their individual desires. Ellena defies the Abbess, insisting on her own inviolable integrity: 'force may send me to the altar, but that it never shall compel me to utter vows which my heart abhors; and if I am constrained to appear there, it shall be only to protest against her tyranny, and against the form intended to sanction it' (p. 92). She insists on her rights as an individual to choose freely in respect to marriage. Vivaldi also resists unjust power of different kinds. He defies the domestic tyranny of his father, noting, 'there are some few instances in which it is virtuous to disobey' (p. 30).

However, while Vivaldi thus seems to resemble Valancourt, who sets individual desire over social obligation, he in fact helps reconcile the two. His experiences transform a sense of personal grievance and injustice into an awareness of social injustice. As in *Caleb Williams*, self-interest produces and is transcended by social consciousness. So in his entrance to the Inquisition he undergoes a revelation:

While meditating upon these horrors, Vivaldi lost every selfish consideration in astonishment and indignation of the sufferings, which the frenzied wickedness of man prepares for man. . . . 'Is this possible!' said Vivaldi internally, 'Can this be in human nature! – Can such horrible perversion of right be permitted. Can man, who calls himself endowed with reason, and immeasurably superior to every other created being, argue himself into the commission of such horrible folly, such inveterate cruelty, as exceeds all the acts of the most irrational and ferocious brute. Brutes do not deliberately

177

slaughter their species; it remains for man only, man, proud of his prerogative of reason, and boasting of his sense of justice, to unite the most terrible extremes of folly and wickedness!'

(p. 198)

Called in front of the Inquisition, he appears detached from his own situation and selfish concerns:

He felt less apprehension for himself, than indignation of the general injustice and cruelty, which the tribunal was permitted to exercise upon others; and this virtuous indignation gave a loftiness, a calm heroic grandeur to his mind, which never, for a moment, forsook him, except when he conjectured what might be the sufferings of Ellena.

(p. 305)

Vivaldi here seems an oddly Godwinian hero,[7] a revolutionary who here has achieved a revolution of sentiment through the achievement of enlightened objectivity and detachment. Feeling is itself purified of its contaminated root in self-interest, to become pure disinterested sympathy for others, conferring upon Vivaldi a degree of nobility that the more selfish Valancourt lacks. In Vivaldi, individual desire has been sublimated into social duty. However, by an odd coincidence typical of Radcliffe, this transformation will produce the satisfaction of individual desires. The opposition between self-love and social duty is in fact an illusion created by the abuse of parental authority.

Like Lewis's Lorenzo, Vivaldi wants to expose hypocrisy, threatening the silent Schedoni: 'I know and will proclaim you to the world. I will strip you of the holy hypocrisy in which you shroud yourself; announce to all your society the despicable artifices you have employed, and the misery you have occasioned. Your character shall be announced aloud' (p. 104). But Vivaldi himself does not achieve this revolution; in the end, he is the vehicle for the plot against Schedoni planned by his ex-accomplice Nicola di Zampari. Evil tidily destroys itself, in a vicious circle in which Schedoni commits suicide and takes his enemy with him. Vivaldi is thus somewhat ineffectual as an active revolutionary; he is an actor rather than author of a plot to expose evil. This is partially because the text constantly reminds us that characters cannot see the consequences of their own actions, for they do not have complete knowledge of the relations that govern this world. Olivia helps Ellena, unaware that in so doing she is rescuing her own child (p. 384); Schedoni's trick of sending Spalatro to Rome backfires, as it is 'the means of bringing his crimes before the public' (p. 362). Vivaldi's plot might have been disastrous; Radcliffe teases us several times by reminding us what his feeling would have been if he'd believed he was accusing his beloved's father. The revolution Vivaldi plans gets outside of his control, although without the devastating consequences of Lorenzo's plot, because it comes into the power of the continuing authority of the Inquisition which is itself untouched by the revolution. While Lewis condemns the Church as a place for hypocrisy, Radcliffe takes the institution associated with gothic oppression, and revises it as an image for a more benign authority, a social institution able to contain and direct individual action.

In *The Monk*, individual desires and social requirements were irrevocably opposed, even though it is suggested ultimately that individual desires are produced by social, if not also supernatural, forces. Correcting this plot, and returning to the model of *Udolpho*, *The Italian* moves towards a world in which social duty, loyalty to the family, tradition, and individual desire are reconciled. The reconciliation is achieved by the removal of false figures of authority, and the gradual emergence of good models already present in the system. Schedoni turns out to be a false father, so that Ellena is not contaminated by her origins: she is the child of the innocent victim not his criminal victor, the descendent of the good brother not the bad, as the text trots out the familiar themes of fraternal rivalry, jealousy, fratricide, and a usurpation of both property and wife. Furthermore, the evil false father is destroyed by a plot he himself created that gets out of his control; the mother, by her own evil passions that turn upon her. The death of the bad parents is countered by the recovery of the true good parent: Ellena's mother Olivia, who is discovered – surprise! – not dead, but in a convent, and who, by another predictable coincidence, turns out to be Ellena's earlier rescuer.

As in Walpole, the text moves towards a future in which the elimination of one past makes possible the recovery of another. As in both *Otranto* and *Udolpho*, a poisonous past disappears (and Schedoni neatly poisons himself, suggesting even further than the earlier works the self-destructive quality of evil) so that the future emerges purified. This process of purification, moreover, involves the redemption of both the extremes of tradition and the individual. The good Abbess of Our Lady of Pity (a kind of female version of *The Romance of the Forest*'s Rousseauean La Luc) is an example of a proper leader and spiritual authority, affording 'a striking instance of the influence, which a virtuous mind may acquire over others, as well as of the extensive good that it may thus diffuse' (p. 299). Virtue originates in individuals, who, serving as models for others, gradually influence society. Against her more common image of the evil individual who is isolated from society by self-interest, but whose autonomy turns out to be an illusion, Radcliffe sets up an alternative individualism, compatible with her own self-image, in which the individual, rightly self-governed and self-controlled, becomes an authority figure presiding over a community. Such authority is not incompatible with institutions but can exist within them: so Vivaldi, horrified by the injustice of the inquisitorial system, encounters the good inquisitor, whose fairness and justice surprise him, causing yet another revolution of sentiment in which he realises that virtue and power can be united. As Burke argued, external authority and individual free will are interdependent; it is only the abuse of, on the one hand, institutions and tradition, and, on the other, individual freedom – not their essential natures – that creates an opposition between them. The final revelation of Ellena's origins removes all conflict, suggesting that the law of the father and the desires of the son are both really satisfied by the same act.

This conclusion obviously invites the criticism that Radcliffe solves problems by a retreat to a benign romance world in which conflict turns out to have been mere illusion, a world suggested by *The Italian*'s fairy-tale style ending. For Radcliffe, as for Burke, the antithesis between individual and society, desire and restraint, is itself a fantasy in the mind of the alienated individual. In her creation of the final fantasy world, Radcliffe draws attention once more to her own position as a model for the alternative individualism and authority that emerges at the end of the text.

As Janet Todd notes, the end oddly downplays the anticipated reunion between boy and girl, shifting the focus suddenly to the reunion of servant and master.[8] However, throughout the text, and less directly in her other works, a parallel is established between the narrator's control of her story and the aristocrat's control of servants. As we have seen, from Walpole on, servants play an important and distinctive role in the gothic. According to Walpole, the servants were a sign of his Shakespearean inheritance; they invoke the presence of the Shakespearean lawless and unruly imagination. But, as I noted in relation to *Caleb Williams*, they have important social as well as literary resonances. Todd sees the representation of servants as a response to an emerging transformation of master–servant relations, in which an earlier feudal relation based on loyalty and love was being transformed into a purely economic relation. The gothic's idealisation of the devoted servant is part of its nostalgia for the good old days before commerce debased all human relations. In *The Italian*, Paulo is an extreme version of this ideal, a servant who wants to die for his master. Like other of Radcliffe servants he is extremely oral, being both tediously loquacious and perpetually hungry.[9] In their attention to material needs, the servants are seen as all appetite; the master–servant relationship is analogous to the rule of body and matter by mind, as they require the aristocrats to restrain them. The threat of lower class subversion, a real possibility in the 1790s, as is seen in concern with servants' insubordination and betrayal of their masters to the government, is never directly expressed in Radcliffe's gentile world. In its most threatening form it appears in the figures of the banditti, those subterranean presences of *Udolpho* and all of Radcliffe's stories, who represent dangerous 'lower' forces – the lower classes and the imagination, or what we would call subconscious. These forces are more commonly present in benign, as sublimated, forms. Like most other servants, Paulo has absolutely no self-control; he is constantly erupting, bursting out of bonds, including those of imposed silence which he finds the most oppressive constraint of all. He provides a comic version of revolutionary energy; a symbol of the lower forces of society, the body, and also, as servants are associated with both the supernatural and knowledge repressed from the upper classes, of the lower faculty of the imagination or subconscious. He is raw nature which must be shaped and ordered by aristocratic art, both for his own and for social good.

The fact that Paulo's speech in particular must be controlled is significant. An important function of servants in gothic novels is to tell stories, often in order to convey information to which other characters, because of aristocratic codes of discretion and indirection, have no access. It was because of this association with low forms such as ghost stories that Locke found them improper companions for children, evincing a middle-class distrust of servants found also in Godwin. Servants are, moreover, frequently represented as a medium which cannot artistically shape the message it conveys, but spews it out in disjointed, disordered form, in which ideas, as if straight from the subconscious, are related by pure association rather than reason. Their perpetual inability to get to a point is a kind of comic version, like the players at the fair, of Radcliffe's own method of creating suspense.

Schedoni's guide's narrative of the story of the Barone di Cambrusca is an important example, which spans many pages. The guide is a version of Paulo; a lesser one, anonymous (suggesting his lack of identity except as a device), and whose relation to Schedoni is – appropriately, considering the villain's view of the basis of relations – purely commercial. The relevance of the guide's story to the main plot is never made clear; we suspect (well-conditioned in gothic paranoia to make everything connect) that the evil Baron will turn out to be Schedoni. We want all bad men to be the same, and Schedoni himself, reacting strongly to the story, suggests such an identification. In fact the Baron turns out to be the similar sounding but apparently quite distinct and ultimately irrelevant Count di Bruni. However, this story is less about the evil it refers to than about how to tell stories, as the episode turns into a battle for authorial control between a lower-class employee and his authoritarian master.[10] While the guide takes his time telling the story, in the circuitously digressive way typical of associative lower-class speech, Schedoni tries to impose order and telos on it, urging him to 'be brief' (p. 279), 'speak to the point' (p. 280); 'Well! this history will never have an end!' (p. 281). For the guide, such hurry is unnatural to the nature of the material he has; he complains 'As if a story could be told in two words' (p. 279). He notes, moreover, that in fact Schedoni's constant demands for the point interrupt the story, keeping it from reaching its end: 'You never will let me finish, Signor'; finally Schedoni breaks in, 'I have listened too long to this idle history. . . . I will hear no more of this absurdity' (p. 285), and the story stops. The attempt to impose too much linear order on the material leads to its abrupt conclusion; by wanting the point too much, Schedoni, and the readers who suffer with him, never get one at all.

Such episodes are typical of the gothic's general self-consciousness about the ways in which stories get told, and offers a defence of Radcliffe's own method. In his fight here for authorial control, as in his penetration into the minds of others, Schedoni is a satanic author. By making him a master of suspense and indirection, Radcliffe, like Godwin and Lewis, suggests the possible doubling between a satanic character and his creator. Even more than Caleb, however, Schedoni is clearly the opposite of his creator, a demonic author whose creation becomes destruction, as he re-presses rather than sublimates the guide's unfiltered narrative. The repressed, as always, returns. Like both of Lewis's male figures, he is a plotter who creates forces beyond his control: seeking to use the Inquisition against his enemies, he finds himself destroyed by its machinery.

The text concludes with a re-establishment of law and order that serves as a corrective not only of Schedoni's machinations, but also Lewis's. In recognition of his loyalty, Vivaldi offers Paulo inde-pendence which the servant vehemently rejects, choosing to stay with his master. The lower order recognises its need for the higher, as its guarantee of true freedom. By focusing on this reunion, Radcliffe reinforces the similarity of the relationship between the lord and his servant and the author and her text. As the proper feudal lord is a benevolent authority who controls his employee with love and kindness, so the author has to order her material, taking charge of it responsibly but without simply imposing on it a tyrannical will. Art's rule over nature must liberate not enslave it.

The end is a masterpiece of authorial control, precisely because of its creation of an impression of total imaginative freedom. As a concluding scene it is somewhat surprising. After all, the text opened with the narrative frame, which served as a model for readers' detached relation to what they will witness. Such a frame can be useful as a disclaimer of authorial responsibility, as it creates the fiction that the author is simply a medium and not the origin of the work. The end, however, fails to return to and neatly close the framing device, creating an odd and rather messy asymmetry, in which expected repetition does not occur. Nor does the text conclude, as *Udolpho* had, with an authoritative moral that asserts the writer's control over the interpretation of her own text. It ends with a carnivalesque scene, which recalls from the narrative past the earlier scene at the fair, as well as the carnival Vivaldi saw when he entered Rome. Paulo becomes the 'master of revels', a Saturn-alian lord of misrule, who in his joy confuses all natural and syntactical order and hierarchy:

who, I say, would have guessed we should ever be let loose

183

again! who would have thought we should ever know what it
is to be happy! Yet here we are all abroad once more! All at
liberty! And may run, if we will, straight forward, from one
end of the earth to the other, and back again without being
stopped! May fly in the sea, or swim in the sky, or tumble over
head and heels into the moon!

(p. 414)

Revealing his Shakespearean ancestry, Paulo becomes a mixture of
Puck and Bottom,[11] whose famous speech he extends, turning the
world upside down. When 'a grave personage near him' corrects
his metaphorical confusion, he rebukes all order '"Pshaw!" replied
Paulo, "who can stop, at such a time as this, to think about what he
means!"' (p. 415).

The text appears to end on a carnivalesque note in which
purpose is subordinated to pleasure, didactic moral to aesthetic
delight – a celebration of language and the lawless imagination
without meaning. Yet, like all carnivals, this is clearly a moment of
licensed subversion, a moment of freedom that is possible because
the status quo has been securely re-established. In Coral Ann
Howells's reading, the author's final imaginative freedom contrasts
with, and is dependent upon, her heroine's concluding containment within the bonds of marriage.[12] But for Radcliffe, as for
Burke, freedom requires order and restraints, found only in
external systems of authority such as the author herself. Such
systems promise the reconciliation of all things the body of the text
had separated: male and female, duty and desire, art and nature,
past and present, moral and aesthetic, master and servant, control
and freedom. The locus for reconciliation is the fairy tale but also
Burkean world in which nature has been transformed into art: 'a
scene of fairy-land' (p. 412), with beautiful grounds and a palace
which 'resembled a fabric called up by enchantment, rather than
a structure of human art' (p. 413). The text ends with a picture of
nature properly mastered and so completed by art, and particularly Radcliffe's art. Imaginative freedom and play, such as Paulo's,
is possible because of the presence of a benign, rather than Satanic
or rather Schedonic, authority ensuring its containment. The
harmony of the scene is not broken by the intrusive author's voice
revealing the moral, as both moral and voice have been completely
internalised into the final vision.

Despite its emphasis upon aesthetic pleasure, the end suggests a serious moral about the artist's individual responsibility to take control of her vision, the shaping process by which she, like God, transforms the world. The narrative of *The Italian* is itself a battle for authorial control. Against both forces from below (raw nature, a revolutionary lower class, and a disorderly imagination) and those from above (tyrannical authorities such as Schedoni and Lewis who abuse power), Radcliffe reasserts a middle-class golden mean of moderation. Whereas for Lewis revision is parody, a breaking and fragmentation of earlier narratives, for Radcliffe it involves the restoration and reintegration of the original and purer source. The end recovers her own plot from the usurping male author, an act of restoration which, like the British myth of the Ancient Constitution, posits a pure original source that has been corrupted and abused, but which can be revived and reformed. In more familial terms, 'Mother' Radcliffe chides the naughty child who took her plot and let it get out of his control. Lewis's story is turned into the premature, which is to say juvenile, form of Radcliffe's work. The two works are thus related antithetically, but also through a developmental line, in which Lewis' plot is absorbed into Radcliffe's narrative of progress.

The relation between the two texts further suggests that of biblical typology, in which the later New Testament corrects and fulfils the earlier Old Testament. Lewis's text becomes a shadowy type of Radcliffe's truth.[13] But if Radcliffe gives the true, revealed version of the narrative, it is because it remains hidden. While Lewis's text is a realisation of the dangers implicit in Radcliffe's work, a making public of horrors she keeps secret and private, Radcliffe reasserts her ability to choose to control and veil those horrors with her art. Lewis extends Godwin's, not to mention Milton's, explorations of the satanic sides of his own enterprises, and so demonises all authority, including his own. His transformation of creation into destruction anticipates that shown in *Frankenstein*. While Radcliffe denounces false authority, including evil authors like Schedoni, she refuses to repudiate all authority and power, but offers herself as an alternative. Her conclusion is a powerful image for authority so absolutely sure of its own control that it can permit license.

This was, however, Radcliffe's last public word during her lifetime; her final statement before she detached herself totally from her art and retreated into her own private world. Like Prospero again, she renounced her magic. Scott described her exit as a grand theatrical gesture, in which 'like an actress in full possession of applauded powers, she chose to retreat from the stage in the blaze of her fame.'[14] Ironically, the attainment of power marks also its abdication. Scott suggested that her withdrawal was caused by her realisation that she could not sustain her power over her own form: 'Mrs. Radcliffe . . . may have been disgusted at seeing the mode of composition, which she had brought into fashion, profaned by a host of servile imitators, who could only copy and render more prominently her defects, without aspiring to her merits.'[15] The image of the bourgeois author as noble lord, graciously ordering his material and servants, was an illusion she could not maintain and which was destroyed by the later imitators who usurped her plot. While Radcliffe was an important authority for later writers, she too had created a force she could not control.

Part IV

1   The Artist as Goth

the books most pernicious in their effects that ever were
produced, were written with intentions uncommonly elevated
and pure.

(Godwin, *Enquirer*, p. 138)

We can never certainly foresee the future destination and
propensities of our children.

(ibid., p. 55)

The publication of *The Monk* has often been identified as both
cause and effect of a degeneration of taste, in which readers'
craving for thrills demanded increasingly graphic forms of realisation. While the seeds of the gothic were sown earlier, it wasn't
until the 1790s that, in J.M.S. Tompkins felicitous appropriation of
an organic metaphor, 'Like the beanstalk, it shot up overnight into
redundant vegetation'.[1] A cult of sentiment grew into a craving for
sensationalism, as Radcliffe's gothic based on suspense and the
refusal to realise terror was succeeded by Lewis's gothic in which
all horrors were gruesomely literalised. For Edith Birkhead the
gothic's premature flowering and rapid decay was a natural evolution, in which the possibilities of the form, realised too completely,
produced its own destruction. With gothic logic, desire satisfied
produced disgust or at best ennui: 'When the novel of terror thus
throws restraint to the winds, outrageously o'ersteps the modesty
of nature, and indulges in a farrago of frightfulness, it begins to
defeat its own purposes, and to fail in its object of freezing the
blood.'[2]

In its own rapid transformation, the gothic reflects the dynamics
with which it has often been associated, in which an originally
revolutionary force becomes a reactionary one. The defamiliarisation of conventions, which, according to the Romantics, enables us
to see the world anew, becomes itself a new convention. Created as
an alternative to mechanistic order, the gothic itself became stale
and mechanical. By 1798 it was already causing despairing outcries
like that of one critic: 'The worst passions of men, poison, daggers,
fire, and lust, horror, dismay, and the Inquisition, are dragged
before us in every shape that can be thought of. . . . In the name of
humanity, let us leave carcases to decay in the earth, and the spirit
to the Almighty's good direction', lest young persons' tastes become totally 'vitiated by scenes of depravity and wickedness too

189

often to be found pourtrayed by the hand of real Genius.'[3] The gothic had quickly turned into a Frankenstein's monster, produced by the grave robbing of literary tradition, in which old plots were dug up, dismembered, then half-heartedly stitched together and mechanically revived in lurid new forms which debauched the reader's taste and wasted the author's genius.

As I have been suggesting, *Frankenstein* is a central metaphor for the gothic genre as it thematises, and ultimately demonises, its own creation. I want to conclude by looking at this work of Mary Shelley, who was herself the result of Godwin and Wollstonecraft's union. Shelley's family life reads like a gothic romance, in which the heroine is the heir of an authoritarian and absent (not to mention philosophical) father, and a dead, idealised mother (who could not be resurrected by any romantic fiat). Both text and author are the product of a complex set of familial relations: Shelley's relation to her remote father, her dead mother (whose name she inherited), her overly idealistic husband, and her dead daughter.[4] For all these intimate and overdetermining relations, she felt herself abandoned by those she loved. Looking back on her childhood, she remembered feeling neglected, as: 'My Father, from age and domestic circumstances, could not "*me faire valoir*".'[5] Her husband was detached from her by his own romantic ideals. She was more conclusively separated from her mother whom she encountered only through books, in an unsettling realisation of the situation in *Maria*, in which the mother, fearing she will die, leaves her story as a voice from beyond the grave for her child to read. While her parents created individuals whose desires forced them to break away from conventions at the ultimate expense of relations with others, their lonely daughter, who through her birth and marriage knew the pains of social ostracism, creates a story of heroic and tragic isolation set against a desire to return to relations. Like Charles in *St Leon*, the conservative child of revolutionary outsiders tries to return to the original paradise rejected by her parents, to come full circle; but for Shelley, paradise has indeed been lost.

Frankenstein gives us many versions of the story of development: that of the monster, Victor, Safie, Walton. One of its most famous, however, is not inside the text, but on its periphery, in the preface Shelley wrote for the 1831 edition, and which has become as much a part of the Frankenstein myth as the text itself.[6] She claims to be writing in order to respond to the question of what a nice young teenage girl was doing with a monster like that: 'How I, then a young girl, came to think of, and to dilate upon, so very hideous an idea?'[7] Such a question reflects the new romantic interest in the author's motives and intentions as the origins of the text. In Godwin's preface to *St Leon*, he notes that although a friend had advised him to keep quiet about himself, as readers 'never give themselves any trouble about the author', he realised that 'The present race of readers' is different: 'They are understood to be desirous to learn about something of the peculiarities, the "life, character, and behaviour" of an author', and 'are willing to learn from his own testimony what trains of thought induced him to adopt the particular subject and plan of the work'.[8] In the later preface to *Caleb Williams* he similarly assumes the reader's interest in the author, and explains the origins of the text in his desire for fame and originality. Mary also thinks it necessary to offer an explanation of the source of the text, to account especially for the discrepancy noted by readers between the adolescent female creator and her 'hideous progeny' (*Frankenstein*, p. 10).

In Shelley's opening statement she provides a story of the text's origins, however, which serves to undercut her own originality. Shelley begins with her own childhood. The preface is a fascinating *Bildungsroman* or *Kunstlerroman*, which first describes Shelley's growth from being the child of her parents to the wife of her husband, and then turns to the development of the tale, which becomes the natural telos of her organic maturation. For Shelley, development is a process of continuing relations rather than increasing independence, as she moves from being 'the daughter of two persons of distinguished literary celebrity' (ibid., p. 5), to becoming the wife of a famous poet. Unlike her father, she didn't desire fame, being rather 'very averse to bringing myself forward in print' (p. 5); she wrote to please her family, as a duty that was part of her inheritance: 'My husband . . . was from the first, very anxious that I should prove myself worthy of my parentage, and enrol myself on the page of fame' (p. 6). For Shelley, the aim of writing is not to assert individuality, but to insert oneself into a family.

This narrative of her own origins is followed by the famous description of the genesis of the text. As has often been noticed, her representation of the events that led to the creation of *Frankenstein* has the effect of subordinating the author to her parents, her husband, and Byron, and finally even a dream, the classic source of gothic inspiration from Walpole on. The effect of this preface is to diminish Shelley's control over her own text: early critics saw her as simply the passive vessel or transparent medium for the ideas of others. Recent critics have tended to see this self-representation as a part of Shelley's ambivalence about authorship and authority.[9] In her preface and dedication, she is careful to position herself as a created being, dependent upon and grateful towards others, who avoids satanic defiance of parental authority. Her dedication to Godwin acknowledges her debt to her father. The epigram from *Paradise Lost* x. 743–5 suggests her literary debt to Milton also. While the fallen Adam's bitter condemnation of God for creating him without his consent looks forward to the monster, who will also quote Milton, it thus already introduces the difference between the character and the author, who appears grateful to others for having created her. Moreover, the preliminary material suggests that the origins of the text pass beyond the author, through a chain which defers authority. As she explains it:

> Every thing must have a beginning, to speak in Sanchean phrase; and that beginning must be linked to something that went before. . . . Invention, it must be humbly admitted, does not consist in creating out of void, but out of chaos; the materials must, in the first place, be afforded: it can give form to dark, shapeless substances, but cannot bring into being the substance itself.
>
> (p. 8).

Creation is not origination but combination, a bringing together of diverse elements that she has inherited from her parents, husband, and her literary ancestors.

Shelley's speaking 'in Sanchean phrase' of herself as a creator is further suggestive of her self-representation. The section of Cervantes' novel to which Shelley is alluding in her quotation is one in which Sancho defends his loyalty to the master he knows is mad: 'I can do nothing else; I have to follow him; we're of the same village; I've eaten his bread; I love him dearly; I'm grateful to him; he gave me his ass-colts; and what is more, I'm faithful; and so it's impossible for anything to part us except the man with the pick and the shovel.'[10] The bonds between master and servant are a complicated mixture of blind devotion, feudal servility, character, and, apparently, fate. Mary represents herself as a loyal Sancho to her parents' and husband's idealistic Don Quixote, especially in

192

1831 when she longs for her now unattainable romantic knight errant. The author is not an aristocratic knight and hero, but merely the hero's loyal and subservient sidekick.

Shelley's preface thus establishes the text as a product of an ideal community, a time 'when I was not alone; and my companion was one who, in this world, I shall never see more' (p. 10). She associates the text with a lost relation that she recreates nostalgically by writing her preface. In fact, her husband not only substantially revised the original manuscript, but also wrote the preface to the first edition of 1818, in which he, speaking as the author, offered an authoritative interpretation of its meaning: 'the exhibition of the amiableness of domestic affection, and the excellence of universal virtue' (p. 14). The writing of the original text had been in part a collaborative effort, in which Percy Shelley's role was that of the gothic master, ordering the disorderly speech of his faithful servant, and giving it meaning. It is only the death of the husband that frees the wife to present her text in her own words and to repossess her identity as author. It is therefore suggestive that she offers not an interpretation of her text, but a description of its origins which downplays her own control over its construction. Shelley's death gives Mary control over her own meaning, which she appears not to want. Similarly, it offers her a freedom and independence that she hates, as she longs for the relations of her past. While the text was written in the midst of a community, her preface originates in a new fallen time, in which she finds herself a solitary author, now isolated as will be both her creator Frankenstein in the act of creation, and the monster himself. It gives us a story for development, similar to those of Victor and Walton, in which a sentimental past of ideal domestic life and community is set in opposition to a gothic present of isolation. Like the text and its monster, the author presents herself as created through others: child of famous parents, wife to a famous husband, now mother of a famous text. Identifying herself as both daughter and mother, she herself reconciles the poles of creator and created that the text will split into gothic doubles. She is the ideal obedient daughter and wife, and a non-authoritarian parent, who both acknowledges her text and yet sets it free, as she bids it 'go forth and prosper' (p. 10), and have a life free from its source.

Shelley thus also creates an image for an author very different from that of the prevalent contemporary view of the Promethean artist, which she will draw on inside her text subtitled 'The Modern

Prometheus'. For her husband, who had his own interest in the figure of Prometheus, the poet is a god who recreates the world with his redemptive imagination, which 'transmutes all that it touches . . . its secret alchemy turns to potable gold the poisonous waters which flow from death through life; it strips the veil of familiarity from the world, and lays bare the naked and sleeping beauty which is the spirit of its forms'.[11] As we will see, in the figure of the Promethean Victor Frankenstein some of these images of poetic creativity are themselves transmuted. But for Percy Shelley, creation also involves submission to forces beyond human control; the poet is both a god and 'an instrument over which a series of external and internal impressions are driven', 'an Aeolian lyre'.[12] This passive aspect of creation appears in Mary Shelley's represent-ation of herself. One reason suggested recently for her view of authority and creativity is the fact that this author was a mother.[13] While, for the male artist, creation can be modelled on the artificial acts of a patriarchal God, for the female, creation is associated with childbirth, of which Shelley had already some experience. Like her own mother, Shelley identifies writing and mothering.

Through the outer frame with which the 1831 text opens, Shelley introduces a contrast between herself and Victor as creators. In the text, however, male creation is identified with science, thus marking the transformation of the gothic villain, the Godwinian philosopher, into the mad scientist whose descendants include Drs Moreau and Jekyll.[14] Victor is represented as a Baconian scientist, who seeks knowledge as power over the natural world.[15] The goal of this scientific quest is the domination of nature that will em-power man, as he dreams of controlling nature in order to 'banish disease from the human frame, and render man invulnerable to any but a violent death' (p. 40). Like Bacon, Victor imagines a utopian world in which matter has been totally conquered by mind. The text, however, shows that nature has a mind of its own which rebels against human systems of control.

Later versions and revisions of *Frankenstein* (which also insist on awarding Victor the title of 'Dr' Frankenstein, perhaps a sign of our declining faith in the medical profession) have often read the story as the revenge of nature upon the technology that has repressed it. While this reading is partially anachronistic, a product of our own increasing distrust of the march of progress, the text does reflect the shifting role of science in the eighteenth and nineteenth centuries. For radicals such as Godwin, science had been celebrated originally as a means of achieving freedom, both from the tyranny of nature and, as science was the province of the middle class, from social domination.[16] With the consequences of the Industrial Revolution increasingly evident, however, it became denounced as a new tyranny which alienated men from nature and themselves. Even Godwin saw that machines, invented to free men, could turn them into slaves; as: 'A mechanic becomes a sort of machine; and his limbs and articulations are converted, as it were into woods and wires. Tamed, lowered, torpified into his character, he may be said perhaps to be content.'[17] For the Romantics, as for Burke, scientific analysis reduces nature to a machine, and is thus destructive of a natural, organic order. In his *Reveries*, one of the many books which Shelley was reading during the composition of *Frankenstein*,[18] Rousseau expresses the romantic distrust of science as an agent of division and murderous dissection. The Solitary Walker refuses to analyse nature because of what it would involve: 'So I should have to study them dead, to tear them apart, remove their bones, dig deep into their palpitating entrails! What a terrible sight an anatomy theatre is! Stinking corpses, livid running flesh, blood, repellent intestines, horrible skeletons, pestilential vapours.'[19] Scientific knowledge does not heal isolation and alienation, but creates further divisions; as in the case of Caleb, who was himself 'a sort of natural philosopher',[20] it sets subject over object as victor over victim. However, at the same time that scientific models for knowledge were becoming suspect, they were gaining wider significance. Partially through the alliance between science and the middle class, the objective rational scientist became a predominant emblem for a norm of human identity that is defined in terms of independence and detachment. For Locke, already, the model for the adult is 'the scientific observer',[21] an image recalled in Godwin's writings as well. As Leonda Schiebinger has pointed out, in contrast to earlier representations of scientists, our modern idea is of 'an isolated individual . . . profoundly alone . . . [a] self-sufficient individual'.[22] The scientist is the epitome of the alienated autonomous individual, the loner *par excellence*, a cerebral questor who, in his laboratory (the new castle that in films becomes the central image for *Frankenstein*) has to detach himself not only from the objects of his analysis but from all relationships.

The scientist is thus the logical extension of the Godwinian individual, whose quest for knowledge requires his isolation. Moreover, he is a version of Godwin himself, whose methodology drew

195

on that of Baconian science. Shelley's story begins with the end of the *Enquiry Concerning Political Justice,* where Godwin also dreams of conquering nature, of creating a static world of immortals in which natural procreation will be unnecessary.[23] In its representation of Godwin, moreover, it revises *St Leon,* which Shelley reread in 1815. The scientist begins his career as an alchemist, reading Paracelsus and Albertus Magnus, and searching for 'the philosopher's stone and the elixir of life' (p. 40). According to him, however, his development involves a break from its original impulse, when he learns from his teachers that the older methods are mere superstition. As Waldman tells him, while the alchemist dreamed of transforming nature, it is only the new practical scientist who can truly conquer it:

> 'The ancient teachers of this science,' said he, 'promised impossibilities and performed nothing. The modern masters promise very little; they know that metals cannot be transmuted, and that the elixer of life is a chimera. But these philosophers, whose hands seem only to dabble in dirt, and their eyes to pore over the microscope or crucible, have indeed performed miracles. They penetrate into the recesses of nature, and show how she works in her hiding places. They ascend into the heavens: they have discovered how the blood circulates, and the nature of the air we breathe. They have acquired new and almost unlimited powers; they can command the thunders of heaven, mimic the earthquake, and even mock the invisible world with its own shadows.'
>
> (pp. 47–8)

As I noted earlier, modern science detaches itself from alchemy, ridiculed as primitive superstition, in order to define itself. Victor's own career reproduces this pattern, and leads him beyond St Leon. However, as critics have noted, Victor's scientific enterprise is not clearly different from the work of alchemy.[24] Shelley's story suggests that modern science, superficially detached from its dark and murky past, becomes another version of it, just as the enlightened rational man, such as Godwin, liberated from the superstition that inhibited the thought of the past, recreates them in new monsters.

On the surface, Victor's scientific and detached relation to the world is contrasted with that of his friend Clerval. While Victor feels himself alienated from nature, Clerval is depicted as being in harmonious sympathy with it, 'a being formed in the "very poetry of nature'" (p. 158). The quote here from 'Tintern Abbey' identifies Clerval with the Wordsworthian nature poet. The two friends thus appear as the opposites of science and art, and the tale suggests a revision of Wollstonecraft's discussion of the dangers of separating male reason from female feeling. Reason, which Percy Shelley calls 'the calculating faculty' which perceives differences and dissects, becomes demonic when separated from the imagination – for Shelley, the synthetic and sympathetic faculty which perceives similarities and brings things together.[25]

As Victor represents a detached individual who sees the world in polar opposites, it is appropriate that his story begins with a quest for a literal pole, and another loner, Walton, who has usually been considered as his double. Walton's exploration to the north is thus set up as another version of Victor's scientific conquest of nature. In both cases, their goals require that they leave a familiar domestic sphere for a strange, barren, foreign territory. Walton's past youth with his sister, 'my best years spent under your gentle and feminine fosterage' (p. 20), provides a striking contrast with his present journey. However, Walton sees his desire for discovery, and 'love for the marvellous' as inspired by his early reading of Coleridge's 'Ancient Mariner': 'I have often attributed my attachment to, my passionate enthusiasm for, the dangerous mysteries of ocean, to that production of the most imaginative of modern poets' (p. 21). He picks up and literalises the old *topos* that makes poetry analogous to sailing, a *topos* also used by Coleridge, and by Shelley in 'Alastor', another poem indirectly alluded to in Mary's text.[26] In so doing, however, analogy is transformed into causality, as poetry is set up as the cause of a search for new lands. To reinforce the parallelism, what Walton discovers is not the north pole, but another Ancient Mariner, Victor Frankenstein. At the extreme part of the world he thus finds part of what he is really searching for: a friend, 'the company of a man who could sympathise with me; whose eyes would reply to mine' (p. 19). For this quester, it is only in the strange world that the familiar can be recovered in the form of a mirror image of the self.

This meeting suggests the text's presentation of enlightened scientist or explorer and Romantic poet as mirror images of each other, related by both sequence and analogy. In Mary Shelley's own life a similar genealogical succession was apparent in the relation between her father and her husband, who saw himself as Godwin's philosophical heir. The representation of the scientist as alchemist identifies Victor also with Percy Shelley, who in his youth was interested in alchemy. Those early interests were carried over to his adulthood; as noted earlier, he appropriated alchemy as an image for poetic creation. Victor's apparent opposition, or at best 'complementarity', to Clerval thus also hides a deeper identification, as Clerval is called 'the image of my former self' (p. 158). Here the echo of Wordsworth's 'Tintern Abbey' suggests an analogy between *Victor* and the Wordsworthian poet, so that Clerval is identified with Dorothy Wordsworth (an analogy which also reinforces the doubling between Clerval and Elizabeth, who both represent a traditionally female feeling, in contrast to Victor's male reason). The lines suggest further that the two opposites are also linked sequentially, as stages in a single process of development. The poet and scientist/explorer are different stages of the same thing, in which an originally ideal harmony with nature leads naturally to alienation from it. The poet is not the alternative to the dissector, but an early version of him. *Frankenstein* looks back to Lewis's representation of creation as murderous, and forward to later nineteenth-century writers who demonise their own creation; in *Dorian Gray*, Henry Wotton is described as an aesthetic dissector, whose art preys on life.[27]

Like the philosopher's stone, art and science are offered as twin means of uniting opposites, of healing the rupture between the human and the natural, which in fact are the cause of this gap.[28] As Burke anticipated, the modern assumption of an essential opposition itself means that the desired reconciliation will be disastrous, a monstrous merging of unlike things, rather than a recovery of a lost unity. The monster himself suggests this perverse and unresolved confusion of antitheses. Although the monster is an artificial creation of Victor's mind, it is also identified, through imagistic associations with the moon and mountains, and through its play on Rousseau's type of innocent noble savage, with the natural world.[29] The natural setting for the reunion of the two main characters and their stories is the mountain, traditionally associated with biblical epiphany (such as Mount Sinai, where the revolutionary leader Moses met God) and romantic revelation. In Radcliffe, mountains are part of the sublime, terrifying because they signify division, although one that is revealed to be necessary in a world of excess identification. In Shelley, the mountain becomes an image not for division but for a reunion between the human and the natural, subject and object, that the human fears will cause his own annihilation. As in Radcliffe, response to nature is a clue to character; moreover, Victor's relation to the monster is mirrored by his relation to the landscape. From a distance, he is first inspired 'with a sublime ecstasy' by the mountains hidden by clouds whose mystery lures him on: 'Still I would penetrate their misty veil' (pp. 97, 96). As in his early experiments, the mystery of nature provokes his desire to know it, which is here represented as a sublimated form of sexual aggression. But as he ascends the labyrinthine path and reaches 'a scene terrifically desolate', from which he can look down at the valley below, he is filled with a distressing sense of human powerlessness. As the sublime is an experience of forces beyond one's control, Victor realises: 'we are moved by every wind that blows, and a chance word or scene that that word may convey to us' (p. 97). The creator who sets himself up as a god, suddenly becomes a despairing version of the Aeolian harp. Even more specifically, the description recalls Percy Shelley's image of power as Mont Blanc, in which the human mind is reduced to a role in which it 'passively/Now renders now receives fast influencings' ('Mont Blanc', 36–7). The moment of human helplessness is reinforced at a textual level as Frankenstein is suddenly made to quote Percy Shelley's 'Mutability' (p. 98). Nature is the point at which human identity and authority break down, including the author's, as it is not clear whose voice – Victor's, Mary's, or Percy Shelley's – is speaking here.

The 1831 preface, with its portrayal of the origins of the text in forces outside of the individual author, reinforces the question of authority and control within the text, raised also by Shelley's editorial role, and the presence of Godwinian, and also Miltonic, subtexts. Like *Caleb Williams*, a central question for interpretation is whose story is it? Frankenstein's quest first appears inset into Walton's story. As a tale of flight and pursuit, the beginning replays elements from the end of *Caleb Williams*, which was also, according to Godwin, the genesis of the tale. We meet Victor chasing his victim; a situation to which we will return as the frame closes, by which time, however, as at the end of *Caleb Williams*, it is unclear as to who is chasing whom. From the initial meeting which enables the two narratives, inner and outer, to meet, the text, like *Caleb Williams*, then goes backwards to explain the causes that led up to this situation. The movement of the text thus also duplicates Victor's own goal, as it is a scientific search for causes: here to explain the origins of this deadly antagonism.

Mary Shelley's preface drew attention to an apparent contradiction between author and text. Her description of the origins of the text showed how a shy, quiet girl could produce such a monstrosity. Victor's story similarly attempts to explain the origins of an even greater opposition between creator and created, cause and effect. Frankenstein locates his own origins in a purely private realm, a sentimental happy valley of innocent childhood that superficially resembles that of Radcliffe's Emily. Like hers, too, it contains elements of a Rousseauian ideal, here drawn more directly from Rousseau's accounts of his own sheltered childhood which preceded his fall and exile from paradise.[30] Victor's father was a bureaucrat who retired from public service to devote himself entirely to his private life when he married, late in life, the daughter of an old friend. Partially through its physically present father, the family is completely cut off from the outside public world; even more than Radcliffe's La Vallée, it is separated from everything outside of itself.[31] For Victor, this is a time of complete safety and freedom. In sharp contrast to Victor himself later, the Frankensteins seem responsible and model enlightened parents, who have a 'deep consciousness of what they owed towards the being to which they had given life' (p. 34). As a result, Frankenstein says:

> No human being could have passed a happier childhood than myself. My parents were possessed by the very spirit of kindness and indulgence. We felt that they were not the tyrants to rule our lot according to their caprice, but the agents and creators of all the many delights which we enjoyed. When I mingled with other families, I distinctly discerned how peculiarly fortunate my lot was, and gratitude assisted the development of filial love.
>
> (p. 37)

The Frankenstein home is a refuge from political life and all conflict and strife, a place of purely benevolent relations. The description of this familial ideal looks back to St Leon's brief domestic bliss, but it seems founded neither on a fall, nor even, as in the case of St Aubert, on a need to protect oneself from a corrupt outside world, but on an innocent desire to enjoy the happiness of the private realm without the distraction of larger social responsibilities.

Looking back, Frankenstein describes his childhood as paradise on earth. Yet in it he also sees the origins of his fall. It is both a time of untainted innocence and the source of corruption, as he tells Walton:

> I feel exquisite pleasure in dwelling on the recollections of childhood, before misfortune had tainted my mind, and changed its bright visions of extensive usefulness into gloomy and narrow reflections upon self. Besides, in drawing the picture of my early days, I also record those events which led, by insensible steps, to my after tale of misery: for when I would account to myself for the birth of that passion, which afterwards ruled my destiny, I find it arise, like a mountain river, from ignoble and almost forgotten sources; but, swelling as it proceeded, it became the torrent which, in its course, has swept away all my hopes and joys.
>
> (p. 38)

While in the first sentence his childhood is represented as a time *before* corruption entered the world, in the second it suddenly appears as the time *in which* corruption subtly originated. As in the case of Emily and Shelley herself, a sentimental childhood is set in opposition to a gothic maturity; yet here the relationship is even more strikingly both antithetical and causal. The relation, or rather apparent disjunction, between the two parts of Victor's life, his past and present, cause and effect, has often puzzled readers. What went wrong that paradise itself should be the source of such a disaster? Why did this dream of reason produce nightmares? Godwin reminds us that parents cannot be totally responsible for their children's lives, the creator cannot control the fate of his creations, but Victor's story seems every parent's nightmare, in which well-intentioned parental benevolence backfires, producing, if here indirectly, monsters.

Victor suggests that the steps of his fall were so gradual and insensible that he couldn't see them at the time. As in *The Monk*, tracing the cause of evil and determining when a disastrous course of action becomes irrevocable is difficult. Like Victor, however, readers have wanted to identify a source of evil, searching his past for incriminating signs. His representation of an ideal childhood has been suspected of hiding more antagonistic feelings, especially towards his father.[32] While a cloistered environment for a child was idealised by Rousseau, it was attacked by Locke, Godwin, and Wollstonecraft, for the reason demonstrated by Lewis: the overprotected child does not learn to prepare him or herself for entrance into the world and so is left open to deception. The text plays on the gothic theme of the dangers of cloistering, which also anticipates Freudian readings in which all such protection is really repression.[33] The attempt to recreate paradise in the bourgeois family destroys it. The tight network of Frankenstein's family, and especially his all-encompassing and possessive relation with his 'more than sister' Elizabeth (p. 36), suggests a hidden incestuous element at the heart of this nuclear family.[34] By turning in upon itself, perhaps also neglecting its larger social obligations, the family doesn't wall monsters out, but ends up producing its own.

While Victor's childhood, like all childhoods, is clearly not as perfect as he remembers in retrospection, readings that attempt to trace what went wrong to Victor's formative years reproduce a tendency in this text to blame parents for their children's faults. *The Monk* played with a similar assignation of responsibility, which itself was a commonplace of romantic education theory, which 'typically placed the blame for an adolescent's misconduct at the door of a negligent (though often well-meaning) parent'.[35] If, according to Locke, the child is not at first responsible for its actions, the parent must be, and as the first actions we learn determine later ones by becoming habitual, then the parent is ultimately responsible for *all* the child's actions. The child is thus not accountable for its own actions, and the present is determined by the past. Most commonly, as we have already seen in Wollstonecraft and Lewis, the gothic lays blame on the mother: Beckford's Vathek has a tyrannical mother, Godwin's Tyrrel an overly permissive one. In Charlotte Dacre's 1806 *Zofloya*, the villainess has been misraised by an irresponsible and overpassionate mother, and in *Dracula*, Lucy's weak mother is partially responsible for her daughter's death. In *Frankenstein*, however, failed fathers are seen as more accountable for their children's fate: Beaufort, Clerval, and Safie's fathers, as well as Victor himself and his father.[36] The theme of Godwin's *Caleb Williams* and *St Leon* is taken up, at least partially to indict the remote Godwin himself.

Like the Godwinian hero, too, Victor sees himself not only as a product of determining childhood circumstances, but as the victim of impulses he cannot control. The lessons of M. Waldman influence him, being 'words of fate, announced to destroy me. . . . I felt as if my soul were grappling with a palpable enemy' (p. 48). Uncontrollable energies also erupt inside him, such as the passion

which arose 'like a mountain river, from ignoble and almost forgotten sources' (p. 38) until it raged out of control. He becomes
divided between what he claims are his natural desires and these
impulses. While, like Rousseau, he is disgusted by dissection and
revolts against the act of creation – 'often did my human nature
turn with loathing from my occupation' (p. 55) – he continues,
drawn by 'a resistless, and almost frantic, impulse' that 'swallowed
up every habit of my nature' (pp. 54–5). Nostalgic for his paradisial home, he still assumes that he must leave it in order to fulfil
his ambition:

> I was now alone. In the university, whither I was going, I must
> form my own friends, and be my own protector. My life had
> hitherto been remarkably secluded and domestic; and this
> had given me invincible repugnance to new countenances. I
> loved my brothers, Elizabeth, and Clerval; these were 'old
> familiar faces'; but I believed myself totally unfitted for the
> company of strangers. Such were my reflections as I com-
> menced my journey; but as I proceeded, my spirits and hopes
> rose. I ardently desired the acquisition of knowledge. I had
> often, when at home, thought it hard to remain during my
> youth cooped up in one place, and had longed to enter the
> world, and take my station among other human beings. Now
> my desires were complied with.
>
> (p. 45)

Victor's equation of maturation with detachment from confinement suggests a greater ambivalence towards his perfect childhood.
Moreover, it reverses his father's journey from the public to the
private realms, but depends upon an equally rigid boundary between
them. Victor's privileging of the former recalls *St Leon*, where
public duty and heroism is elevated and private desire denounced
as restricting and emasculating. The gothic's reworking of the
opposition between individual desire and social or religious duty
suggests the continuity between a Puritan work such as *Pilgrim's
Progress*, in which the hero must renounce his family and travel
alone, and romantic works that represent the artist as similarly
subject to higher laws, which demand that he reject all normal ties.
The journey of the poet in 'Alastor' begins when he must leave
'His cold fireside and alienated home / To seek strange truths in
undiscovered lands' (pp. 76–7). For the poet, whose 'calling' is
creation, home is the place where the true artist is not in fact at

home. The Romantic artist seeks foreign places, sublime and bleak landscapes, apocalyptic worlds of fire and ice,[37] in which extreme spots he, like Walton, hopes to find an image for himself. Like the gothic villain, the Romantic poet is only at home when in exile; alienation is his 'natural' state. It is poetically just, if nothing else, that Keats, Shelley, and Byron all died abroad.

Victor therefore assumes an opposition between creativity and domesticity, which is later proved when the former destroys the latter. However, he originally believes also that the two can be finally united; he imagines going away to school as a preliminary step in a pattern of development, in which he leaves his family and Elizabeth in the belief that he will finally return home. Science and marriage are thus not essentially incompatible, but themselves can be joined by sequence. The projected shape for his own career thus follows a dialectical pattern of exile and return. However, this circle is broken in the middle, when the effects of his scientific projects make return impossible. This pattern of failed reconciliation is echoed in the act of scientific creation itself. In Baconian science (which in this again follows a hidden alchemical pattern), the analysis and dissection of nature is only a prelude to its reconstruction and synthesis according to human ideals of order. Separation of nature is only the first stage in its reunion at a higher level. Such a model (which anticipates Hegel) underlay Godwin's attempt to take apart a mystified social order and put it back together in rational terms. As a creator, however, Frankenstein seems better at the dismemberment or deconstruction of old bodies than at the construction of something new. The dissected parts are joined together artificially but do not cohere:

> How can I describe my emotions at this catastrophe, or delineate the wretch whom with such infinite pains and care I had endeavoured to form? His limbs were in proportion, and I had selected his features as beautiful. Beautiful! – Great God! His yellow skin scarcely covered the work of muscles and arteries beneath; his hair was of a lustrous black, and flowing; his teeth of a pearly whiteness; but these luxuriances only formed a more horrid contrast with his watery eyes, that seemed almost of the same colour as the dun white sockets in which they were set, his shrivelled complexion and straight black lips.
>
> (p. 57)

Taking in the animated whole with his eyes, Frankenstein once more takes it apart, to suddenly realise for the first time that the parts form a whole that disgusts him.

Victor's perception here is a kind of parody of the blazon form of courtly love, drawn upon also by Lewis, in which the lover takes the object of his attention apart piece by succulent piece.[38] The erotic model reinforces the association of the monster throughout the text with not only nature but also women.[39] Intertextually, this association is underlined by the similarity between the stories of Wollstonecraft's Jemima and the monster, both denounced by society as monsters, and whose stories stand at the heart of their respective texts. Within the text, furthermore, the night after the creation, Frankenstein has a dream in which he meets Elizabeth, and tries to kiss her only to have her turn into the corpse of his dead mother.[40] As the dream suggests, with its shift between desire and disgust, life and death, mother and lover, the monster represents to Victor a confusion of the differences that are essential for his identity. Made up of bits and pieces, born out of death, the monster uncannily relates but also potentially blurs all boundaries between discrete categories: animate/inanimate, nature/art, living/dead, male/female, human/non-human, and mother/lover.[41] However, at the same time, as Victor's opposite he ironically creates his creator; the scientist constructs his own autonomous scientific identity when he builds a monster who, made up of bits and pieces, appears to embody the lack of autonomy and individuation. The autonomous detached modern self depends upon its opposite for self-definition.

The monster therefore also reveals that an identity dependent upon absolute oppositions is unstable, as he represents both polar difference and the merging and hideous convergence of differences. Victor's creation of this monster suggests that the rational analytic mind that divides absolutely can only imagine reconciliations as monstrous regression to a state of undifferentiation. It seems hardly surprising that Frankenstein interprets the monster's prophetic words, 'I shall be with you on your wedding night' (p. 168), spoken after Frankenstein retracts his promise to create a monstrous mate, as signifying his own death. He foresees his wedding which would unite the two sexes as an apocalyptic last battle that will result in his own death – an expectation that makes him a less than cheerful groom.

Victor's assumption that his marriage will be his death suggests how in the text women also both represent difference and threaten it, by establishing relationships that undermine male autonomy. Frankenstein's mother, especially, is associated more with death than life. She first enters the story when she is found by Frankenstein's father, kneeling over the coffin of her dead father. Alphonse chooses to memorialise this scene in a painting, as a tribute to daughterly devotion. But it fixes the mother forever in association with death, and it is significant that this portrait is the first thing that Victor sees, looming large at him, when he returns home after the murder of William. That murder too is connected with the influence of a picture of the dead and now deadly mother: it is her miniature portrait that first attracted the monster, and on hearing the tragic news, Clerval exclaims: 'Poor William! . . . dear lovely child, he now sleeps with his angel mother!' (p. 73). Return to the mother prevents male development and maturation rather definitely in this case. As Nancy Chodorow has argued, while female development builds upon a continuing identification with the mother, for men the attainment of identity requires detachment. For the male, therefore, women may represent an earlier state in which differences are not distinguished, which the male fears returning to as a form of regression. *Frankenstein* suggests that male identity depends less upon the oedipal killing of the father to become him, than upon killing the mother to *not* become her. As Judith Wilt argues, the mother as origin of life reveals the illusory nature of autonomy. The fiction of male self-creation requires the murder of the source who could expose the derivative nature of individuality.[42]

The death of his mother therefore marks Victor's exodus to university and the beginning of his scientific career. Detached from a female past, he is able to create himself as a scientist. Yet the scientist is both the opposite of the mother and a parodic version of her. As critics have noted, Victor's usurpation of divine powers of creation is also a male appropriation of the female ability to give birth.[43] He thus breaks from a female past to recreate it in grotesque forms.

The creature's development replays and reverses that of his creator. Where Victor begins in a domestic world of the family from which he must separate himself to become an artist and adult individual, the monster, like Rousseau's Emile and noble savage, begins in isolation; his goal is to establish relations with others. Made up of diverse parts, he wants to be a part of a larger group.

Whereas Frankenstein attempts to take the role of the autonomous creator and father of a new race, his creature and son seeks
to return to the community and family that his source has rejected.
His story is a quest for relations, an attempt to discover how he fits
into the world. The monster's development involves a kind of
self-raising in which he acquires knowledge by himself. While in
one sense he is an ideal 'self-made' man who educates himself, in
another, having had the advantage of knowing his own beginning
by reading Victor's journal, he is acutely aware that he is not
self-made but the literal fabrication of another. His gradual development follows, as has been noted, Lockean and Hartleyean
psychology. Abstracted from society, he becomes the ideal philosophical subject: the child as true *tabula rasa*. Totally isolated, the
monster is at first unable to distinguish differences, and his initial
education involves learning to discriminate separate things. His
development, however, takes him from one extreme to another:
from a state of undifferentiation into one in which he discovers his
own absolute difference from others. Knowledge is ultimately only
of his own alienation: 'Increase of knowledge only discovered to
me more clearly what a wretched outcast I was' (p. 131). Reading,
his main source of connection with others, only reinforces his
exclusion from a literary community. He seeks his own identity in
the texts he finds:

> As I read, however, I applied much personally to my own
> feelings and condition. I found myself similar, yet at the same
> time strangely unlike to the beings concerning whom I read,
> and to whose conversation I was a listener. I sympathised
> with, and partially understood them, but I was unformed in
> mind; I was dependent on none, and related to none. 'The
> path of my departure was free';[44] and there was none to
> lament my annihilation. My person was hideous, and my
> stature gigantic: what did this mean? Who was I? What was I?
> Whence did I come? What was my destination? These questions
> continually recurred, but I was unable to solve them.
>
> (p. 128)

Paradise Lost especially captures his imagination, as it did Mary
Shelley's, as a model for his own story. He sees himself as both
Adam and Satan, but finally recognises that, as a monster, there is
no absolutely correct part for him in the story: 'I am thy creature;
I ought to be thy Adam; but I am rather the fallen angel, whom

thou drivest from joy for no misdeed. Every where I see bliss, from which I alone am irrevocably excluded. I was benevolent and good; misery made me a fiend. Make me happy, and I shall again be virtuous' (p. 100).[45]

The monster's development thus mirrors as it reverses Victor's, as he tries to move from one state which he finds limiting to another which will give him an identity. It falls into two parts: an innocent Rousseauian childhood in nature, and an evil gothic adulthood in a society that has no place for him. His narrative, like that of Victor, relates these antithetical stages to each other, to explain how the innocent child turned into a child-murderer. His story looks back to those of Jemima, the characters of Godwin, the tradition of robber fiction, and to Rousseau who represented himself as a good person who has been turned by a barbaric society into an outcast and 'monster'.[46] Exiled from other humans, he loses his sense of identity: 'detached as I am from them and from the whole world, what am I?'[47] But, for Rousseau, innocence is found or recovered in the solitude of a Crusoesque state in which every man is an island. The monster, however, is corrupted not by a bad society but by lack of society: 'My vices are the children of a forced solitude that I abhor; and my virtues will necessarily arise when I live in communion with an equal' (p. 147). Like Victor, his corruption is identified with isolation, but an isolation that he, unlike his master, has not chosen. Like Caleb, who was forced to replicate Falkland's solitude, the monster is made into the image of his enemy, even as they become increasingly opposed.

Like Victor, too, the monster locates the source of his fall in forces outside of himself, primarily his irresponsible creator. As Victor felt revulsion for his act of creation, the monster loathes his own mirror-acts of destruction but feels incapable of stopping himself; while he feels 'agony and remorse', 'A frightful selfishness hurried me on' (p. 219), 'I was the slave, not the master, of an impulse, which I detested, yet could not disobey' (p. 220). Emphasising the determinism of action, he alludes to Milton's Satan in his claim that: 'Evil thenceforth became my good. Urged thus far, I had no choice but to adapt my nature to an element which I had willingly chosen. The completion of my demoniacal design became an insatiable passion' (p. 220). For Milton, the basis of reason, and thus free will, is choice; for the monster, caught in a plot which he (and the real author Mary Shelley) sees as modelled on Milton's, there is no choice, only a (literally) prescribed fate that sweeps him on. The monster sees himself as helpless over himself and his fate. Creator and created are thus united by a chain of opposition and identification, as each sees himself as the innocent victim of the other's hostility, and the other as the cause responsible for all evil.[48]

Moreover, this all-consuming relation, like that between Caleb and Falkland, makes all alternative or 'normal' relations impossible. The death of William destroys the domestic world, which Victor had imagined cut off from his experiments. In Radcliffe, the identification between the sentimental and the gothic worlds is suggested, but ultimately denied; La Vallée is a paradise that, though briefly lost, can be recovered; more accurately, it can be recovered as a place of innocence because it *is* briefly lost. Emily encounters demonic forms of domesticity elsewhere, so that her childhood world remains intact. In *Frankenstein*, however, Victor's experiments turn the home into a gothic place of horror; the complete separation of public and private finally causes the elimination of the difference between them, as the sentimental home and family is destroyed by Victor's gothic activities. Leaving home cannot be a prelude to a final return, for it causes the destruction of the private world.

For Frankenstein, the death of Elizabeth and elimination of his hope of marriage is the climax of his narrative, after which it breaks down from a linear recounting of his history into a more disjointed and somewhat confused account of his pursuit of the monster. In the last part of the narrative, he is frequently radically disoriented: 'no distinct idea presented itself to my mind'; his thoughts 'rambled' 'confusedly' as 'I was bewildered in a cloud of wonder and horror' (p. 197). Frankenstein is now in the position of the monster at the beginning of his development, when he could not differentiate things. His attempt to mature into an adult detached from all others results in a regression to an uncanny version of the state of childhood. Dreaming and waking become difficult to distinguish; indeed, as he dreams that the dead are alive, he tries to convince himself that dreams are the reality, and reality a nightmare. The anticipated union of male and female in marriage is replaced with a parodic confusion of all differences.

As these differences disappear, however, Victor attempts to reinforce them in increasingly schematic and antithetical forms. He sees himself in apocalyptic terms as a Christ figure, a resurrecter of the dead who is now led on by a 'good angel', who has prepared a banquet for him in the wilderness, towards an apocalyptic battle in the north with his satanic adversary.

Victor at the end thus recalls Caleb, who also anticipates a revolutionary meeting between truth and falsehood. Like Caleb, too, this last battle is seen as a struggle for narrative control and authority. Walton's peripheral position gives him the power of the last word; while he can be read as a double of Victor, he also could be seen as an objective, detached, Godwinian judge over the story. Yet Victor does not allow him such control; he tells his story to him, and then asks to see Walton's notes, and 'corrected and augmented them in many places' (p. 210). Frankenstein tries to reassert control by acting as the editor of his own story and imposing absolute polarities upon it. Whereas Falkland had Caleb, Wollstonecraft had Godwin, and Mary Shelley had Percy Shelley reworking their narratives, Victor Frankenstein tries to take sole authorial and editorial control over his own text, for fear lest 'a mutilated one should go down to posterity' (p. 210). While he lacks authorial control over his life and creature, he claims it in regards to his own story, in order to ensure how it will be read after his death, when it will give him another version of the immortality he desired.

As Mary Poovey shows, Shelley's later revisions increased the element of determinism in the text, to make Victor present himself as a passive victim of fate.[49] Telling his story is thus a way of both recovering control over his own life at the point when he has lost it (as Caleb also attempted), and also abnegating it, as he constructs a narrative in which he had no authoritative control over himself. In looking back on his life he sees it as totally determined by the character that was his fate, his evil destiny, or evil angel. But what 'determines' his life seems a rather random, arbitrary set of occurrences, parts that only gain significance when, at the end, they are re-membered into a coherent whole. Interpretation becomes fate, an imposition of determinism on every event that occurred through the omniscience of hindsight; reading, even of the self, leads not to self-determination and freedom but bondage.

We have reasons, moreover, to mistrust Victor's interpretive skills, and his ability to read the most basic facts of his own life. In the midst of his own story, Victor is unable to interpret even the most obvious clues given to him: he misreads the monster's words concerning his wedding night (later blaming the monster for blinding him so that he did so), and sees the food and clothing left for him in the north as coming from a guardian angel helping him against his adversary, when it is obvious that his adversary is this angel. Good and evil, angel and devil, thus seem to be products of an obsessive bifurcating mind that senses its own loss of control, and therefore attempts to regain it by imposing absolute and destructive coherence on the world.

Constructing the narrative of his life, moreover, Frankenstein shapes it into a single unified chain leading to an inevitable conclusion in which any alternative was impossible. Yet, as in *The Monk*, the randomness of these apparently determining factors, the possibility of events having gone in another direction, is entertained. Frankenstein's life may be simply a product of arbitrary associations, which he, acting egotistically as not just author but also editor and interpreter of his own tale, has put together and formed into a whole. The most important accident, that comes to be read in retrospect as determining (as well as a case of pathetic fallacy), is the blasting by lightning of the oak tree in the second chapter. The result is a temporary redirection of his energies that he attributes to the intervention of 'the guardian angel of my life', but which was not, alas, equal to his evil demon: 'Destiny was too potent, and her immutable laws had decreed my utter and terrible destruction' (p. 42). Shelley's later revision of the episode emphasises the inefficacy of human choice in a predetermined world. In the first edition, Alphonse explains to his son the principle of electricity; in the second it is 'a man of great research' (p. 41) who does the teaching. The revision produces two different 'explanatory' readings: in the first, it is suggested that the father's explanation is a source of the son's obsession; in the second, it is the father's lack of interest that leaves the son open to dubious, here even unknown and therefore mysterious, influences. What is important is that whichever version one reads can be made to make sense, and to explain what happens. The episode seems overdetermined as representing the cause and source of Victor's interest, transferring guilt onto the parent no matter *what* he does (a hideous moral for all parents). The determination is increased as the tree becomes a metaphor for Frankenstein himself, who throughout the text refers to himself as 'blasted'.[50] An accident – one of nature too – is read as determining his life, so that an analogy seems to have causal power.

From his beginning, Victor imagines that the conclusion of his story and life will be a final and climactic meeting of creator and created. However, as in Radcliffe, the deferral of horror manages to at least partially defuse it. The apocalyptic meeting Victor has been anticipating does not take place, and he dies anticlimactically, not in a deadly battle with his double but simply worn out, alone with Walton. Writing the conclusion of her own text, Shelley does not give us a big bang that would close the text neatly with a morally and aesthetically satisfying struggle between deadly antagonists.[51]

Percy Shelley noted the similarity between the ending of Mary's text and that of her father.[52] In both, it is the child who forgives the parent, and recognises his intrinsic value. In general, too, the text recalls *St Leon*, as a tale of a fall caused by a search for forbidden knowledge that leads to a complete break between father and son. In all three novels the original sin is attributed to the father: Falkland's guilt, St Leon's passion for black magic, Frankenstein's transgression of nature. In *Caleb Williams*, the son's final forgiveness of his persecuting father leads to a reciprocal forgiveness and recognition, yet one that is only the prelude to the (perhaps rather convenient) death of the parent that precludes the need for the establishment of any further relation. In *St Leon*, father and son are separated, as the present has to free itself completely from the sins of the past. The ending of *Frankenstein* seems even bleaker in its representation of the reunion between a father and son who have become pursuer and pursued. By the end it is not clear who is pursuing whom, as both characters see themselves as victim of the other's antagonism. While Victor sees himself as the pursuer of the monster, it is the creature who catches up with his creator. But he arrives too late, to discover that Victor is already dead, and unable to respond, even briefly, to the monster's profession of love and regret. The parent dies unforgiving, denouncing his creation as his demonic adversary to the very end. Moreover, the death of the father does not free his son. The child's fate is bound up with its parent's from whom it cannot be detached, even by death. For Victor, that meant they were locked in an antagonistic struggle in which they were trying to kill each other. The monster, however, reads this relationship as requiring that he kill not his creator but himself. To the father's sadist, the child is a perfect masochist who internalises parental hatred and turns it against himself. Blaming Victor for his fate, he turns at the end to identify Victor as 'my victim' (p. 219). His final statements include praise of his creator, and self-condemnation as his murderer. The monster thus becomes a version of Caleb, who moves from denouncing to praising Falkland, and also of the author Shelley, who paid tribute to her creators in the preface.

Although, or perhaps because, Victor asserts authorial control over his story, it ultimately escapes him. Although the title refers to him, suggesting the conventional novelistic identification of character and text, the text does not just consist of his narrative, but is constructed out of multiple plots, which surround and are surrounded by his story. The doubling of Victor's story in Walton as well as the monster subverts Frankenstein's attempt to keep the narrative referring to him. It seems highly appropriate that most people who haven't read the text but know (in one mangled form or another) the myth, assume that the title refers to the creature rather than the creator. By a strange twist of fate, the monster denied a name, given no proper identity except the one he derives from identification with his creator, has usurped the name of his creator.

Moreover, the breakdown of Victor's linear quest for autonomy and control is contrasted with the creation of the text. At the same time, the creation called *Frankenstein* is set up in identification with and opposition to the monster, as an example of creation as successful combination.[53] Like *Maria*, the novel is a series of multiple narratives. Yet these various parts seem reducible to a central dualism. Kate Ellis sees the narrative structure as combining a linearity associated traditionally with masculinity and a circularity associated with femininity: as a result it 'imposes upon the linear unfolding of the plot line the very sort of order that Mary Shelley is commenting on in the novel as a whole: one that separates "outer" and "inner", the feminine sphere of domesticity and the masculine sphere of discovery'.[54] This separation between outer frame and inner narrative seems to duplicate the dualisms enacted in the text, particularly that between the public and private, male and female, spheres. What is not necessarily clear, however, is the relation between these narrative spheres. Are they set up as opposites, duplicating the antagonism within the text? Or does their relation offer an *alternative* to that within the text, suggesting a model for bridging oppositions through a narrative structure made up of various parts? By deconstructing male myths of personal autonomy, does the text itself set forth a female model of a 'relational identity', based not on detachment but on connections with others?[55]

Within the text, the monster itself is a parodic model of this ideal of relational identity, which, while now claimed by some feminists, looks back to Burke. But the monster is clearly not an alternative to male individualism, because he is a creation of it. The central relation between the monster and Frankenstein comes to a dead end, though not the one that Victor, with his bifurcating mind which can only imagine relations as murderous antitheses, expects. The survivor, who alone lives to tell the tale, is Walton, the figure in the outermost frame with whom the narrative began. The outside of the text is a series of letters home to his sister. While seeking the north pole, therefore, he seems to remain attached to the female domestic world, and a sister with whom he is intimate, but who yet does not satisfy his dream of ideal sympathy and friendship. But this is a rather strange use of the epistolary mode, as not only does it seem impossible for her to reply, but, from the third letter on, he is unable to send the letters to her. A potential dialogue hides what is in fact a monologue in which, as in Maria's letter to her supposedly dead child, the text cannot be sent out to the world but remains with its source.

As I mentioned earlier, Walton is frequently seen as simply a double of Frankenstein. Forced to turn back from his quest, he describes himself as having his hopes 'blasted' (p. 215), an adjective that suggests an identification with Victor. The relation between the two men's stories is left ambiguous, however. Victor is unclear as to his motives for telling Walton his story. At times it seems told as a moral cautionary tale, in which the author tells a story to prevent the hearer (or reader) from repeating an earlier error, in the way that Milton's Raphael told Adam about the war in heaven, St Leon presented his life to the reader, and the Ancient Mariner told his to the Wedding Guest. In this respect the stories are set up as opposites. But Victor veers maniacally from counselling Walton to abandon his quest to begging him to continue both it and his own. Fearing that he will die before his mission of destruction is complete, he asks Walton to fulfil it in his place, only to retract his request: 'No; I am not so selfish.' But he immediately retracts that retraction, 'swear that he [the monster] shall not live' (p. 208), only then to offer himself as a model to be repudiated not followed: 'Peace, peace! learn from my miseries, and do not seek to increase your own' (p. 210). His own story becomes a moral which he no sooner pronounces than withdraws: 'Seek happiness in tranquillity, and avoid ambition, even if it be only the apparently innocent one of distinguishing yourself in science and discoveries. Yet why do I say this? I have myself been blasted in these hopes, yet another may succeed' (pp. 217–18). The relation between Walton and Victor thus seems unclear: are they *parallels*, Walton a mere mirror of Victor, suggesting his obsessed solipsistic mind that reduces all others to versions of himself? Are they *opposites*, in which Walton is a redeemed version of Victor who turns back from his doomed quest, albeit against his will, to the world of relations before it is too late?[56] Or is the relationship *sequential*, one of inheritance, in which Walton, having learned nothing from the story save the confirmation of his already established romantic ideals, will carry on Victor's task elsewhere? One never knows the consequences of stories, as authors cannot control the effects their texts have on readers.

Shelley's tale is ambiguous in its conclusion partially because it 'weds' both male and female, radical and reactionary, forms of gothic narrative to suggest their essential interdependence. While Ellis identifies the outside frame with the male narrative of discovery and the inner one with the female narrative of domesticity, the associations of the two stories can also be reversed. Victor's inner story follows the trajectory of the revolutionary male gothic, which tells of the isolation and ultimately complete alienation of the hero. Beginning in a familiar domestic world, the hero, like Walton after him, goes to a strange world. In the end he cannot return to his original home because his quest has destroyed it. Walton's outer story is, however, the story of exile and return, of a circular defamiliarisation and refamiliarisation that is typical of the conservative Radcliffean female gothic. He goes out into a strange land, but the needs of the community, the crew he is forced to be responsible for despite his own desires, bring him back to his homeland. The fact that his narrative contains Victor's might lead us to see the novel as indicating the overriding triumph of relations. However, we do not see Walton's return any more than we see the monster's self-annihilation. The last image, and last words, are that of the monster disappearing, 'lost in darkness and distance' (p. 223). The familiar world that endures at the end exists only outside the circles of the text, in the figure of Margaret Saville, Walton's sister, the text's destiny as its reader.

But it also is represented by another woman whose initials are also M.W.S.,[57] the text's source and author, who places her own story at the outermost circle of the text. The relation between creator and created in the text appears to be a parody of the author's relation both to her sources and to her creation, the text itself.

However, by the end of the tale, the author's personal relations, idealised in the preface, have also been transformed. Shelley's opening praise for her sources is undercut within the text by her indirect critique of them. The 1831 preface sets up the altruism of a dutiful daughter and responsible mother – who did not write at first because of her domestic duties, 'the cares of a family' (p. 6) – as an alternative to the irresponsible parents in the text, who themselves refer to irresponsible fathers outside of the text: her literary fathers, Rousseau and Milton, and, more specifically, Godwin and Shelley. The text thus sets a male drive for self-assertion and autonomy against a female need to construct relations, and shows the first destroying the second. The text thus also inverts the original relation established in the preface, as after positioning herself deferentially in a subordinate relationship to her various sources, Shelley's deference itself becomes a mark of her superiority to them.

Whereas Wollstonecraft tried to deconstruct sexual difference, Shelley reaffirms it and transvalues it. As a solution it seems an ambiguous one. Mary Poovey claims that, in her idealisation of female selflessness, Shelley reveals her own obedience to a conservative ideology of femininity. James Carson argues, in contrast, that it is in fact a sign of her inheritance from radicals who used a Christian ethics of self-sacrifice to oppose growing commercialism.[58] Her apparent construction of an ethics of care as an alternative to an ethics of egotistical conquest has made her attractive to feminists.[59] But this solution further reproduces the problem attacked in the text. Even as it claims to be based on relations with others, her self-definition depends, like Victor's, on her absolute difference from them, which suggests that the relations she offers as an alternative to alienation and isolation are only a nostalgic fantasy.

Since Gilbert and Gubar especially, Shelley has been identified with her creature, who represents also the experience of the woman author in a male literary tradition. However, Shelley can equally be identified with her own villain, Victor, whose creation, through its distortion of mothering, seems to mirror and parody her own. Like Victor, she claimed that her creation originated in forces beyond her control, which contradicted her true nature and desires. Poovey has read Shelley's conflict as a kind of reversed version of the classic struggle between desire and duty. For Shelley, family duty dictated that she be an individual, and follow her own desires; while, according to her self-representation, her true desire was to efface herself. For Poovey, what Shelley identified as her authentic self was in fact the ideology of the 'proper lady', so that Shelley herself enacts the Godwinian tragedy in which the individual is possessed by social forces. As in *The Monk*, the conflict between natural desires and social duty is complicated if natural desires are themselves artificial constructs. While her own mixing of radical and conservative ideologies again identifies her with the monster (who, as Lee Sterrenberg has shown, conflates both sides of the revolutionary arguments), it also allies her with Victor, who from one perspective is a radical revolutionary, from another a tyrannical patriarch.[60]

Like Victor, too, Shelley seems better in tearing apart than in building up: while quite canny in deconstructing the dangers inherent in male creativity, she can't put the pieces back together into a coherent image for an alternative female creativity. While, for Wollstonecraft, mothering and writing are linked as radical tools for social reformation, for Shelley, who was both a child whose birth had caused her mother's death and a mother who had watched her daughter die, both are equally ambiguous tools of deadly creation.[61] While her text might offer an alternative model for a female textual identity, it is disparaged as 'hideous' (p. 10).[62] Moreover, from this stage of premature authorhood, Shelley, like that other precocious child Lewis, did not develop creatively very far. She remained trapped in gothic widowhood, worshipping an idealised past which she fictionalised in her later, less successful works.[63] As in the case of Lewis, this arrested creative development was justified by her early representation of the impossibility and indeed undesirability of human creation and authorial control. For Mary Shelley, her parents' progressive ideal of self-determination had become the gothic inherited family curse, a sign of essential alienation from which she wants to escape into a fantasy of relations. As in the case of St Leon's son Charles, the irresponsibility of the parent forces the child into premature and thus unnatural independence. While Godwin had urged parents to teach children to think for themselves, his daughter dreamed for her single surviving child: 'Oh my God, teach him to think like other people.'[64]

2 The Rise of Gothic Criticism

~❧~

> We cannot exist without generating evil. The more active and
> earnest we are, the more mischief shall we effect.
>
> (Godwin, *Enquirer*, p. 72)

Anne Mellor has argued that the 1831 revisions of *Frankenstein*
reflect not Victor's determinism but Shelley's own increasing fatal-
ism and gloomy sense of the unfolding of a relentless Godwinian
Necessity. In this, Pamela Clemit notes, she was typical of the
radical spirit at the time, which by the early nineteenth century
had lost faith in its own narratives of progress and revolutionary
change through reason.[65]

Part of the increasing popularity of the gothic in the twentieth
century stems from our own increasing distrust of the enlightenment myths that we have suspiciously inherited. The progress of
gothic criticism in this century, however, has taken a somewhat
circuitous and scenic route from its own origins. Critical work on
the gothic began early in this century with the painstaking recovery
of the past by Edith Birkhead, Eino Railo, Michael Sadlier, and,
especially, J.M.S. Tompkins and Montague Summers. In most there
is still a somewhat apologetic tone, reflecting a slight embarrass-
ment in their own interests in the lurid subject. Edith Birkhead, for
example, ends her study by trivialising her subject as a form that
doesn't 'reflect real life, or reveal character, or display humour'
(which she presumably thinks are things really worth doing), but
is 'full of sentimentality, and it stirred the emotions of pity and
thrill' but only in order finally 'to produce a thrill'.[66]

The monumental Montague Summers, however, both defiantly
and authoritatively insisted that readers take the gothic seriously as
an art form. With Walpolean flamboyance he inverted traditional
aesthetic hierarchies, claiming that, far from being a low form of
popular art, the gothic was 'an aristocrat of literature', and warned
his readers that 'all men of taste, all cognoscenti, all who can have
the slightest claim to literary knowledge or are fond of books have
read at least *The Mysteries of Udolpho*, *The Italian*, *The Monk*, and
Melmoth the Wanderer'.[67] Summers is a modern Walpole, the scholar
as antiquarian and necromancer, whose work is to resurrect the
dead. His works are a literary Strawberry Hill, made up of eccentric
descriptions of gothic oddities (many of which would have been
better left to rot in peace than resurrected). His slant is intensely and

218

frankly conservative; he emphasises the fact that the greatest gothic writers were against the French Revolution. He describes both the gothic and Romanticism as reactionary modes, which suggest an aspiration for something beyond the deadening familiarity of this world, a longing for the past that Summers clearly shared. The gothic is thus clearly escapist, but for Summers imaginative escapes are essential to life:

> To escape thus from mundane reality is a primitive desire, and, in itself, it is excellent and good. The world, if we had not our dreams, would, God knows, be a very dull place. Of course, as precisians will never fail to tell you, there is a danger in dreams. But, if we had not dreams, life, I take it, would be far more dangerous; in fact, it would not be worth living at all. We call our dreams Romance, and it was just this that the Gothic novelists gave to their readers.[68]

For Summers, art offers a refuge from reality; but it can only do so as long as it is separate from reality. He denounces critics who confuse art and life when they claim that the gothic was as subversive as the French Revolution, reminding us, that 'a revolution in literature . . . is a very different thing from a social Revolution'.[69] His particular enemy is surrealism, which he accused of 'having confused and deliberately commingled the two'.[70] While surrealism claimed to be the true heir to the gothic, Summers saw it as its gothic double, its antithesis not its descendent: 'the dark dream, an evil dream and delerious vision, which is a dark reality' that one should not seek, but 'beware'.[71] It stands for a confusion between art and life that the gothic itself, he believes, never entertains. Moreover, surrealism, with its use of 'automatic writing, which is in itself a very dangerous experiment' and 'the expression of thought without the control of reason',[72] denies the artistic control and authority that Summers assumes as he analyses the craft of his authors. While with barren modern scepticism it denies the existence of the supernatural, it submits humans to internal powers they cannot control.

⋅ While later critics have been enormously indebted to Summers, they have also been generally intensely irritated by his pomposity. Like the gothic servant, he is often long-winded and rambling. Ironically, too, the method he denounced was partially largely responsible for the gothic's modern gain in prestige. Surrealism marked the turn to applications of emerging psychoanalytical theory to the gothic, which became examinable in a more orderly and scientific way as an example of the subconscious emerging, the repressed returning, to reveal a truth underneath the oppressive surface of appearances. The truth rises not when we are in control, but when we lose it; for André Breton, it is the point at which 'human reason loses control that the most profound emotion of the individual has the fullest opportunity to express itself'.[73] Freud's concept of the 'uncanny', through which something once familiar becomes estranged from us, is often invoked to explain the gothic's defamiliarisation of reality.[74] Psychoanalytical vocabulary has often seemed helpful also in describing the oedipal nature of the gothic, obsessed as it is with family rivalry, and with a satanically ambiguous villain whose self-sufficiency is both his glory and his damnation. It suggests a tension between a lower nature and interfering systems of repression, which internalises the gothic conflict between individual and society, and so provides a link between psychology and social forces. With its theory of an under-lying reality, psychoanalysis helped give the gothic a new 'profundity', by seeing it as the revelation of the private life of either the individual or his culture that had been buried by habit, the conscious will, and forces of individual and social repression.

If psychoanalytical terms are useful in discussing the gothic, this is not, however, because they provide a key to unlock the mysteries of the gothic but rather, as some recent critics have noted, because psychoanalysis is itself a gothic, necromantic form, that resurrects our psychic pasts.[75] As Ian Watt notes, 'a sense of the mysterious and immobilising power of the past is one of the characteristic features both of psychoanalysis and Gothic fictions', which both represent 'the individual . . . as essentially imprisoned by an om-nipotent but unseen past'.[76] Moreover, psychoanalysis posits a model for development which moves from a state of undiffer-entiation with the world to one of separateness, even opposition towards it, as autonomy is gained through the oedipal crisis. Thus, like Protestant individualism, it privileges autonomy and self-deter-mination as the sign of maturity. But it also makes such autonomy impossible, by suggesting the power of the personal past to determine, unconsciously, one's actions in the present. Freud, the modern mad scientist (as the recent *Silence of the Lambs* makes clear with its monstrous psychiatrist-villain), is interested in analysing deviations from rather than successful realisations of the norm of development. Like the gothic, psychoanalysis tells us that the free individual is in fact caught up in an overdeter- mined chain of relations; moreover, the temptation to remain or return to previous stages impedes individual change. Rather than being a tool for explaining the gothic, then, psychoanalysis is a late gothic story which has emerged to help explain a twentieth-century experience of paradoxical detachment from and fear of others and the past. Both are symptoms of the alienation peculiar to a modern bourgeois society.[77]

Nearing the end of this century, the gothic has undergone a gradual revolution in prestige, in which also the grounds of evaluation and assessment of its achievement have reversed. While a late aesthete like Summers admired the form for its autonomy and independence from, even aristocratic indifference towards, reality, critics today locate its significance in its revelation of social conditions. Freed from the shackles of New Criticism which imprisoned us in the autonomous verbal structure, we are free to see the gothic, as it clearly must be seen, in its broader social as well as literary context. Since I became interested in the gothic, about ten years ago now, I have watched in amazement and sometimes horror as the bulk of gothic criticism has swelled with increasing rapidity to its present monstrous dimensions. In the last few years psychoanalytical methods have been increasingly succeeded by Marxist and feminist approaches (although many of these incorporate earlier psychoanalytical readings). Early loose, impressionistic readings have evolved into attempts to analyse the form with more rigorous and scientific precision. The study of the gothic has increased as part of critical interrogations of the authority of the canon, reflecting further the recent focus on literature as a product of social forces, and on its relationship particularly to issues of class and gender. The gothic has seemed relevant to attempts to theorise the relation between art, politics, history, and sexuality.[78] Perhaps this is because our modern mistrust of causality as an adequate mode for explaining the relations between these different forces leaves us in a gothic world, made up of effects without agents, creations without creators, ideological constructs that have taken on lives of their own.

Scholarship is always a necromantic enterprise; today it tends to revive the dead to dismember it, in the hope of recreating both past and present. From its beginning the gothic has suggested the limits of causality and modern systems for understanding relations, and offered itself as a form of 'cultural self-analysis'.[79] Like other previously marginalised forms, it is therefore being used today to critique established norms: the canon, gender roles, and the traditional ideals of western individualism which took form during the seventeenth and eighteenth centuries. The gothic exposes the limits of modern rational ideals of both human and textual autonomy, coherence, self-control, and Lockean notions of personhood. A form whose monstrous corporate identity transgresses traditional generic categories seems appropriate for new attempts at boundary negotiations. The current analysis of ideological systems seems, however, even as it attacks our enlightenment inheritance, to reproduce at times a naive Godwinianism, for it implies that revelation is itself reformation and revolution, as if by exposing errors, ripping away idolatrous black veils, the truth will be seen. Like Godwinians, we tend to view everything as constructs we can take apart to remake in our own image. Unlike Godwin, however, we no longer believe that truth is under the veil, as, like Radcliffe, we know that all we will find is more art, constructs that we have made. But, like Lewis, that makes us think that not only is art a fraud, but life is, as reality is not real but a series of artificial Baconic idols.

For us, however, freedom from bondage in such illusions comes from reading, particularly criticism, which institutionalises the (originally anti-institutional) Protestant tradition of self-scrutiny, turning it into a larger psychoanalysis of cultural motives and impulses. Like Godwinian self-scrutiny and Freudian analysis, reading may be seen as a way of gaining power over and so breaking away from the past. Interpretation gives us an illusion of control, especially as it has itself become increasingly idealised as a more authentically heroic and creative act than writing, a means of an ideal communal construction of the text that offers an alternative to the rampant possessive individualism of artistic creation. Even so, we are sensitive to the possibility, illustrated already in Godwin, that reading will itself become an assertion of power. The gothic critic can always turn into a rational villain who, as Fred Botting suggests, extends Victor's quest by ripping apart old texts, 'to produce new and hideous progenies that have lives of their own', and battling for narrative authority, to realise 'a unifying will to dominate and control the text'.[80] The gothic gives us an ancestor for our current obsessive self-criticism and self-scrutiny of past and present motives. Like other ironic and parodic art forms, it appeals to a postmodern sensibility because of its demonisation of creation and authority, its blatant confession of its own inability to create anew, or originate. One possible consequent danger is that we will repudiate all power, authority, even action, for its gothic potential.[81] Important as it is to pull apart, it is dangerous to confuse it with building up. The problem with choosing Goths as a model is that, like their descendent Frankenstein, they were, as Wren described them, 'rather Destroyers than Builders',[82] and it is always easier to deconstruct than to reconstruct. But the gothic seems an appropriate genre for our own dark enlightened age, another best and worst of times, so ahead of itself that it calls itself 'postmodern', in which we believe that by dismantling the past and remaking it in our own image we will really get ahead, and yet are simultaneously sceptical of all plots of progress. At a time in which change has become so rapid that it seems a truly gothic force over which we have no control, we flee from a sense of an ending to a culture of recycling which we hope will preserve us from the horrors of loss, closure, and death.

Notes

PART I

1 *Monthly Review*, quoted from Eino Railo, *The Haunted Castle: A Study of the Elements of English Romanticism*, London, Routledge, 1927, p. 104.

2 Mary Shelley, *Frankenstein, or, The Modern Prometheus*, Oxford and New York, Oxford University Press, 1980, p. 8. All further citations will be from this edition.

3 Robert D. Hume, 'Gothic versus Romantic: a Reevaluation of the Gothic Novel', *PMLA*, 1969, vol. 84, p. 283.

4 J.M.S. Tompkins, *The Work of Mrs. Radcliffe and Its Influence on Later Writers*, New York, Arno Press, 1980, p. 74. Radcliffe's admirer and heir, Sir Walter Scott, also noted and accepted calmly this subordination: 'The force, therefore, of the production, lies in the delineation of external incident, while the characters of the agents, like the figures in many landscapes, are entirely subordinate to the scenes in which they are placed; and are only distinguished by such outlines as make them seem appropriate to the rocks and trees, which have been the artist's principle objects' (*Scott's Lives of the Novelists*, London, J.M. Dent, n.d., p. 225).

5 See Elizabeth Napier, *The Failure of Gothic: Problems of Disjunction in an Eighteenth-Century Literary Form*, Oxford, Clarendon Press, 1987, especially pp. 34–7, and p. 136.

6 Robert Keily, *The Romantic Novel in England*, Cambridge, Harvard University Press, 1972, pp. 41, 116.

7 William Patrick Day, *In the Circles of Fear and Desire: A Study of Gothic Fantasy*, Chicago, University of Chicago Press, 1985; Robert Miles, *Gothic Writing 1750–1820: A Genealogy*, London and New York, Routledge, 1993, p. 3.

8 See, for example, Miles's study, op. cit., p. 224. David Punter's important study focuses on the gothic as a literature reflecting the alienation of modern capitalist life, in which the subject is divided from his work, nature, from others, and himself; see *The Literature of Terror: A History of Gothic Fictions from 1765 to the Present Day*, London, Longman, 1980.

9 Ian Watt, 'Time and Family in the Gothic Novel: *The Castle of Otranto*', *Eighteenth Century Life*, 1986, vol. 10, no. 3, p. 165.

10 *New Monthly Magazine*, 1826, quoted from Elizabeth MacAndrew, *The*

Notes

Gothic Tradition in Fiction, New York, Columbia University Press, 1979, p. 126.
11 Scott, op. cit., p. 198.
12 Review of *Emmeline, the Orphan of the Castle*, in *Analytical Review*, 1 July 1788; extract reprinted in Ioan Williams (ed.), *Novel and Romance 1700–1800: A Documentary Record*, London, Routledge, 1970, p. 355.
13 Quoted from T.M. Raysor (ed.), *Coleridge's Miscellaneous Criticism*, London, 1936, pp. 195–6.
14 James Beattie, *On Fable and Romance* (1783); extract reprinted in Williams, op. cit., p. 327.
15 Edith Birkhead, in *The Tale of Terror: A Study of the Gothic Romance*, London, Constable, 1921, describes an 1837 short story called 'The Story-Haunted', which crudely treats this theme, relating 'the sad fate of a youth brought up in a solitary library reading romances to his mother' (p. 188). After his mother dies, appropriately in an agony of terror brought on by her reading, the young man goes out into a real world for which he is totally unequipped, as he sees it too literally through books. Wilde's *Picture of Dorian Gray* is a more complexly self-critical treatment of the issue, which is not, however, confined to the gothic, but begins as an attack on the gothic's ancestor, the romance, appearing in literature from *Inferno* v through *Don Quixote* and *Mme Bovary* to the present.
16 See also Janice Radway's discussion of modern gothic romance, *Reading the Romance: Women, Patriarchy and Popular Culture*, Chapel Hill and London, University of North Carolina Press, 1984.
17 On the parallels between the gothic and carnival, see also Miles, op. cit., pp. 4–9. The two are linked further by their play on the grotesque.
18 Keily, op. cit., p. 252.
19 Scott, op. cit., p. 220. Miles further argues that the gothic's frequent failure to tidy things up neatly is its success, its refusal to reproduce an ideology that claims that everything is in its lawful place (op. cit., p. 83).
20 Wendy Tamar Heller, *Dead Secrets: Wilkie Collins and the Female Gothic*, New Haven, Yale University Press, 1992, pp. 2–3. On the dual interpretations of the gothic by female readers especially, see Juliann E. Fleenor (ed.), *The Female Gothic*, Montreal, Eden, 1983, pp. 24–6.
21 Punter, op. cit., p. 97; see also pp. 402–27.
22 Kenneth W. Graham, 'Afterword: Some Remarks on Gothic Origins', in Kenneth Graham (ed.) *Gothic Fictions: Prohibition/Transgression*, New York, AMS Press, 1989, p. 260. See also his essay in this volume, 'Emily's Demon-Lover: The Gothic Revolution and *The Mysteries of Udolpho*', pp. 163–71. Psychoanalytical readings tend to support the argument that the gothic is subversive, by claiming that the gothic represents the eruption of the subconscious energies that can subvert the official order of the super-ego or dominant culture; see Rosemary Jackson's *Fantasy: The Literature of Subversion*, New York and London, Methuen, 1981.
23 Coral Ann Howells, *Love, Mystery, and Misery: Feeling in Gothic Fiction*, London, Athlone Press, 1978, p. 6.
24 Keily, op. cit., p. 36.

Notes

25 See Terry Lovell, *Consuming Fiction*, London, Verso, 1987, pp. 55–72, who analyses perceptively some of the problems with the current critical bifurcation which tends to focus on determining whether the gothic is radical or reactionary.

26 Wylie Sypher, 'Social Ambiguity in the Gothic Novel', *Partisan Review*, 1945, vol. 12, p. 60.

27 Hume, op. cit., pp. 289–90.

28 Day, op. cit., pp. 74, 192.

29 Napier, op. cit., p. 40. See also, pp. 4–6, 39. Napier also argues that the gothic's tendency to parody its own values signifies its crippling insecurity (p. 41).

30 See Kate Ferguson Ellis, *The Contested Castle: Gothic Novels and the Subversion of Domestic Ideology*, Urbana and Chicago, University of Illinois Press, 1989.

31 See Ian Watt, *The Rise of the Novel: Studies in Defoe, Richardson and Fielding*, Berkeley, University of California Press, 1967; on the novel and causality, see also Patricia Tobin, *Time and the Novel: The Genealogical Imperative*, Princeton, Princeton University Press, 1978, pp. 3–28, 51–52.

32 See especially Punter, op. cit., pp. 197, 402–27.

33 See C.B. Macpherson, *The Political Theory of Possessive Individualism: Hobbes to Locke*, Oxford, Oxford University Press, 1962, and Charles Taylor, *Sources of the Self: The Making of the Modern Identity*, Cambridge, Mass., Harvard University Press, 1989, who maps the rise of the modern 'punctual self'. See also Susan R. Bordo's discussion of the 'birth' of the modern world as a kind of philosophical oedipal crisis, in which a masculine autonomous self detached itself from the feminine world with which it had been previously identified (*The Flight to Objectivity: Essays on Cartesianism and Culture*, Albany, State University of New York Press, 1987).

34 On the gothic's Protestant inheritance, see Victor Sage, *Horror Fiction in the Protestant Tradition*, London, Macmillan, 1988. The gothic's apparent attack on Catholicism conceals not only a nostalgia for the 'mother' church, the source from which Protestantism emerged through its own revolution, but also, as Sage argues, a distrust of its own impulses, especially as realised by non-conformists.

35 Bram Stoker, *Dracula* (1879), Toronto and New York, Bantam Books, 1981, p. 32. The identification of the vampire and lawyer is telling of a traditional distrust of the law. In general, Dracula is a strange hybrid of past and present; moreover, like the gothic form itself, he is both transgressive and deeply law-abiding – bound by what seem rather ludicrous rules artificially constructed by his author which limit his behaviour, including those that make him conform to certain social proprieties: like any normal entrepreneur, he can only come to England by legally buying the land.

36 See Peter L. Thorslev, Jr, 'Incest as Romantic Symbol', *Comparative Literature Studies*, 1965, vol. 2, pp. 41–58.

37 See Richard Hurd, *Letters on Chivalry and Romance* (1762), ed. Hoyt Trowbridge, Los Angeles, William Andrews Clark Memorial Library,

Notes

1963, p. 120. Recovery makes possible a developing sense of literary genealogy and a national tradition, apparent also in Clara Reeve's *Progress of Romance*, which traces the rise of the present novel out of the past romance (*The Progress of Romance, Through Times, Countries, and Manners with Remarks on the Good and Bad Effects of it, on them Respectively, in a course of Evening Conversations*, 2 vols, Colchester, W. Keymer, 1785).

38 For the gothic's place in the construction of a national identity, see Ian Duncan, *Modern Romance and Transformations of the Novel: The Gothic, Scott, Dickens*, Cambridge, Cambridge University Press, 1992.

39 Quoted from H.T. Dickinson, 'The Eighteenth-century Debate on the "Glorious Revolution"', *History*, 1976, vol. 61, p. 39.

40 On the different meanings of the word, see Ronald Paulson, *Representations of Revolution (1789–1820)*, New Haven and London, Yale University Press, 1983, pp. 36–8.

41 See Alfred E. Longueil, 'The Word "Gothic" in Eighteenth Century Criticism', *Modern Language Notes*, 1923, vol. 38, pp. 453–60, and Arthur O. Lovejoy, 'The First Gothic Revival and the Return to Nature', *Modern Language Notes*, 1932, vol. 47, pp. 419–46.

42 Samuel Kliger, *The Goths in England: A Study in Seventeenth and Eighteenth Century Thought*, Cambridge, Mass., Harvard University Press, 1952; Mark Madoff, 'The Useful Myth of Gothic Ancestry', in Roseann Runte (ed.), *Studies in Eighteenth Century Culture*, vol. 8, Madison, University of Wisconsin Press, 1979, pp. 337–50.

43 Robert, Lord Molesworth, 'The Principles of a Real Whig' (1711), quoted from H.T. Dickinson (ed.), *Politics and Literature in the Eighteenth Century*, London, J.M. Dent, 1974, p. 24.

44 On the mythic significance of the idea of 'The Norman Yoke', see Christopher Hill, *Puritanism and Revolution: Studies in Interpretation of the English Revolution of the Seventeenth Century*, Harmondsworth, Penguin, 1958, pp. 58–125; on modern idealisation of the feudal world, see also Raymond Williams, *The Country and the City*, New York, Oxford University Press, 1973, especially pp. 35–45.

45 Keily, op. cit., p. 9.

46 On the influence of Machiavelli in the idea of the old gothic constitution, see J.G.A. Pocock, *The Machiavellian Moment: Florentine Political Thought and the Atlantic Republican Tradition*, Princeton and London, Princeton University Press, 1975. Machiavelli seems a suspect source for any attempts to recover purity; through Elizabethan villains, he is an ancestor of the rational philosopher gothic villain.

47 See M.H. Abrams, *Natural Supernaturalism: Tradition and Revolution in Romantic Literature*, New York, W.W. Norton, 1971.

48 Clara Reeve, *Memoirs of Sir Roger de Clarendon*, 3 vols, London, Hockham & Carpenter, 1793, vol. 1, pp. xvi–xvii.

49 *The Works of Lord Macaulay*, vol. 2, London, Longmans, Green & Co., 1914, p. 314.

50 ibid., pp. 318, 317.

51 ibid., p. 314.

52 ibid., p. 330.

53 Horace Walpole, quoted from Scott, op. cit., p. 194.

54 Horace Walpole, *The Castle of Otranto* (1764), in E.F. Bleiler (ed.), *Three Gothic Novels*, New York, Dover, 1966, p. 18. All further quotations, henceforth referenced in the text, are from this edition.

55 Quoted from Watt, 'Time and Family', p. 162. As self-appointed historian of the present, Walpole's job was to turn it into the past. On the relation of his nostalgia to wider eighteenth-century attitudes, see Fredric V. Bogel, *Literature and Insubstantiality in Later Eighteenth-Century England*, Princeton, Princeton University Press, 1984, especially pp. 108–35.

56 David D. McKinney, 'The Castle of My Ancestors: Horace Walpole and Strawberry Hill', *British Journal for Eighteenth-Century Studies*, 1990, vol. 13, pp. 199–214.

57 See Isaac Kramnick, *Bolingbroke and his Circle: The Politics of Nostalgia in the Age of Walpole*, Ithaca and London, Cornell University Press, 1968, pp. 111–87.

58 See, for example, his disjointed speech pp. 68–70 which is punctuated by constant interruptions, both from outside and from Manfred himself, who criticises his own mode of presenting information: 'your mode of interruption has disordered me'; 'pardon me gentlemen, I am too warm'; and while he tries to urge himself on, 'but to the point', he in fact delays himself and keeps himself from reaching it. See further below (pp. 122–4) for Radcliffe's revision of this tactic.

59 Macaulay, giving the devil his due, saw this ability to combine and unite disparate things as Walpole's strength. He compared it to the conceits of the seventeenth-century metaphysicals: 'Like theirs, it [Walpole's wit] consisted in an exquisite perception of points of analogy and points of contrast too subtle for common observation', he 'startles us by the ease with which he yokes together ideas between which there would seem, at first sight, to be no connection' (op. cit., p. 331).

60 See Jess M. Stein, 'Horace Walpole and Shakespeare', *Studies in Philology*, 1934, vol. 31, pp. 51–68. Throughout the eighteenth century, Shakespeare was associated with nature; see also Lovejoy, op. cit., pp. 441–2. The gothic shows how the establishment of a native English tradition depends upon an antithesis between England and France. The British association of Britain with freedom and France with tyranny colours all comparisons of their mutual cultures, from their literary giants to their attitudes towards nature; the difference between Shakespeare and Voltaire echoes the contrast between the wild English gothic garden in which nature flourished freely (according to the British gardeners, who also used it as an image for Britain and its government), and the artificial French neoclassical gardens which repressed nature.

61 See Leo Spitzer, 'Notes on the Poetic and Empirical "I" in Medieval Authors', *Traditio*, 1946, vol. 4, pp. 414–22.

62 Quoted from Summers, *The Gothic Quest: A History of the Gothic Novel*, New York, Russell & Russell, 1964, p. 182.

63 Basil Willey, for example, says that *Caleb Williams*: 'still reads like a work composed under an afflatus or imaginative "possession"' (*The Eighteenth Century Background: Studies on the Idea of Nature in the Thought of the Period*, Boston, Beacon Press, 1961, p. 214). The effect may stem

from the fact that many gothic masterpieces – such as Walpole's, Godwin's, Brockden Brown's, Beckford's *Vathek*, Lewis's *Monk*, and *Frankenstein* – were written quickly.

64 Percy Bysshe Shelley, 'A Defence of Poetry', in Donald H. Reiman and Sharon B. Powers (eds), *Shelley's Poetry and Prose*, New York and London, W.W. Norton, 1977, p. 480; on this image for creation, see M.H. Abrams, 'The Correspondent Breeze: A Romantic Metaphor', reprinted in *The Correspondent Breeze: Essays on English Romanticism*, New York and London, W.W. Norton, 1984, pp. 25–43.

65 See Scott, op. cit., p. 191, who notes how Walpole was a fake dilettante who laboured to make his labour seem effortless.

66 On the Revolution as the cause of 'a new sense of the way one action or event follows another – a new sense of plot or sequence and new examples of serial structure', see Paulson, op. cit., p. 49; see also pp. 1–7, 55, and 225.

67 Reprinted in Alfred Cobban (ed.), *The Debate on the French Revolution 1789–1800*, London, Nicholas Kaye, 1950, p. 64.

68 Edmund Burke, *Reflections on the Revolution in France* (1790), ed. J.G.A. Pocock, Indianapolis and Cambridge, Hackett, 1987, pp. 27–8. All further quotations, henceforth referenced in the text, will be from this edition.

69 On Burke's fear of undifferentiation and role as 'guardian of the boundary', see also Paulson, op. cit., p. 73; Isaac Kramnick, *The Rage of Edmund Burke: Portrait of An Ambivalent Conservative*, New York, Basic Books, 1977; and David Punter, '1789: The Sex of Revolution', *Criticism*, 1982, vol. 24, p. 203. The creation of differences in regards to revolutions underlies Burke's argument in his later defence of himself against the charge of inconsistency, in which he attacked the argument that if he defended the American revolution he was bound to defend *all* revolutions.

70 Burke's model for this process of channelling rather than repressing human energies through external forces is again from nature:

> To destroy any power growing wild from the rank productive force of the human mind is almost tantamount, in the moral world, to the destruction of the apparently active properties of bodies in the material. It would be like the attempt to destroy (if it were in our competence to destroy) the expansive force of fixed air in nitre, or the power of steam, or of electricity, or of magnetism. These energies always existed in nature, and they were always discernible. They seemed, some of them unserviceable, some noxious, some no better than a sport to children, until contemplative ability, combining with practic [*sic*] skill, tamed their wild nature, subdued them to use, and rendered them at once the most powerful and the most tractable agents in subservience to the great views and designs of men.
>
> (*Reflections*, p. 139)

71 Edmund Burke, *A Philosophical Enquiry into the Origin of Our Ideas of the Sublime and Beautiful* (1757), ed. James T. Boulton, Notre Dame and London, University of Notre Dame Press, 1958, p. 68.

72 Edmund Burke, *An Appeal From the New to the Old Whigs*, ed. and intro. John M. Robson, Indianapolis and New York, Bobbs-Merrill, 1962, pp. 96–7. All further quotations, henceforth referenced in the text, will be from this edition.

73 Tom Paine, *Rights of Man* (1791), intro. Eric Foner, Harmondsworth, Penguin, 1984, p. 182. For Rousseau, unveiling is an image for the enlightenment; see Jean Starobinski, *La Transparence et l'obstacle*, Paris, Gallimard, 1971. We will see this rhetoric of revelation extended by Godwin and attacked by Radcliffe.

74 Mary Wollstonecraft, *A Vindication of the Rights of Woman* (1792), ed. Carol H. Poston, New York and London, W.W. Norton, 1975, p. 150.

75 See Paulson, op. cit., pp. 60–5, and Kramnick, *The Rage of Edmund Burke*, pp. 153–4, who sees this as partially an attack on Rousseau's claim that in his *Confessions* he 'Dared to strip man's nature naked' (p. 155). As Kramnick notes, 'Nakedness becomes symbolic in the *Reflections* for the end of the traditional order' (p. 153), the chaos of a world without limits or art to restrain individuals. Burke again differentiates himself from 'naked' individuals, by padding his speech with allusions to Shakespeare's *King Lear*, which provides an important subtext for both the discussion of naked human nature and that of the proper exercise of authority.

76 On Burke's ambivalent relation with the middle class which he both denounced and epitomised, see Kramnick, *The Rage of Edmund Burke*.

77 Edmund Burke, *Letter to a Member of the National Assembly (1791)*, in *The Works of Edmund Burke*, 9 vols, Boston, Charles Little, 1839, vol. 3, p. 311.

78 On this imagery, see Paulson, op. cit., pp. 72–3; Chris Baldick, *In Frankenstein's Shadow: Myth, Monstrosity and Nineteenth-Century Writing*, Oxford, Clarendon Press, pp.17–21.

79 Quoted from T.M. Raysor (ed.), op. cit., pp. 11–12.

80 Quoted from Keily, op. cit., p. 30.

81 J.M.S. Tompkins, *The Popular Novel in England, 1770–1800*, (1932), Lincoln, Nebraska, University of Nebraska Press, 1963 rpt, p. 274, who sees a source in Mme de Cenlis's popular *Adele et Theodore*, translated in 1782.

82 The return of the dead becomes increasingly invoked in more grotesque and literal forms, especially in today's vampires and cannibal zombie dead. The reciprocal preying of past and present emerges, however, already in the mid-nineteenth century. Dickens's gothic *Tale of Two Cities*, set during the French Revolution, obsessively replays the theme of the murderous return of the past and battle with the present: from the figure of the imprisoned Dr Monette who is 'recalled to life' to the 'resurrectionist', that is, body-snatcher, Jerry Cruncher. This resurrection of the dead is itself a symbol for the Revolution, which is recalled to life as a contradictory merging of opposites: both 'the best of times' and 'the worst of times'. In its complete identification of opposites, it also conflates time, as the past becomes 'a time very much like the present'. The dead past is the enemy of the living present because it comes back as a version of the present; the disappearance of historical difference is a much greater threat than difference itself.

Notes

83 Quoted from Summers, op. cit., p. 38.

84 John Locke, *Some Thoughts Concerning Education* (1693), ed. and intro. John W. and Jean S. Yolton, Oxford, Clarendon Press, 1989, p. 196. All further quotations, henceforth referenced in the text, will be from this edition.

85 Paulson, op. cit., pp. 57–73.

86 On this as a general narrative principle, see Peter Brooks, *Reading for the Plot: Design and Intention in Narrative*, New York, Vintage, 1985, especially pp. 90–112; Patricia A. Parker, *Inescapable Romance: Studies in the Poetics of a Mode*, Princeton, Princeton University Press, 1979.

87 See also Brooks, op. cit., p. 103, who discusses the double function of plot, which both gets us to and defers an end.

88 See Railo, op. cit., p. 69, and Birkhead, op. cit., p. 119. On Beckford's perverse Peter Pan fantasies, see Keily, op. cit., pp. 45–60.

89 Scott, op. cit., p. 227.

90 Stoker, op cit., p. 320. Dracula is usually seen as a demonic parent, or Christ, especially in the scene with Mina where he presses her to his breast and makes her suck his blood, in a parody both of communion and a mother–child symbiosis which further inverts gender roles. But Stoker also compares them in a simile to 'a child forcing a kitten's nose into a saucer of milk to compel it to drink' (p. 298), making Dracula the evil child, who imposes his power on those weaker than himself. The image of the demonic child, the antithesis of the Rousseauian ideal, appears in the gothic from Beckford's Vathek through Bronte's Heathcliff, to the present, where, since the *Exorcist*, it has become increasingly, and suggestively, omnipresent.

91 Paul A. Cantor, *Creature and Creator*, New York, Cambridge University Press, 1984, pp. 111, 113–14.

92 See the moral cautionary stories illustrating this point in both *Education*, p. 197, and *An Essay Concerning Human Understanding* (1690), vol. I, New York, Dover, 1959, pp. 531–5.

93 See Locke's *Essay*, vol. I, p. 533. For Locke, irrational associations, 'the wrong and unnatural combinations of ideas' (p. 534), are the basis of almost all error.

94 Stoker, op. cit., p. 361.

95 Quoted from Victor Sage (ed.), *The Gothick Novel*, London, Macmillan, 1990, p. 113.

96 See Marianne Hirsch, *The Mother/Daughter Plot: Narrative, Psychoanalysis, Feminism*, Bloomington, Indiana University Press, 1989, pp. 50–8.

97 See Norman N. Holland and Leona F. Sherman, 'Gothic Possibilities', *New Literary History*, 1976–7, vol. 8, pp. 279–94, who see the gothic as returning the reader to an early stage of psychic development, before the establishment of individual identity through the discovery of the opposition between self and other. The loss of stable boundaries can be both pleasurable, recalling an earlier symbiotic union, and terrifying, by its threat to the separate self. In his more recent work, 'Narrative and Psychology in Gothic Fiction' (in Kenneth Graham (ed.), op. cit., pp. 1–27) David Punter argues also that the gothic represents a denial of loss and change and rejection of maturation.

Notes

98 See Ellen Moers, *Literary Women: The Great Writers*, New York, Oxford University Press, 1977, pp. 90–110; Ellis, op. cit.; Fleenor (ed.), op. cit.; Miles, op. cit., pp. 50–81.

99 On this as a basic female narrative form, see Elizabeth Abel, Marianne Hirsch, and Elizabeth Langland (eds), *The Voyage In: Fictions of Female Development*, Hanover, NH, University Press of New England, 1983, pp. 9–11, and Marianne Hirsch, op. cit.

100 On mother–daughter relations in the gothic and their implications for female identity, see also Claire Kahane, 'The Gothic Mirror', in Shirley Nelson Gardener, Claire Kahane, and Madelon Sprengnether (eds), *The (M)other Tongue: Essays in Feminist Psychoanalytic Interpretation*, Ithaca, Cornell University Press, 1985, pp. 334–51. Many recent feminist readings of this difference draw on the work of Nancy Chodorow, who explained this asymmetry in sexual development and identity as the natural product of a modern capitalist society in which mothers are the primary caretakers of children. While both the male and female child's first relationship is thus with a woman, the male child is forced to repudiate his first identification, to set himself off as different from the mother, as he develops; for the female child, however, development may be even more problematic, as sexual identity is achieved by the continuation of the original identification with the mother. The asymmetry Chodorow notes thus supports antithetical gender roles: masculine identity is defined by difference, the rebellion against identification, female is defined by sameness, and submissive obedience. The stereotypical male has too rigid a sense of his own isolation; the female, too little sense of her own difference from others. Nancy Chodorow, *The Reproduction of Mothering: Psychoanalysis and the Sociology of Gender*, Berkeley, University of California Press, 1978.

101 On the difference between these two aesthetic ideologies, see Terry Eagleton, *Marxism and Literary Criticism*, Berkeley and Los Angeles, University of California Press, 1976, pp. 64–6. In Coleridge's account of the composition of the *Lyrical Ballads* (a work linked to the gothic by the common source of the ballad tradition, and also attacked by early reviewers as infantile art), however, defamiliarisation and familiarisation were seen as complementary parts of the romantic project – which may account for conflicting interpretations of Romanticism as a revolutionary and reactionary movement; see Samuel Taylor Coleridge, *Biographia Literaria* (1817), in James Engell and W. Jackson Bate (eds), *Coleridge's Collected Works* vol. 2, Princeton, Princeton University Press, pp. 6–7.

102 See also Baldick, op. cit., pp. 10–29.

103 Timothy J. Reiss, *The Discourse of Modernism*, Ithaca and London, Cornell University Press, 1982. Eric Rothstein has also discussed the role of analogy in eighteenth-century epistemology and narrative structure; see *Systems of Order and Inquiry in Late Eighteenth-Century Fiction*, Berkeley, University of California Press, 1975. For Rothstein, the gothic was a kind of generic throwback, which resisted the increasing tendency of realistic novels to rely 'more on causality (linear plot), less on analogical panorama' (p. 243).

Notes

104 Dustin Griffin, *Regaining Paradise: Milton and the Eighteenth Century,* Cambridge, Cambridge University Press, 1986, p. 2.

105 Roger Sharrock, 'Godwin on Milton's Satan', *Notes and Queries,* 1962, vol. 207, p. 464; William Godwin, *Enquiry Concerning Political Justice* (1798), ed. Isaac Kramnick, Harmondsworth, Penguin, 1976, p. 309.

106 *De Profundis,* in *Complete Works of Oscar Wilde,* intro. Vyvyan Holland, London and Glasgow, Collins, 1966, p. 922. *Dorian Gray* is partially a working out of the paradox in Wilde's aesthetic claims that art is both totally cut off from life, an aesthetic realm which has no influence, and life's model – as he himself exemplified.

107 *Letter,* p. 306; see also pp. 304–13 for Burke's attack on Rousseau as a philosophical monster, who manifested 'a love of his kind and hatred of his kindred' (p. 307). See also Kramnick, *The Rage of Edmund Burke,* pp. 153–5.

108 Jean-Jacques Rousseau, *Reveries of the Solitary Walker* (1782), trans. and intro. Peter France, Harmondsworth, Penguin, 1979, p. 27. All further quotations, henceforth referenced in the text, will be from this edition.

PART II

1 Godwin and the Gothic of Revolution

1 William Godwin, *Enquiry Concerning Political Justice* (1793), ed. and intro. Isaac Kramnick, Harmondsworth, Penguin, 1976, p. 693. All further citations, henceforth referenced in the text, will be from this edition.

2 See especially James T. Boulton, *The Language of Politics in the Age of Wilkes and Burke,* Westport, CT, Greenwood, 1975; and Marilyn Butler, 'Godwin, Burke, and *Caleb Williams*', *Essays in Criticism,* 1982, vol. 32, pp. 237–57.

3 See Isaac Kramnick, 'Religion and Radicalism: English Political Theory in the Age of Revolution', *Political Theory: An International Journal of Political Philosophy,* 1977, vol. 5, pp. 505–34.

4 William Godwin, *The Enquirer, Reflections on Education, Manners and Literature in a Series of Essays* (1797), New York, Augustus M. Kelley, 1965, pp. 10–11. All further quotations, henceforth referenced in the text, will be from this edition.

5 See Mark Philps, *Godwin's Political Justice,* Ithaca, Cornell University Press, 1986, pp. 15–57, who stresses Godwin's debt to the dissenting tradition of individual conscience in which he was raised.

6 *Thoughts on Man;* quoted from George Woodcock, *William Godwin: A Biographical Study,* Montreal and New York, Black Rose, 1989, p. 234.

7 William Hazlitt, *Lectures on English Poets and The Spirit of the Age: or Contemporary Portraits,* intro. Catherine Macdonald Maclean, London, J.M. Dent & Sons Ltd, 1967, p. 202.

8 For an analysis of Godwin's style and its relation to Burke's, see Boulton, op. cit., pp. 210–26, and Butler, op. cit., pp. 242–3. Language

itself had been a political issue since the seventeenth century, as the Protestant distrust of forms of representation included figurative language as distorting of meaning.

9 On the relation between the two works, see especially David McCracken, 'Godwin's Literary Theory: The Alliance between Fiction and Political Philosophy', *Philological Quarterly*, 1970, vol. 49, pp. 113–33; Philps, op. cit., pp. 103–19; and Pamela Clemit, *The Godwinian Novel: The Rational Fictions of Godwin, Brockden Brown, Mary Shelley*, Oxford, Clarendon Press, 1993, pp. 35–69.

10 See also Tilottama Rajan, 'Wollstonecraft and Godwin: Reading the Secrets of the Political Novel', *Studies in Romanticism*, 1988, vol. 27, pp. 221–51.

11 In an undated manuscript he wrote, anticipating Shelley, that 'I am convinced that imagination is the basis of social morality. It is by dint of feeling, and of putting ourselves in fancy, into the place of other men, that we can learn how we ought to treat them, and be moved to treat them as we ought'; cited from Gary Kelly, *The English Jacobin Novel, 1780–1805*, Oxford, Oxford University Press, 1976, p. 236.

12 See especially the essays 'Of an Early Taste for Reading', pp. 29–35, 'Of Choice in Reading', pp. 129–46, and 'Of Learning', pp. 351–67.

13 William Godwin, *Caleb Williams* (1794), ed. and intro. David McCracken, Oxford and New York, Oxford University Press, 1970, Appendix, p. 338. All further citations, henceforth referenced in the text, will be from this edition.

14 McCracken, op. cit., pp. 126–7.

15 This rather eclectic group of works included Richardson's *Clarissa* and *Sir Charles Grandison*, Bage's *Hermsprong*, Mackenzie's *Man of Feeling*, Rousseau's *La Nouvelle Héloise*, Radcliffe's *Romance of the Forest* and newly published *Mysteries of Udolpho*, as well as the *Newgate Calendar* and *Lives of the Pirates*; see Kelly, op. cit., pp. 191–2. Despite Godwin's disclaimer over influence, most of what he read got into his works.

16 For Leslie Stephens this made it a generic freak, 'a kind of literary curiosity – a monstrous hybrid between different species'; see *Studies of a Biographer*, vol. 3, second series, London, Buckworth & Co., 1902, p. 154. The kindest thing Stephens says of the work, or of Godwin for that matter, is that it 'gains interest by a fortunate confusion' (p. 154).

17 See Burton R. Pollin, *Education and Enlightenment in the Works of William Godwin*, New York, Las Americas Publishing Co., 1962.

18 Quoted from Woodcock, op. cit., p. 22. The school was never opened as Godwin failed to attract any pupils.

19 In identifying curiosity as an essential human characteristic, Godwin agrees with Burke; see *A Philosophical Enquiry into the Origin of Our Ideas of the Sublime and Beautiful* (1757), ed. James T. Boulton, Notre Dame and London, University of Notre Dame Press, 1958, p. 31. For Burke, however, curiosity is 'superficial', 'it always has the appearance of giddiness, restlessness and anxiety', unless it is properly controlled.

20 Quoted from Woodcock, op. cit., p. 10. He spent all his time reading and later remembered worrying, 'What shall I do, when I have read through all the books that there are in the world?'; quoted from Basil

Willey, *The Eighteenth Century Background: Studies on the Idea of Nature in the Thought of the Period,* Boston, Beacon Press, 1961, p. 212; see also pp. 213–14. He kept an obsessive list of his reading as if to prove that he *had* read everything.

21 Hazlitt, op. cit., p. 191.

22 Exodus was a common model for revolutionaries, including Milton, who identified with Moses, a poet–prophet leading his people towards a promised land (which they ultimately were too fearful to enter, and chose to return to Egyptian slavery); see Michael Walzer, *Exodus and Revolution,* New York, Basic Books, 1985.

23 On the relation of this to Godwin's text, see Ian Ousby, '"My servant Caleb": Godwin's *Caleb Williams* and the Political Trials of the 1790s', *University of Toronto Quarterly,* 1974, vol. 94, no. 1, pp. 47–55.

24 See Godwin's distinction of the noble form of curiosity from the ignoble, the latter being 'an obstinate, self-willed principle, opening veins of its own choosing, wasting itself in oblique, unprofitable speculations, and refusing to bring its energies to bear upon a pursuit pointed out to it by another', *Enquirer,* p. 53.

25 Godwin later tried to pacify dog-lovers by depicting a faithful dog in *St Leon,* a text which also redeems the despised servant in the figure of the loyal Hector.

26 On this medieval model for knowledge, see Ernst Cassirer, *The Individual and the Cosmos in Renaissance Philosophy,* trans. Mario Domandi, Philadelphia, University of Pennsylvania Press, 1963. On the emergence of Baconian science, see below, pp. 101–3, 194–6 esp..

27 *Letter to a Member of the National Assembly* (1791), in *The Works of Edmund Burke,* 9 vols, Boston, Charles Little, 1839, vol. 3, p. 311.

28 Falkland's dehumanisation further repeats Satan's notorious 'degradation' from the epic hero of the first book into the caricature and emblem of evil in Book X.

29 See Appendix II, pp. 340–1. On the repressed erotic element of the text, suggested by the echoes of *Clarissa,* see Ronald Paulson, *Representations of Revolution (1789–1820),* New Haven and London, Yale University Press, 1983, pp. 230–5, who also discusses the relation in terms of Girard's theory of imitative desire; and Alex Gold, Jr, 'It's Only Love: The Politics of Passion in Godwin's *Caleb Williams',* *Texas Studies in Literature and Language,* 1977, vol. 19, pp. 135–60.

30 On doubling in the text, see also William Patrick Day, *In the Circles of Fear and Desire: A Study of Gothic Fantasy,* Chicago, University of Chicago Press, 1985, pp. 137–9.

31 On the role of analogy in the story, see also Eric Rothstein, *Systems of Order and Inquiry in Late Eighteenth-Century Fiction,* Berkeley, University of California Press, 1975.

32 See Butler, op. cit.; Kelly, op. cit., p. 194; Boulton, op. cit., pp. 227–32; David McCracken, 'Godwin's Reading in Burke', *English Language Notes,* 1970, vol. 7, pp. 264–70; Clemit, op. cit., pp. 39–45.

33 For a reading of the religious implications of surveillance in the text, see Rudolf F. Storch, 'Metaphors of Private Guilt and Social Rebellion in Godwin's *Caleb Williams',* *English Literary History,* 1967, vol. 34,

pp. 188–207. James Thompson, 'Surveillance in William Godwin's *Caleb Williams*', in Kenneth W. Graham (ed.), *Gothic Fictions: Prohibitions/Transgressions*, New York, AMS Press, 1989, gives a Foucauldian reading of the text, arguing that 'the gothic novel and above all *Caleb Williams* dramatise the real source of terror in the industrial age of discipline and surveillance: the penetration of state apparatus into the everyday lives of individuals' (p. 192). The gothic's representation of paranoia, the fear that one is being watched, reflects the burden of constant self-scrutiny, which internalises both religious and social forms of surveillance, and turns the self into its own cruel, and inescapable, monitor: a gothic double that is both victor and victim, pursuer and pursued.

34 See especially pp. 186–9, where Caleb extends Rousseau's claims that the mind is its own place: 'This type of reverie can be enjoyed anywhere where one is undisturbed, and I have often thought that in the Bastille, and even in a dungeon with not a single object to rest my eyes on, I could still have dreamed pleasantly' (*Reveries of the Solitary Walker* (1782), trans. and intro. Peter France, Harmondsworth, Penguin, 1979, p. 90).

35 See Jacqueline T. Miller, 'The Imperfect Tale: Articulation, Rhetoric, and Self in *Caleb Williams*', *Criticism*, 1978, vol. 20, no. 4, pp. 366–82, who reads the text as the story of 'a man who never succeeds in becoming his own author' (p. 372). She sees Caleb as a mere imitator of Falkland, noting that his work as a servant appropriately involves copying from his master's manuscript (p. 373).

36 On the endings, and theories of Godwin's possible motives for revision, which range from political prudence to anxiety over Richardson's influence, see D. Gilbert Dumas, 'Things as They Were: The Original Ending of *Caleb Williams*', *Studies in English Literature 1500–1900*, 1966, vol. 6, pp. 575–97; Mitzi Myers, 'Godwin's Changing Conception of *Caleb Williams*', *Studies in English Literature 1500–1900*, 1972, vol. 12, pp. 591–628; Kenneth W. Graham, 'Narrative and Ideology in Godwin's *Caleb Williams*', *Eighteenth-Century Fiction*, 1990, vol. 2, no. 3, pp. 215–28; and McCracken, 'Godwin's Reading in Burke'.

37 See also Seamus Deane, *The French Revolution and Enlightenment England 1789–1832*, Cambridge, Mass., Harvard University Press, 1988, pp. 83.–7, who sees Godwin's view of the punitive power of the conscience as influenced by Holbach.

38 Quoted from Clemit, op. cit., p. 42.

39 Montague Summers, *The Gothic Quest, A History of the Gothic Novel*, New York, Russell & Russell, 1964, p. 403, whose contempt for the character complemented his loathing of the author whom he saw as 'an Utopian fantast' and hypocrite whose 'life was in contradiction to his dreams' (p. 403).

40 Kenneth W. Graham, 'The Gothic Unity of Godwin's *Caleb Williams*', *Papers on Language and Literature*, 1984, vol. 20, pp. 47–59.

41 See B. Sprague Allen, 'The Reaction Against William Godwin', *Modern Philology* September 1918, vol. 16, no. 5, pp. 57–75, for gory details.

42 In this, the anti-Godwinian novel extends Burke's tracing of the

Revolution to a conspiracy of intelligentsia which, while originally set up against tyrannies, became a new tyranny. So the translator of *Horrid Mysteries* exposes the hypocrisy of secret societies, 'that pretend to reform the defects of government, while selfish views are concealed under the imposing outside of philosophy and patriotism' (*Horrid Mysteries: A Story Translated from the German of the Marquis of Grosse by Peter Will* (1797), London, The Folio Press, 1968, p. xvii).

2 The Reveries of a Solitary Woman

1 William Godwin, *Caleb Williams* (1794), ed. and intro. David McCracken, Oxford and New York, Oxford University Press, 1970, p. 1.

2 Mary Wollstonecraft, *Maria, or the Wrongs of Woman* in Gary Kelly (ed. and intro.), *Mary and The Wrongs of Woman* (1798), Oxford, Oxford University Press, 1976, p. 73. All further citations, henceforth referenced in the text, will be from this edition.

3 Mary Wollstonecraft, *A Vindication of the Rights of Women* (1792), ed. Carol H. Poston, New York and London, W.W. Norton, 1975, p. 5. All further citations, henceforth referenced in the text, will be from this edition.

4 Mary Wollstonecraft, *Thoughts on the Education of Daughters* (1787), in Janet Todd and Marilyn Butler (eds), *The Works of Mary Wollstonecraft*, London, William Pickering, 1989, vol. 4, pp. 42, 37.

5 Typically, Wollstonecraft's own rational discourse here exposes its religious (and elsewhere sentimental) origins, as Wollstonecraft transfers to reason a phrase which originally referred to God. For the enlightened Protestant, reason, a version of the individual conscience, assumes the role of God.

6 As many critics have noted, Wollstonecraft's discourse is not as rational as she thinks; see, for example, James T, Boulton, *The Language of Politics in the Age of Wilkes and Burke*, Westport, CT, Greenwood, 1975, pp. 167–76. Moreover, her identification with enlightenment values, and desire to simply extend the rights of male individualism which she identifies as human nature, has made her problematic for current feminists, some of whom see her as merely replacing one ideological identity with another; see Janet Todd, *Feminist Literary History*, New York, Routledge, 1988, pp. 103–17; Anna Wilson, 'Mary Wollstonecraft and the Search for the Radical Woman', *Genders*, 1989, vol. 6, pp. 88–101; and Mary Poovey, *The Proper Lady and the Woman Writer*, Chicago, University of Chicago Press, pp. 55, 79–80, esp.

7 See Boulton, op. cit.; Ronald Paulson, *Representations of Revolution (1789–1820)*, New Haven and London, Yale University Press, 1983, pp. 79–87, who discusses Wollstonecraft's identification of Burke with gothic systems of sexual oppression; and Poovey, op. cit., pp. 56–68.

8 See Mary Wollstonecraft, *Vindication of the Rights of Men* (1790), Gainesville, Florida, Scholars' Facsimiles & Reprints, 1960, pp. 112–17 especially, where Wollstonecraft attacks Burke's identification of sublimity with masculinity and beauty with femininity as degrading to women. Her critique of chivalric paternalism as part of Burke's 'gothic

notions' (p. 10) mirrors the message of much female gothic: that systems claiming to shelter women are in fact the source of their oppression, refuges are always prisons.

9 See especially Gary Kelly, 'Godwin, Wollstonecraft and Rousseau', *Women and Literature*, 1975, vol. 3, pp. 21–6.

10 On Wollstonecraft as Romantic wanderer, see Richard Holmes (ed. and intro.), *Mary Wollstonecraft and William Godwin: A Short Residence in Sweden and Memoirs of the Author of 'The Rights of Woman'*, Harmondsworth, Penguin, 1987, pp. 26–8.

11 *Memoirs*, in Holmes, ibid., p. 249.

12 As we will see, Wollstonecraft is usually attracted to what she condemns; her response to Milton's couple is more complex than she implies, as it appears in her letters as a model for her relationships with both Imlay and Godwin. See, for example, her letter to Godwin of 15 September 1796, in which she reassures him that 'I shall be angry if you sweeten grammatical disquisitions after the Miltonic mode', an allusion to *Paradise Lost*, IV, 492–502; in Ralph Wardle (ed.) *The Letters of William Godwin and Mary Wollstonecraft*, Lawrence, Kansas, University of Kansas Press, 1966, p. 35.

13 See Spencer, op. cit., pp. 22–33, and Poovey, op. cit., pp. 35–47.

14 Tilottama Rajan, 'Wollstonecraft and Godwin: Reading the Secrets of the Political Novel', *Studies in Romanticism*, 1988, vol. 27, p. 241.

15 ibid., p. 236.

16 On Wollstonecraft's transformation of her own life into her art see also Mitzi Myers, 'Pedagogy as Self-Expression in Mary Wollstonecraft: Exorcising the Past, Finding a Voice', in Shari Benstock (ed.), *The Private Self: Theory and Practice of Women's Autobiographical Writing*, Chapel Hill, University of North Carolina Press, 1988, pp. 192–210, who sees all of Wollstonecraft's works as 'experiments in selfhood' (p. 195); on *Maria* as the union of the personal and the political, see Mitzi Myers, 'Unfinished Business: Wollstonecraft's *Maria*', *Wordsworth Circle*, 1980, vol. 11, no. 2, pp. 107–14. Poovey, op. cit., pp. 97–8, 103–6, notes also, however, how Wollstonecraft's identification with her characters creates difficulties in the sustaining of a consistent distance between the character and an overriding narrative voice.

17 On Wollstonecraft's use of the gothic as a means of representing societal oppression of the individual, see Rajan, op. cit., pp. 221–51; Marilyn Butler, 'The Woman at the Window: Ann Radcliffe in the Novels of Mary Wollstonecraft and Jane Austen', in *Women and Literature*, 1980, vol. 1, pp. 128–48. Butler notes that Wollstonecraft's use of both sentimental and gothic forms exposes her 'inclination to choose fictional styles which cannot do other than communicate the obsessive inwardness she deplores' (p. 144.)

18 Rajan, op. cit., p. 228.

19 See Jean-Jacques Rousseau, *Reveries of the Solitary Walker* (1782), trans. and intro. Peter France, Harmondsworth, Penguin, 1979, p. 90, and Godwin, *Caleb Williams*, pp. 186–7. For Caleb, however, the stoic transcendence of circumstance is not adequate and deepens his craving for others.

20 See Paulson, op. cit., pp. 166–7.

21 This opposition between a teleological quest and a seductively entrapping bower is an old one in the epic and romance tradition; Ulysses' return is impeded by Circe and Calypso who try to detain him from returning to his home and true identity. For Ulysses, however, the problem is a purely personal one. The tension is turned into an opposition between private pleasure and public duty with the *Aeneid*, however, where Aeneas's desire for Dido conflicts with his duty to found Rome. In later romances, such as those of Ariosto, Tasso, and Spenser, the tension is moralised by the representation of the bower as an illusion that emasculates the male. It is precisely this reading of the tension between duty and pleasure as reality and fiction that, with the rise of capitalism and the mythologising of one's 'calling', gets incorporated further into the opposition between the public world and the private (in which women, after all, read and write fictions). The private world is the world of love and the imagination; while it is designed potentially to refresh one for the arduous work of public life, it is seen as dangerous when turned into an end in itself. Although the private is idealised in capitalism, as the world in which the individual is in his castle, when he is his true self – stripped of the public social roles that distort by misrepresenting his identity – it is also suspected; see also below, pp. 98–100, 203–4 esp.

22 'Individuality is of the very essence of intellectual excellence. He that resigns himself wholly to sympathy and imitation can possess little of mental strength or accuracy. The system of his life is a species of sensual dereliction. He is like a captive in the garden of Armida; he may revel in the midst of a thousand delights; but he is incapable of the enterprise of a hero, or the severity of a philosopher. He lives forgetting and forgot' (William Godwin, *Enquiry Concerning Political Justice* (1794), ed. and intro. Isaac Kramnick, Harmondsworth, Penguin, 1976, p. 757).

23 See Godwin, *Caleb Williams*, pp. 179–80. The story is repeated in *Maria*, also, in the tales of a young inmate of the asylum, who was driven mad by her jealous husband (p. 88). Society destroys male and female individuality in different ways, taking from men the freedom to move outside; women, who have already had that right taken away from them, lose the ability to move inside – that is, to reason.

24 See J.M.S. Tompkins, *The Popular Novel in England, 1770–1800*, London, Constable, 1932, who notes that this character developed to bridge the growing gap between men and women: 'to induce some measure of approximation in the ethical ideals and emotional sensitiveness of the two sexes' (p. 149).

25 Like *Caleb Williams*, and the gothic in general, Wollstonecraft's work draws heavily on Richardson.

26 *Memoirs*, in Holmes, op. cit., p. 264. Godwin disliked it for its roughness and lack of unity.

27 See, for example, Poovey, op. cit., pp. 71–81, and Todd, op. cit., p. 108.

28 For an antithetical reading of Wollstonecraft's view on maternity as the triumph of subversive female sexuality, rather than its

containment, see Laurie Langbauer, *Women and Romance: The Consolations of Gender in the English Novel*, Ithaca and London, Cornell University Press, 1990, pp. 93–126. Langbauer's argument (largely directed against Poovey) stems from her assumption that 'Writing about the body is particularly attractive to Wollstonecraft' (p. 105), a statement which might be held true if one revised it to read 'writing negatively'.

29 See also Poovey, op. cit., pp. 97–8, and 103–6; and Butler, op. cit., p. 144.

3 The Chymicall Wedding and the Bourgeois Marriage

1 Charles Nicholl, *The Chemical Theatre*, London, Routledge and Kegan Paul, 1980, pp. 38–9.

2 William Godwin, *Caleb Williams* (1794), ed. and intro. David McCracken, Oxford and New York, Oxford University Press, 1970, p. 326.

3 See Tillotama Rajan, 'Wollstonecraft and Godwin: Reading the Secrets of the Political Novel', *Studies in Romanticism*, 1988, vol. 27, pp. 221–51; and Mitzi Myers, 'Godwin's *Memoirs* of Wollstonecraft: The Shaping of Self and Subject', *Studies in Romanticism*, 1981, vol. 20, pp. 299–316 on Godwin's editorial role.

4 Quoted from Richard Holmes (ed. and intro.), *Mary Wollstonecraft and William Godwin: A Short Residence in Sweden and Memoirs of the Author of 'The Rights of Woman'*, Harmondsworth, Penguin, 1987, p. 43.

5 See Holmes, op. cit., pp. 276–7; Holmes (pp. 12–17) turns them into an image for the union of enlightenment and romanticism.

6 Quoted from Myers, op. cit., p. 311.

7 William Godwin, *Travels of St Leon* (1799), London, Henry Colburn and Richard Bentley, 1831, p. x. All further citations, henceforth referenced in the text, will be to this edition.

8 On the bourgeois use of this image, see Jean H. Hagstrum, *Sex and Sensibility: Ideal and Erotic Love from Milton to Mozart*, Chicago, University of Chicago Press, 1980.

9 Burton R. Pollin has noted Godwin's debt to Italian sources in his introduction to Godwin's *Italian Letters or The History of the Count de St Julian*, Lincoln, University of Nebraska Press, 1965, pp. xiii–xiv.

10 Gary Kelly, 'Godwin, Wollstonecraft and Rousseau', *Women and Literature*, 1975, vol. 3, pp. 24–6, argues that Rousseau became more influential on Godwin after his wife's death because of his association of the two.

11 See, for example, Gary Kelly, *The English Jacobin Novel, 1780–1805*, Oxford, Oxford University Press, 1976, p. 216.

12 See Isaac Kramnick, *The Rage of Edmund Burke*, New York, Basic Books, 1977, pp. 126–65, who shows further how Burke associates the bourgeoisie with unrestrained masculine aggression and the aristocracy with female traits and values, an association whose pejorative possibilities Wollstonecraft notes.

13 G.J. Barker-Benfield, 'Mary Wollstonecraft: Eighteenth-Century

Commonwealthwoman', *Journal of the History of Ideas*, 1989, vol. 50, pp. 108–9. In this, the radicals anticipate Freud's argument that civilisation requires discontent: immediate satisfaction of desire inhibits the work that culture needs in order to progress towards deferred gratification.

14 ibid., p. 111.

15 *Short Residence*, in Holmes, op. cit., p. 195.

16 Nicholl, op. cit., p. 1.

17 ibid., p. 3.

18 ibid., p. 4.

19 ibid.

20 See ibid., especially pp. 38–9.

21 ibid., p. 41.

22 Samuel Taylor Coleridge, *Biographia Literaria* (1817), in James Engell and W. Jackson Bate (eds), *Coleridge's Collected Works*, Princeton, Princeton University Press, 1983, vol. 2, p. 17; Coleridge is himself appropriating and secularising John Davies' description of the soul. On the image of the Romantic artist as alchemist, see Jay Macpherson, *The Spirit of Solitude: Conventions and Continuities in Late Romance*, New Haven and London, Yale University Press, 1982, pp. 183–218, who relates the figure also to Faust and Milton's 'Il Penseroso'.

23 Percy Bysshe Shelley, 'Defence of Poetry', in Donald H. Reiman and Sharon B. Powers (eds), *Shelley's Poetry and Prose*, New York and London, W.W Norton, 1977, p. 505.

24 Nicholl, op. cit., pp. 2–3, who notes the deeper similarities between the two modes that science needed to repress in order to create itself. In *Reflections on Gender and Science*, Evelyn Fox Keller sees the battle between modern science and alchemy as crucial to the emergence of modern notions of identity. Alchemy was revived during the years of the Civil War, to be repudiated after the Restoration as (paradoxically in light of *St Leon*'s values) effeminate and soft. She relates the birth of a 'hard' and 'masculine' science to the revolution of sexual relations; the scientific revolution was both cause and effect of: 'the polarization of gender required by industrial capitalism. In sympathy with, and even in response to, the growing division between male and female, public and private, work and home, modern science opted for an even greater polarization of mind and nature, reason and feeling, object and subject' (*Reflections on Gender and Science*, New Haven, Yale University Press, 1985, p. 63). See also Susan R. Bordo, *The Flight to Objectivity: Essays on Cartesianism and Culture*, Albany, State University of New York Press, 1987.

25 See Nicholl, op. cit., pp. 7–14.

26 See also Charles Webster, *From Paracelsus to Newton: Magic and the Making of Modern Science*, London, Cambridge University Press, 1982.

27 On the radicals' appropriation and revision of alchemical ideas, see also Marie Roberts, *Gothic Immortals: The Fiction of the Brotherhood of the Rosy Cross*, London and New York, Routledge, 1990, especially pp. 27–34.

28 In a comic tone, Jane Austen, in *Northanger Abbey*, suggests that the

gothic world is held off by modern means of surveillance that sound rather like an equally gothic spy system. Henry Tilney tells Catherine no gothic goings-on are possible in England, because everything we do here is out in the open; atrocities possible in foreign countries are impossible in England, 'in a country like this, where social and literary intercourse is on such a footing; where every man is surrounded by a neighbourhood of voluntary spies, and where rods and newspapers lay every thing open' (*Northanger Abbey* (1818), Harmondsworth, Penguin, 1972, pp. 199–200). Austen would have been quite conscious of how in small towns neighbourly attention was similar to snooping.

29 *Horrid Mysteries: A Story Translated from the German of the Marquis of Grosse by Peter Will* (1797), London, The Folio Press, 1968, pp. xvi–xviii.

30 In the episode in which his house is burnt he is also Priestley, whose treatment by a barbaric mob recalls that of the alchemist John Dee; see Nicholl, op. cit., p. 43. Roberts notes, too, his basis in Godwin's friend Holcroft (op. cit., 27–31)

31 Nicholl, op. cit., p. 41

PART III

1 From Here to Here: Radcliffe's Plot of Female Development

1 Sir Walter Scott, *Scott's Lives of the Novelists*, London, J.M. Dent, n.d., pp. 214, 224, 244, 213, 219.

2 Quoted from Devendra Prasad Varma, *The Gothic Flame: Being a History of the Gothic Novel in England: its Origins, Efflorescence, Disintegration, and Residuary Influences*, New York, Russell & Russell, 1957, p. 85.

3 See Percy Bysshe Shelley, 'Defence of Poetry', in Donald H. Reiman and Sharon B. Powers (eds), *Shelley's Poetry and Prose*, New York and London, W.W. Norton, 1977, p. 486: 'A Poet is a nightingale, who sits in darkness and sings to cheer its own solitude with sweet sounds; his auditors are as men entranced by the melody of an unseen musician, who feel that they are moved and softened, yet know not whence or why.' Poetry is thus both self-contained and influential. Shelley's image for the poet looks back again to Milton's 'Il Penseroso' – also echoed by the critic above, who recalls Milton's description of the solitary man who listens to the nightingale and himself walks 'unseen' ('Il Penseroso', 65). As we will see, Milton's 'penseroso' vision is important for Radcliffe's idea of art and the artist.

4 David Durant, 'Ann Radcliffe and the Conservative Gothic', *Studies in English Literature, 1500–1900*, 1982, vol. 22, pp. 526, 528.

5 See also Mary Poovey's reading of the role of sentiment in this text in 'Ideology and *The Mysteries of Udolpho*', *Criticism*, 1979, vol. 21, no. 4, pp. 307–30. On St Aubert as version of the Rousseauian teacher, see Alan Richardson, 'From *Emile* to *Frankenstein*: The Education of Monsters', *European Romantic Review*, 1991, vol. 1, no. 2, pp. 147–8.

6 Ann Radcliffe, *The Mysteries of Udolpho* (1794), ed. and intro. Bonamy Dobrée, Oxford and New York, Oxford University Press, 1966, p. 5. All

further citations, henceforth referenced in the text, will be from this edition.

7 See, for example, p. 15, where Emily fancifully speculates that the little lights she sees in the evening are fairies; St Aubert gently disillusions her by explaining the natural phenomenon of glow worms but picks up the game to say 'we shall see fairies, perhaps; they are often companions'. Emily then recites her crudely Shakespearean poem 'The Glow-Worm'; as Radcliffe herself will show further, art is the proper place through which one can contain the natural human need for mysteries and supernatural forces. On the influence of Milton's poem on eighteenth century descriptions of twilight, see Dustin Griffin, *Regaining Paradise: Milton and the Eighteenth Century*, Cambridge, Cambridge University Press, 1986, pp. 72–82; for the broader implications of this genre as a means of suggesting the imagination's power to create suspense and unite opposites, see Patricia A. Parker, *Inescapable Romance: Studies in the Poetics of a Mode*, Princeton, Princeton University Press, 1979, especially pp. 12, 187–91, 197–9, 225, 265–6.

8 See Edmund Burke, *A Philosophical Enquiry into the Origin of our Ideas of the Sublime and Beautiful* (1757), ed. James T. Boulton, Notre Dame and London, University of Notre Dame Press, 1958, p. 111. The difference is one of relation – we love our mothers but fear our fathers. See also Isaac Kramnick, *The Rage of Edmund Burke: Portrait of an Ambivalent Conservative*, New York, Basic Books, 1977, pp. 93–8, who discusses both the class and gender associations of the two categories, as Burke identifies the sublime with the male and the middle class, and the beautiful with the female and the aristocracy. In Radcliffe's *The Italian* (1797), ed. and intro. Frederick Garber, Oxford and New York, Oxford University Press, 1981, pp. 158–9, the hero and heroine rhapsodise over the landscapes that appeal to them and whose union foreshadows their own:

'See,' said Vivaldi, 'where Monte-Corno stands like a ruffian, huge, scared, threatening, and horrid! – and in the south, where the sullen mountain of San Nicolo shoots up, barren and rocky! From thence, mark how other overtopping ridges of the mighty Apennine darken the horizon far along the east, and circle to approach the Velino in the north!'
'Mark too,' said Ellena, 'how sweetly the banks and undulating plains repose at the feet of the mountains; what an image of beauty and elegance they oppose to the awful grandeur that overlooks and guards them! Observe, too, how many a delightful valley, opening from the lake, spreads its rice and corn fields, shaded with groves of the almond, far among the widening hills; how gaily vineyards and olives alternately chequer the acclivities; and how gracefully the lofty palms bend over the higher cliffs.'

9 See Mary Wollstonecraft, *A Vindication of the Rights of Woman* (1792), ed. Carol H. Poston, New York and London, W.W. Norton, 1975, pp. 49, 65, 187. The theme is central to *Udolpho*, in the hatred of Laurentini for the

Marchioness, and repeated in the secondary plot, in the Countess de Villefort's jealousy of her younger and prettier stepdaughter Blanche, which caused her to wall her up (temporarily) in the convent. See also Mme la Motte's fear of Adeline in *The Romance of the Forest*.

10 See Jane Spencer, *The Rise of the Woman Novelist: from Aphra Behn to Jane Austen*, New York, and Oxford, Basil Blackwell, 1986, p. 204. Valancourt first appears as a hunter, a disguise he has donned in order to give his otherwise aimless ramblings through nature a purpose. He pretends to have a cause, to be on a male goal-oriented quest, but is in fact, at first, an undirected wanderer. There is an obviously ironic disjunction here between his true, non-predatory and non-teleological nature, and his disguise as a violator of nature. Yet Valancourt is at a number of times also mistaken for a 'banditti', the robbers Emily fears obsessively and who later turn up also disguised as hunters. Despite Valancourt's almost irritating mildness, any husband is a potential banditti who will take from Emily both her property and herself. A prospective lover is difficult to differentiate from real banditti – or from other men, for that matter, as Emily seems often to confuse the man she loves with others, including her father and Du Pont. Later female gothic plays even more on the fine line between the lover and the predator.

11 See, for example, p. 168, where Emily typically projects Valancourt's image into the mountain landscape before her, and then remembers also her father.

12 See David Durant, 'Aesthetic Heroism in *The Mysteries of Udolpho*', *Eighteenth Century Theory and Interpretation*, 1981, vol. 22, pp. 175–88. Durant nicely notes how the text's identification of aesthetic taste with morality traps the reader: 'The reading experience allows one to discriminate between open-minded, astute, moral readers who appreciate *Udolpho* and narrow, apathetic, insensitive, and wicked readers, whose minds are so embedded in the prosaic world as to hate the novel' (p. 187).

13 See Claire Kahane, 'The Gothic Mirror', in Shirley Nelson Gardener, Claire Kahane, and Madelon Sprengnether (eds), *The (M)other Tongue: Essays in Feminist Psychoanalytic Interpretation*, Ithaca, Cornell University Press, 1985, pp. 334–9; Norman N. Holland and Leona F. Sherman, 'Gothic Possibilities', *New Literary History*, 1976–7, vol. 8, p. 283. On the creation of architectural structures that threaten identity, see also Eugenia C. DeLamotte, *Perils of the Night: A Feminist Study of Nineteenth-Century Gothic*, New York, Oxford University Press, 1990, pp. 14–29.

14 The echoes of *Hamlet* in the scenes with Laurentini suggest Laurentini is Hamlet, emphasising the possibility that this woman is the dispossessed heir, driven not merely melancholy but completely mad. The text thus flirts with, though finally denies, the possibility suggested by Kahane and Judith Wilt, that the gothic reveals the denial of his powerful female source by the male individual. See Judith Wilt, '*Frankenstein* as Mystery Play', in George Levine and U.C. Knoepflmacher (eds), *The Endurance of 'Frankenstein': Essays on Mary Shelley's Novel*, Berkeley, University of California Press, 1979, p. 38. For

Kahane, the oedipal surface of gothic narratives conceals a 'deeper' pre-oedipal plot of conflict with the mother, just as Freud's oedipal narrative of development represses the first relation with the mother (op. cit., pp. 335–7).

15 See Nelson C. Smith, 'Sense, Sensibility, and Ann Radcliffe', *Studies in English Literature 1500–1900*, 1973, vol. 12, pp. 577–90, and Poovey, op. cit., pp. 319–22.

16 See also Gary Kelly, '"A Constant Vicissitude of Interesting Passions": Ann Radcliffe's Perplexed Narratives', *Ariel*, vol. 10, no. 2, 1979, p. 55.

17 On plot's retarding function in general, see Peter Brooks, *Reading for the Plot: Design and Intention in Narrative*, New York, Vintage, 1985, pp. 90–112.

18 See, for example, Kelly, op. cit., p. 57; and Coral Ann Howells, *Love, Mystery, and Misery: Feeling in Gothic Fiction*, London, Athlone Press, 1978, p. 48, who sees a similar incoherence in Emily's character as simply 'a linear series of responses to outlandish situations'.

19 See, for example, the privileging of melancholy over mirth in Emily's poem, 'To Autumn', and, especially, the description which recalls both *Paradise Lost* IV and 'Il Penseroso': 'The sun was now set, and recalling her thoughts from their melancholy subject, she continued her walk; for the pensive shade of twilight was pleasing to her, and the nightingales from the surrounding groves began to answer each other in the long-drawn, plaintive note, which always touched her heart' (pp. 584–5). The change appears in Emily as well, softened and matured through suffering into a 'penseroso' type (see especially p. 502), whose nature is also accentuated through the contrast with the 'allegro' Blanche.

20 J.M.S. Tompkins, *The Work of Mrs Radcliffe and Its Influence on Later Writers*, New York, Arno Press, 1980, p. 16.

21 This family also includes a son, who is, however, passed over as a bit of a fop. One way of preventing oedipal rivalry, which could disturb the harmony of the family, is through a focus on the father–daughter rather than father–son relation. St Aubert had two sons – the making of classic conflict, as in Milton and Schiller, not to mention the Bible – who were, however, conveniently eliminated through death. Other gothic novelists will see however the incestuous potential within the father–daughter relation.

22 Edmund Burke, *Reflections on the Revolution in France* (1790), ed. J.G.A. Pocock, Indianapolis and Cambridge, Hackett, 1987, p. 30. M. Quesnel also contains elements of Burke's earlier enemy in India, Warren Hastings, whom Burke attacked for his violent eradication of native traditions.

23 One alternative to such rivalry is set up through Emily's friendship with Blanche. The two girls are described as so similar that it is obvious they are designed to be friends; but they are also set up as the complements common in romance and fiction (including Richardson, Rousseau, and Scott) of the 'allegro' and 'penseroso', light and dark, types. The possibility of rivalry between them is avoided by this difference and by the handy device of doubling heroes, as Henri

is created as an appropriate mate for Blanche. Of course it would obviously have been neater if Blanche had been used to mop up the unlucky Du Pont, who, unlike another rejected suitor, Louis de la Motte in *The Romance of the Forest*, is left out of the happy ending that doesn't conform completely to conventional closure and ideals of narrative tidiness. As his name reveals, Du Pont serves as a bridge, and therefore gets burned.

24 See Montague Summers, *The Gothic Quest: A History of the Gothic Novel*, New York, Russell & Russell, 1964, p. 12.

25 See Durant, 'Ann Radcliffe', pp. 528, 526. See also Kahane, op. cit., p. 340, who notes the frustrating disjunction between the experience of the novel and its closure.

26 Jane Spencer, op. cit., p. 207; see also Poovey, op. cit., pp. 311, 327, DeLamotte, op. cit., pp. 186–92. Radcliffe's plot establishes the pattern extended by the modern female gothic romance, which says that the system that caused conflict can cure it; see Janice Radway, 'The Utopian Impulse in Popular Culture: Gothic Romances and Feminist Protest', *American Quarterly*, 1981, vol. 33, pp. 140–62.

27 Quoted from Ioan Williams (ed.), *Novel and Romance 1700–1800: A Documentary Record*, London, Routledge, 1970, p. 390.

28 Scott, op. cit., pp. 235–6.

29 ibid. pp. 232, 234. See also Scott's comments on the problems with Walpole's natural explanations, ibid., pp. 88–203.

30 However, while the figure behind the veil is not what we expected, it is symbolically relevant. As an image of the denial of the flesh by the focus on the afterlife, it is an extreme version of the counsel offered to Emily by St Aubert, Montoni, and the Count De Villefort on the stoic repression of earthly feeling, of material interest. It suggests one extreme, the total denial of feeling, by which Emily is tempted when she considered entering the convent, but which she will have to avoid, especially as the place where passion is repressed is also where it erupts in its most extreme form. As Laurentini suggests, Udolpho and the convent are mirror images of each other; unrestrained passion and absolute repression are locked together.

31 See Michael Murrin, *The Veil of Allegory*, Chicago, University of Chicago Press, 1969. Romantic writers revised the metaphor of the veil and revelation for their own revolutionary art; see especially Shelley's 'Defence of Poetry', in Reiman and Powers, op. cit., pp. 487 and 505. In Shelley, however, veiling and unveiling are often indistinguishable; like Radcliffe, Shelley often finds, behind his veils and masks, only further masks.

32 Radcliffe's association of the veil with a female body also recalls and revises the image as it was used by Rousseau. See Part I above, pp. 27–8, especially n. 73. In *La Nouvelle Héloise*, especially, St Preux dreams that the dead figure of Julie's mother turns into that of the dying Julie herself, covered with a 'terrible', 'impenetrable veil' that, as she explains, 'No hand can put . . . aside' (*La Nouvelle Héloise*, trans. and abr. Judith H. McDowell, University Park and London, University of Pennsylvania Press, 1968, p. 365).

Notes

33 On the figure of veil, see Elizabeth P. Broadwell, 'The Veil Image in Anne Radcliffe's *The Italian*', *South Atlantic Bulletin*, 1975, vol. 40, pp. 76–87; Ford H. Swiggart, Jr, 'Ann Radcliffe's Veil Imagery', *Studies in the Humanities*, 1969, vol. 1, p. 55; Eve Kosofsky Sedgewick, *The Coherence of Gothic Conventions*, New York, Methuen, 1986, pp. 140–75. On the Miltonic ancestry of this eighteenth-century image, see Dustin Griffin, op. cit., pp. 72–82.

34 See Samuel Johnson, *Lives of the English Poets* (1779), 2 vols, London, Oxford University Press, 1977 rpt, vol. 1, p. 123: 'He saw Nature, as Dryden expresses it, *through the spectacles of books*.' Milton was generally set up as the type for the learned, artificial 'penseroso' author, contrasted with Shakespeare as the 'allegro' unschooled child of nature, and artless genius.

35 Like Radcliffe's other heroines, Emily imagines banditti everywhere, even putting them into her landscape sketches and poems. Their role is partially an artistic convention, as Radcliffe derived them – like her landscapes themselves – from paintings such as those of Salvator Rosa. In terms of spatial metaphors, the banditti who have possessed the subterranean passages of the Chateau le Blanc are, along with the servants, the subconscious of the text. They epitomise the forces that threaten the heroine: unlicensed male power, identified with the savage and hostile nature of the unrestrained sublime and with avarice. Associated with nature, they are thus Radcliffe's version of Natural Man, which owes more to Hobbes than to Rousseau. Moreover, their use of superstition to cloak self-interest allies them both to radical critiques of monarchy and conservative attacks on secret societies.

36 Memory is in this respect set up as analogous to music, which also bridges the division between absence and presence. In *Udolpho*, the various places are again linked by being haunted by mysterious music associated with the return of the dead. Music's necromantic function turns out to be an illusion, however, when the discrepancy between sound and source is finally revealed: the musicians are not angels, but Du Pont and the devilish Laurentini.

37 Radcliffe herself has often been accused of such temporal confusion, especially in her anachronistic settings; see Elizabeth Napier, *The Failure of Gothic: Problems of Disjunction in an Eighteenth-Century Literary Form*, Oxford, Clarendon Press, 1987, p. 21. On memory in the text, see Terry Castle, 'The Spectralization of the Other in *The Mysteries of Udolpho*', in Felicity Nussbaum and Laura Brown (eds), *The New Eighteenth Century: Theory, Politics, English Literature*, New York, Methuen, 1987, pp. 231–53.

38 One could thus read Emily's experience in terms of Peter Brook's Freudian reading of the plot: Brooks argues that narrative repetition is a way of mastering 'uncanny' forces beyond one's control, such as death and loss, and submitting them to our will (see op. cit., pp. 97–100).

39 It is significant that Montoni also goes to jail, where he dies. His fate thus includes an unredeemed version of Valancourt as well as replaying that of the Marchioness, as it appears he was poisoned.

40 See Kahane, op. cit., pp. 35–7, who takes her cue from feminist readings of Freud, which probe beyond Freud's focus on the child's relation to the father in the oedipal stage, and look back to the first relation with the mother as being formative of identity.

41 From the beginning, St Aubert, as opposed to the developer M. Quesnel, has been associated with trees, an image which links him with Burke, for whom the tree is a central image of organic continuity. St Aubert remembers his childhood at his ancestral home as a time of innocent harmony with nature, spent in the chestnut tree the insensitive M. Quesnel is about to cut down:

> How often, in my youth, have I climbed among its broad branches, and sat embowered amidst a world of leaves, while the heavy shower has pattered above, and not a rain drop reached me! How often I have sat with a book in my hand, sometimes reading, and sometimes looking out between the branches upon the wide landscape, and the setting sun, till twilight came, and brought the birds home to their little nests among the leaves!
>
> (p. 13)

The past was a time of perfect reconciliation between the human and natural, and moreover, nature and culture, as the image of the boy reading in the tree suggests. Reading is not a sign of human self-consciousness that alienates it from nature but what connects the human to the natural, as Radcliffe's own text indirectly does by aligning virtue and taste, and so suggesting the Burkean message that human nature is art. At the end, the image of the tree marks further the union of the natural and the divine supernatural, even as the demonic supernatural, through Radcliffe's explanations, has been exorcised.

42 See also Kate Ferguson Ellis, *The Contested Castle: Gothic Novels and the Subversion of Domestic Ideology*, Urbana and Chicago, University of Illinois Press, 1989, pp. 39–41, for interesting suggestions on Milton's association in the gothic with the setting of limits, an association that allies him with Burke rather than Rousseau.

43 *Comus*, 1012–16.

44 It is quoted on pp. 70, 272, 357, 389; Sabrina's song is imitated in Emily's 'To a Sea-Nymph', p. 420; the Lady lost in the woods is recalled on pp. 64–5 and 409. While descriptions of La Vallée draw on Milton's Paradise, other allusions come almost entirely from his early works: 'Il Penseroso' is quoted on pp. 352 and 629, and imitated in Emily's last poems, 'To Autumn' (p. 592) and 'To Melancholy' (pp. 665–6); 'Lycidas' is quoted on p. 475. Radcliffe's use of Milton, like her use of Rousseau, is eccentrically selective; the younger and muted Milton, rather than the powerful father of *Paradise Lost*, seems to be invoked as the Guardian Spirit for Radcliffe's enterprise.

45 Pamela Clemit, *The Godwinian Novel: The Rational Fictions of Godwin, Brockden Brown, Mary Shelley*, Oxford, Clarendon Press, 1993, pp. 17–34, which discusses Godwin's early romance *Imogen* as a revision of *Comus*.

46 Robert Miles, *Gothic Writing 1750–1820: A Genealogy*, London and New York, Routledge, 1993, p. 93. Sheridan LeFanu's *Uncle Silas* draws especially and ironically on *The Tempest* as subtext.
47 See also Kelly, op. cit., pp. 60–1, who discusses Radcliffe's authorial voice as the ideal upheld by the text.

2 Lewis's Gothic Revolution

1 Quoted from Lewis F. Peck, *A Life of Matthew G. Lewis*, Cambridge, Mass., Harvard University Press, 1961, pp. 208–9.
2 Matthew Lewis, *The Monk* (1796), ed. and intro. Howard Anderson, Oxford and New York, Oxford University Press, 1973, p. 53. All further citations, henceforth referenced in the text, will be from this edition.
3 Frederick Schiller, *Ghost-Seer*, in *The Works of Frederick Schiller: Early Dramas and Romances*, trans. Henry G. Bohn, London, Henry G. Bohn, 1853, p. 429. Lewis gives a comic version of this theme in the figure of Jacintha.
4 The gothic is based in a theatrical tradition, especially that of Shakespearean and Jacobean drama; see Coral Ann Howells, *Love, Mystery, and Misery: Feeling in Gothic Fiction*, London, Athlone Press, 1978, pp. 16–24, 62–79. But, as always, it is suspicious of its own ancestry; as Lewis suggests, it also inherits the seventeenth-century Puritan tradition of denouncing the theatre as fraud (discussed by Jonas Barish in *The Antitheatrical Prejudice*, Berkeley, University of California Press, 1981), which it combines with the attack on theatre made by Rousseau in his *Lettre à D'Alembert*.
5 Lewis's relation with his own mother was an intense and complex one; he wrote *The Monk* in part to support her after her divorce from his father; on his early death, in a nicely gothic short-circuiting of genealogical succession, the parent was heir to the child.
6 In this, however, Elvira is true to Locke, who advocates censoring the Bible as inappropriate for the young; see John Locke, *Some Thoughts Concerning Education* (1693), ed. and intro. John W. and Jean S. Yolton, Oxford, Clarendon Press, 1989, p. 213.
7 On voyeurism in the text and its relation to the theme of unveiling, see also Elizabeth Napier, *The Failure of Gothic: Problems of Disjunction in an Eighteenth-Century Literary Form*, Oxford, Clarendon Press, 1987, pp. 115–19. William Patrick Day, *In the Circles of Fear and Desire: A Study of Gothic Fantasy*, Chicago, University of Chicago Press, 1985, pp. 63–9, and Robert Miles, *Gothic Writing 1750–1820: A Genealogy*, London and New York, Routledge, 1993, pp. 57–64, discuss voyeurism and reading in the gothic in general.
8 On this traditional reading of the senses, see Walter Ong, *The Presence of the Word: Some Prolegomena for Cultural and Religious History*, Minneapolis, University of Minnesota Press, 1967, pp. 117–18. This opposition between sight and sound plays an important part in *Frankenstein*, where the monster's hideous appearance is contrasted with his

eloquence, which he believes is the truer representation of his inner nature. If his voice is his true identity, however, it has been greatly influenced by art, especially Milton's.

9 Matilda's staged suicide attempt causes her robe to fall open, sending Ambrosio into raptures:

> She had torn open her habit, and her bosom was half exposed. The weapon's point rested upon her left breast: And Oh! that was such a breast! The Moon-beams darting full upon it, enabled the Monk to observe its dazzling whiteness. His eye dwelt with insatiable avidity upon the beauteous Orb. A sensation till then unknown filled his heart with a mixture of anxiety and delight: A raging fire shot through every limb; The blood boiled in his veins, and a thousand wild wishes bewildered his imagination.
>
> (p. 65)

Just before the desire that is raised here is consummated, the breast appears once more, as the part signalling that the whole it signifies is soon to be attained: 'He sat upon her Bed; His hand rested upon her bosom; Her head reclined voluptuously upon his breast. Who then can wonder, if He yielded to the temptation?' (p. 90). The climax is an authorial striptease, as the curtain falls at the moment of consummation and stays down for a hundred pages of subplot in which the story goes backwards, thus identifying the satisfaction of desire and regression. Concealment here demonstrates less authorial restraint, motivated by discretion and good taste, than Lewis's proof that he can employ the Radcliffean principle that what is not seen completely is most stimulating to the imagination for erotic titillation.

10 Matilda's strategy anticipates that of the (aptly named for this context) modern Madonna, who claims to gain power by taking control of her own sexual displaying.

11 An obvious literary model here is *Paradise Lost*, in which Milton faces the problem of telling a story whose inevitable conclusion everyone knows. By separating the fall into two stages, drawing out of verses of Genesis, he introduces the possibility of discontinuity; at the same time as we know everything that will happen, we are tempted to imagine 'What if? . . .' something else had occurred. An impression of free will is created in a narrative of strict determination. For Milton, however, it is more than merely an impression, as it is vital to his project of justifying God's ways to man to show that Adam and Eve acted freely; for Lewis, however, the illusion of freedom is merely another of art's frauds.

12 In a literal way, too, these subplots took on lives of their own, as they were later published separately – see Montague Summers, *The Gothic Quest: A History of the Gothic Novel*, New York, Russell & Russell, 1964, p. 211.

13 See, for example, pp. 252–4, where thoughts of Ambrosio are mingled with those of Lorenzo. Lewis thus recalls Radcliffe's idea that, for the young girl, hero and villain are difficult to distinguish, while suggesting further the proximity between familial and sexual desire, both of which converge in Ambrosio.

14 See also Robin Lyndenberg, 'Ghostly Rhetoric: Ambivalence in M.G. Lewis's *The Monk*', *Ariel: A Review of English Literature*, 1979, vol. 10, pp. 65–79.
15 See Ronald Paulson, *Representations of Revolution (1789–1820)*, New Haven and London, Yale University Press, 1983, pp. 221–3.
16 See also Kate Ferguson Ellis, *The Contested Castle: Gothic Novels and the Subversion of Domestic Ideology*, Urbana and Chicago, University of Illinois Press, 1989, p. 143.
17 See Daniel P. Watkins, 'Social Hierarchy in Matthew Lewis's *The Monk*', *Studies in the Novel*, 1986, vol. 18, pp. 115–24, especially pp. 116, 121.
18 ibid., p. 122.
19 See André Parreaux, *The Publication of 'The Monk': A Literary Event*, Paris, Michel Didier, 1960.
20 'Reflections on the Novel', in The Marquis de Sade, *The 120 Days of Sodom and Other Writings*, trans. Austryn Wainhouse and Richard Seaver, New York, Grove, 1966, p. 109.
21 Quoted from Summers, op. cit., p. 213.
22 Quoted from Peck, op. cit., p. 24.
23 Quoted from ibid., p. 25.
24 Quoted from ibid., p. 25. Lewis was parodied in the 1798 *The New Monk* in which the book that the heroine's mother censors was *The Monk* itself; see Summers, op. cit., p. 246.
25 Quoted from Peck, op. cit., p. 25.
26 Quoted from Summers, p. 214.
27 Lyndenberg, op. cit., p. 67.
28 ibid., p. 66.
29 David Punter, 'Social Relations of Gothic Fiction', in David Punter, David Aers, and Jonathan Cook (eds), *Romanticism and Ideology: Studies in English Writing 1765–1830*, London, Routledge, 1981, pp. 113–14; see also Napier, op. cit., pp. 120–6.
30 Lyndenberg, op. cit., p. 68.
31 ibid., p. 65.
32 Quoted from ibid., p. 66. On the relation between writing and desire, see also Wendy Jones, 'Stories of Desire in *The Monk*', *English Literary History*, 1990, vol. 57, pp. 129–50.
33 ibid., p. 67.
34 See Summers, op. cit., p. 215.
35 Quoted from Lyndenberg, op. cit., p. 77.
36 Quoted from Merritt Y. Hughes (ed.), *John Milton: Complete Poems and Major Prose*, Indianapolis, Odyssey Press, 1957, p. 727.
37 ibid., p. 75.
38 ibid., p. 75.
39 On Lewis's view of the creator as destroyer, see also Keily, op. cit., pp. 102–3.

3 'A way thus dark and circuitous': The Revolution Comes Full Circle

1 Ann Radcliffe, *The Italian or the Confessional of the Black Penitents: A Romance* (1797), ed. and intro. Frederick Garber, Oxford and New York, Oxford University Press, 1981, p. 346. All further citations, henceforth referenced in the text, will be from this edition.
2 Quoted from Eino Railo, *The Haunted Castle: A Study of the Elements of English Romanticism*, London, Routledge, 1927, p. 97.
3 For another discussion of the relation between the three texts, see David Punter, *The Literature of Terror: A History of Gothic Fictions from 1765 to the Present Day*, London, Longman, 1980, pp. 70–97.
4 See also Syndy M. Conger, 'Sensibility Restored: Radcliffe's Answer to Lewis's *The Monk*', in Kenneth W. Graham (ed.), *Gothic Fictions: Prohibition/Transgression*, New York, AMS Press, 1989, pp. 113–49, for a reading of the relation between the two texts, which discusses also Radcliffe's adherence to the then fashionable belief that faces express character (pp. 133–5).
5 Peter Brooks argues that narrative repetition reassures us that the story will not 'short-circuit', reach a disastrous, as premature, ending; see *Reading for the Plot: Design and Intention in Narrative*, New York, Vintage, 1985, pp. 103–4. In Lewis, however, *all* closure is too soon. In her revision, Radcliffe thus reasserts the difference between proper (her own) and improper (Lewis's) models for narrative development and arrival at a conclusion.
6 Dante's story itself is circular, as the end of poem is the beginning of writing. It suggests the Christian view of time which combines a linear and teleological model for narrative with a circular and repetitive one, turning history into a progressive circle. Radcliffe's narratives rework this biblical model.
7 Compare p. 198 cited above, with the epigram to *Caleb Williams* which sets out 'Things as They Are':

> Amidst the woods the leopard knows his kind;
> The tyger preys not on the tyger brood:
> Man only is the common foe of man.

8 Janet Todd, 'Posture and Imposture: The Gothic Manservant in Ann Radcliffe's *The Italian*', in Janet Todd (ed.), *Women and Literature* vol. 2, Rutgers, Rutgers University Press, 1982, pp. 25–38.
9 See especially *Udolpho's* Annette, whose constant terror is that she will either be silenced or starved.
10 See also, for example, the dialogues between De la Motte and Peter in *The Romance of the Forest*.
11 On the use of Shakespeare and Milton as authorities at the endings of Radcliffe's texts, see also Coral Ann Howells, 'The Pleasure of the Woman's Text: Ann Radcliffe's Subtle Transgressions in *The Mysteries of Udolpho* and *The Italian*', in Graham (ed.), op. cit., pp. 158–61.
12 Ibid., pp. 160–1.
13 See Northrop Frye, *The Great Code: The Bible and Literature*, New York and London, Harcourt Brace Jovanovich, 1982, pp. 78–88.

14 Sir Walter Scott, *Scott's Lives of the Novelists*, London, J.M. Dent, nd, p. 223.
15 ibid.

PART IV

1 J.M.S. Tompkins (1932), *The Popular Novel in England, 1770–1800*, Lincoln, Nebraska, University of Nebraska Press, 1963 rpt, p. 243.
2 Edith Birkhead, *The Tale of Terror: A Study of The Gothic Romance*, London, Constable, 1921, p. 157.
3 *Gentleman's Magazine*, September 1798, reprinted in Ioan Williams (ed.), *Novel and Romance 1700–1800: A Documentary Record*, London, Routledge, 1970, p. 448.
4 Recently there has been a large number of important discussions of *Frankenstein* as a reworking of Shelley's personal and literary relations to her family; see especially Ronald Paulson, *Representations of Revolution (1789–1820)*, New Haven and London, Yale University Press, 1983, pp. 242–3, and the following essays in George Levine and U.C. Knoepflmacher (eds), *The Endurance of 'Frankenstein': Essays on Mary Shelley's Novel*, Berkeley, University of California Press, 1979: Lee Sterrenburg, 'Mary Shelley's Monster: Politics and Psyche in *Frankenstein*', pp. 143–71; U.C. Knoepflmacher, 'Thoughts on the Aggression of Daughters', pp. 88–122; Peter Dale Scott, 'Vital Artifice: Mary, Percy, and the Psychopolitical Integrity of *Frankenstein*', pp. 172–204; see also William Veeder, *Mary Shelley and 'Frankenstein': The Fate of Androgyny*, Chicago and London, University of Chicago Press, 1986, and Anne K. Mellor, *Mary Shelley: Her Life, Her Fiction, Her Monsters*, New York and London, Routledge, 1989. On her relationship with her husband, see also P.D. Fleck, 'Mary Shelley's Notes to Shelley's Poems and *Frankenstein*', *Studies in Romanticism*, 1967, vol. 6, pp. 226–54; Christopher Small, *Ariel Like a Harpy: Shelley, Mary and 'Frankenstein'*, London, Gollancz, 1972, pp. 100–21, and Margaret Homans, *Bearing the Word: Language and Female Experience in Nineteenth-Century Women's Writing*, Chicago and London, University of Chicago Press, 1986, pp. 103–19. Homans also discusses Shelley's relations with her mother and daughter; see also Ellen Moers, *Literary Women: The Great Writers*, New York, Oxford University Press, 1985, pp. 90–9.
5 Cited in Knoepflmacher, op. cit., p. 94. A later, unpublished novel, *Mathilda*, took revenge on Godwin for his coldness, by depicting a father's incestuous passion for the daughter who uncannily resembles the mother who died giving her life.
6 This is especially true of film adaptations since the 1935 *Bride of Frankenstein* (which doubles Mary Shelley and the bride). In recent years, the representation of the creation of the text has taken on a life of its own, as the subject of such films as Ken Russell's outrageous *Gothic*, and the terrifyingly dreadful *Rowing with the Wind*.
7 Mary Shelley, *Frankenstein, or, The Modern Prometheus* (1818), Oxford and New York, Oxford University Press, 1980, p. 5. All further citations, henceforth referenced in the text, will be from this edition.

Notes

8 William Godwin, *Travels of St Leon* (1799), London, Henry Colburn and Richard Bentley, 1831, p. vi. See also Percy Shelley's review of *Frankenstein*, in which he claimed that readers were bound to wonder 'what could have been the series of thoughts . . . which conduced, in the author's mind, to the astonishing combinations of motives and incidents, and the startling catastrophe, which compose the tale'; in *The Complete Works of Percy Bysshe Shelley*, ed. Roger Ingpen and Walter E. Peck, New York, Gordian, 1965, vol. 6, p. 263.

9 See especially Mary Poovey, *The Proper Lady and the Woman Writer: Ideology as Style in the Works of Mary Wollstonecraft, Mary Shelley, and Jane Austen*, Chicago, University of Chicago Press, 1984, pp. 114–71; Mellor, op. cit., pp. 52–69.

10 Cervantes, *The Adventures of Don Quixote* (1614). trans. J.M. Cohen, Harmondsworth, Penguin, 1950, p. 687. Shelley read *Don Quixote* in 1816; see *Mary Shelley's Journal*, ed. Frederick L. Jones, Norman, Okla., University of Oklahoma Press, 1947, p. 73. Cervantes's text is probably the most famous example of a self-parodying form that satirically treats romance conventions; like the gothic, it shows the dangers of confusing art and life, although suggesting that the lack of confusion has its own perils.

11 Percy Bysshe Shelley, 'A Defence of Poetry', in Donald H. Reiman and Sharon B. Powers, *Shelley's Poetry and Prose*, New York and London, W.W. Norton, 1977, p. 505.

12 ibid., p. 480; see also pp. 503, 506.

13 See Ellen Moers, op. cit., pp. 90–9, who notes further the negative aspects of this model for creation.

14 See J.E. Svilpis, 'The Mad Scientist and Domestic Affections in Gothic Fiction', in Kenneth W. Graham (ed.), *Gothic Fictions: Prohibition/ Transgression*, New York, AMS Press, 1989, pp. 63–87. On the text as a feminist critique of science, see Mellor, op. cit., pp. 89–114.

15 On Shelley's use of Bacon, see Svilpis, op. cit., pp. 65–6, and Patrick J. Callahan, '*Frankenstein*, Bacon, and the "Two Truths"', *Extrapolation*, 1972, vol. 14, pp. 39–48.

16 See Isaac Kramnick, 'Religion and Radicalism: English Political Theory in the Age of Revolution', *Political Theory: An International Journal of Political Philosophy*, 1977, vol. 5, pp. 505–34.

17 William Godwin, *Fleetwood or the New Man of Feeling* (1805), 3 vols, New York, Garland Publishing, 1979 rpt, vol. 1, p. 277.

18 See *Mary Shelley's Journal*, p. 72. After her marriage, Shelley began a rigorous program of reading, which included a rereading of her parent's political tracts and novels, as well as parodies of them (*St Godwin*), and also the works of Locke, Richardson, Rousseau, Goethe (*Clarissa, Confessions, Emile, La Nouvelle Héloise, Reveries, Werther*), and Milton (*On Education, Paradise Lost* and *Regained*, 'Lycidas', *Areopagitica*), and gothic works, including those of Beckford, Charles Brockden Brown, Lewis and Radcliffe; like the monster, she also read Plutarch's *Lives*; see *Journal*, pp. 32–3, 47–9, 71–3, 88–90.

19 Jean-Jacques Rousseau, *Reveries of the Solitary Walker* (1782), trans. and intro. Peter France, Harmondsworth, Penguin, 1979, p. 114. For Shelley's

relation to Rousseau, see Alan Richardson, 'From *Emile* to *Franken-stein*: The Education of Monsters', *European Romantic Review*, 1991, vol. 1, no. 2, pp. 147–62; James O'Rourke, '"Nothing More Unnatural": Mary Shelley's Revision of Rousseau', *English Literary History*, 1989, vol. 56, no. 3, pp. 543–69; and David Marshall, *The Surprising Effects of Sympathy: Marivaux, Diderot, Rousseau, and Mary Shelley*, Chicago and London, University of Chicago Press, 1988. Marshall notes how Shelley would have associated Rousseau with her parents, especially her mother. O'Rourke notes, too, however, that Shelley also associated him with irresponsible parenting, repeatedly attacking him for his abandonment of his children, an abandonment echoed by Victor's negligence.

20 William Godwin, *Caleb Williams* (1794), ed. and intro. David McCracken, Oxford and New York, Oxford University Press, 1970, p. 4.

21 See John Locke, *Some Thoughts Concerning Education* (1693), ed. and intro. John W. and Jean S. Yolton, Oxford, Clarendon, 1989, p. 15.

22 Leonda Schiebinger, 'Feminine Icons: The Face of Early Modern Science', *Critical Inquiry*, 1988, vol. 14, no. 4, p. 688.

23 See William Godwin, *Enquiry Concerning Political Justice* (1794), ed. and intro. Isaac Kramnick, Harmondsworth, Penguin, 1976, especially pp. 776–7.

24 See A.D. Harvey, '*Frankenstein* and *Caleb Williams*', *Keats–Shelley Journal*, 1980, vol. 29, p. 22, and Marie Roberts, *Gothic Immortals: The Fiction of the Brotherhood of the Rosy Cross*, London and New York, Routledge, 1990, pp. 95–110.

25 See 'A Defence of Poetry', in Reiman and Powers, op. cit., especially pp. 480, 502–3.

26 Victor later quotes Coleridge's 'Ancient Mariner' in reference to his own situation (p. 59), thus reinforcing the identification between himself and Walton. The analogy between poetry and a sea voyage is an old one; see Ernst Robert Curtius, *European Literature and the Latin Middle Ages*, trans. Willard Trask, Princeton, Princeton University Press, 1963, pp. 128–30.

27 See Oscar Wilde, *The Picture of Dorian Gray* (1891), ed. and intro. Isobel Murray, Oxford and New York, Oxford University Press, 1981, pp. 55–6. In the nineteenth century the aesthetic relation to life was parodied as a predatory one; a famous caricature represented Flaubert in the act of pinning Mme Bovary on a fork. See C.J. Rawson, 'Cannibalism and Fiction: Reflections on Narrative Form and "Extreme Situations"', part 1, *Genre*, 1977, vol. 10, pp. 667–711.

28 See also Paul de Man's critique of the romantic symbol as a uniter of subject and object which in reality reinforces the abyss between them; 'The Rhetoric of Temporality, ' in Charles S. Singleton (ed.), *Interpretation: Theory and Practice*, Baltimore, Johns Hopkins University Press, 1969, pp. 173–209.

29 As Laura Killian pointed out to me, the monster can thus also be seen as a critique of Rousseau's idea of Natural Man, which shows that the ideal is itself a human, and monstrous, construct. Shelley thus continues the critique of Rousseau begun by her mother, in which the exposer of ideology is revealed to be the fabricator of another pernicious fiction about our essential natures. It is important that the

monster himself does not identify with nature, which he finds frighteningly cold and hostile. Part of his monstrosity is his resistance to the categorical differences Victor imposes; he is alienated from both the human and natural orders.

30 See O'Rourke, op. cit.

31 See also Kate Ferguson Ellis, 'Monsters in the Garden: Mary Shelley and the Bourgeois Family', in Levine and Knoepflmacher (eds), op. cit., pp. 136–8.

32 See, for example, John A. Dussinger, 'Kinship and Guilt in Mary Shelley's *Frankenstein*', *Studies in the Novel*, 1976, vol. 8, pp. 42–5, 50–2; Laura P. Claridge, 'Parent–Child Tensions in *Frankenstein*: The Search for Communion', *Studies in the Novel*, 1985, vol. 17, pp. 17–18. The suspicion is especially tempting for Freudian readers trained to unearth repressed oedipal anxiety and see the father as the real monster of the story.

33 See also Eugenia C. DeLamotte's reading of the ambivalence of all enclosures for women especially, in *Perils of the Night: A Feminist Study of Nineteenth-Century Gothic*, New York, Oxford University Press, 1990, pp. 153–65. Homes and prisons, madhouses, convents, are difficult to differentiate, as any refuge can turn out to be a trap.

34 See also Ann Mellor's reading of the text as indicative of Shelley's ambivalent idealisation of the bourgeois family she never was a part of; op. cit., pp. 44, 189.

35 Claridge, op. cit., p. 14.

36 See also ibid., pp. 15–18.

37 On this imagery, and its relation to the romantic representation of extremes that meet, see Andrew Griffin, 'Fire and Ice in *Frankenstein*', in George Levine and U.C. Knoepflmacher (eds), op. cit., pp. 49–76.

38 Recent feminist readings have analysed the blazon as a form through which the male subject constructs himself as a unified whole against the fragmented female. He puts himself together by taking a girl apart, attaining integrity by denying it to the female, who becomes instead his polar and incoherent 'other'; simultaneously, he overcomes the power of desire to act as a fragmenting form, that could reduce the poet to pieces; see Nancy Vickers, 'Diana Described: Scattered Woman and Scattered Rhyme', *Critical Inquiry*, 1981, vol. 8, pp. 265–79; Patricia A. Parker, *Literary Fat Ladies: Rhetoric, Gender, Property*, London and New York, Methuen, 1987, pp. 126–54.

39 See especially Sandra Gilbert and Susan Gubar, *The Madwoman in the Attic: The Woman Writer and the Nineteenth-Century Imagination*, New Haven, Yale University Press, 1979, pp. 21–47; Homans, op. cit., pp. 100–19; Christine Froula, 'When Eve Reads Milton: Undoing the Canonical Economy', *Critical Inquiry*, 1983, vol. 10, pp. 321–47; Mellor, op. cit., pp. 118–21.

40 The dream recalls and inverts the generational confusion in that of Rousseau's St Preux, in which the dead Julie's mother turns into her daughter, covered by a terrible veil; see above, Part III, section 1, n. 32.

41 See also Paulson, op. cit., p. 247. On Shelley's drawing on the traditional association of the monstrous with a terrible mixing of unlike

Notes

things, see Chris Baldick, *In Frankenstein's Shadow: Myth, Monstrosity and Nineteenth-Century Writing*, Oxford, Clarendon Press, 1987, pp. 13–16, 34–6. As Baldick and Sterrenberg both note, such an association underlay Burke's representation of the Revolution as a chaotic confusion of differences.

42 See Judith Wilt, '*Frankenstein* as Mystery Play', in George Levine and U.C. Knoepflmacher (eds), op. cit., p. 38. On the murder of the maternal principle in the text, see also, Homans, op. cit.

43 See for example, Mellor, op. cit., pp. 115–26.

44 It seems significant that the monster is able also to quote Percy Shelley, whose poem 'Mutability' here and elsewhere provides another literary subtext.

45 See also Gilbert and Gubar's important argument that the monster plays the part of Milton's Eve, and the author herself, as Shelley shows that to be female in the male literary tradition is to be a monstrous outcast; op. cit., pp. 230–4.

46 Rousseau, op. cit., p. 27.

47 ibid.

48 See also Paul Cantor, *Creature and Creator*, New York, Cambridge University Press, 1984, especially p. 131.

49 See Poovey, op. cit., pp. 133–7.

50 See pp. 90, 190, 223, 218, and 160 especially, where he is 'a blasted tree; the bolt has entered my soul'. The word is itself further over-determined by intertextual resonances. It echoes Maria's lament that marriage has 'blasted' her; Mary Wollstonecraft, *Maria, or The Wrongs of Woman*, in *Mary and The Wrongs of Woman* (1798), ed. and intro. Gary Kelly, Oxford, Oxford University Press, 1976, p. 138; as well as Caleb's self-representation, *Caleb Williams*, p. 10; and St Leon's lament, *St Leon*, p. 466. See also Byron's representation of Rousseau, in *Childe Harolde* III, 78–80 (quoted from Pamela Clemit, *The Godwinian Novel: The Rational Fictions of Godwin, Brockden Brown, Mary Shelley*, Oxford, Clarendon Press, 1993, pp. 156–7):

His love was passion's essence: – as a tree
On fire by lightening, with the ethereal flame
Kindled he was, and blasted.

In film versions, the interest in the seminal lightning bolt is continued but displaced to the actual act of creation, which always gets a lot of cinematic attention.

51 Films, however, usually feel they have to give it to us, seduced by Victor's obsessive rhetoric.

52 See Percy Bysshe Shelley, *Complete Works*, vol. 6, pp. 263–5. Percy's role in the creation of the text has been subject to some speculation; see especially Mellor, op. cit., pp. 58–69, 219–24. Not only did he also write the preface, but he wrote an early review. Like Victor, with whom he clearly sympathised, he seemed intent on controlling the interpretation of the story. The moral he offers is a Godwinian one, concerning the working of Necessity, and production of evils that 'flow irresistibly from certain causes fully adequate to their production'.

257

Like St Leon, too, the text suggests society's scapegoating of great men: 'often in society, those who are best qualified to be its benefactors and its ornaments are branded by some accident with scorn, and changed, by neglect and solitude of heart, into a scourge and curse.'

53 See also Devon Hodges, '*Frankenstein* and the Feminine Subversion of the Novel', *Tulsa Studies in Women's Literature*, 1983, vol. 2, pp. 155–64.
54 Ellis, op. cit., p. 124.
55 See, for example, Hodges, op. cit. On Shelley's own idealisation of a relational identity, see Mellor, op. cit., pp. 178–9.
56 See, for example, Claridge, op. cit., p. 24, who sees Walton as 'a successful, if subdued, modern Prometheus', as he assumes the 'responsibilities of the mature adult' and returns to 'the goal of communion with others'.
57 See Mellor, op. cit., p. 54.
58 James P. Carson, 'Bringing the Author Forward: *Frankenstein* through Mary Shelley's Letters', *Criticism*, 1988, vol. 33, especially pp. 434–7.
59 See also Mellor, op. cit., p. 205, who notes, however, that throughout her works Shelley has a tendency to kill off women who embody her own ideal.
60 See Sterrenberg, op. cit., and Clemit, op. cit., p. 162.
61 Ellen Moers reads the text as a nightmare version of what it means to be a mother. Specifically, she connects it to Shelley's dream in which she had imagined 'that my little baby came to life again, that it had only been cold, and that we rubbed it before the fire, and it lived' (quoted from Moers, op. cit., p. 96). Where Wollstonecraft created a romance fantasy of a mother bringing her child back from the dead, for Shelley that narrative becomes a horror story. See also Homans, op. cit., pp. 111–14, and Baldick, pp. 30–3, who reads Victor as a version of the author's fear about her own role as author and parent.
62 See also Hodges, op. cit., p. 162.
63 On Shelley's later works, which are obsessively and fantastically autobiographical, see also Mellor, op. cit., pp. 141–69, and Poovey, op. cit., pp. 143–71.
64 Quoted from Robert Keily, *The Romantic Novel in England*, Cambridge, Harvard University Press, 1972, p. 172.
65 See Mellor, op. cit., pp. 170–6; Clemit, op. cit., pp. 148–54. While Mellor thus disagrees with Poovey, the two arguments needn't be mutually exclusive, but again might suggest the identification between Mary and Victor, who both revise an original version of their stories from a situation of alienation.
66 Birkhead, op. cit., p. 223.
67 Montague Summers, *The Gothic Quest: A History of the Gothic Novel*, New York, Russell & Russell, 1964, p. 397. In this he is obviously Radcliffe's heir, who claims that aesthetic taste reveals individual worth.
68 ibid., p. 198.
69 ibid., p. 398.
70 ibid., p. 398. See in general his last chapter, pp. 382–411.
71 ibid., p. 409.

72 ibid., pp. 408, 387.
73 Quoted from Victor Sage (ed.), *The Gothick Novel*, London, Macmillan, 1990, p. 112.
74 Sigmund Freud, 'The Uncanny', in *On Creativity and the Unconscious*, New York, Harper & Row, 1958, pp. 122–61. I have preferred, however, to use the original theory of defamiliarisation associated with Romantic art, and outlined in the *Lyrical Ballads*.
75 See especially William Patrick Day's reading of Freud, in *The Circles of Fear and Desire: A Study of Gothic Fantasy*, Chicago, University of Chicago Press, 1985, pp. 177–90.
76 Ian Watt, 'Time and Family in the Gothic Novel: *The Castle of Otranto*', *Eighteenth Century Life*, 1986, vol. 10, no. 3, p. 167.
77 See especially David Punter's work, *The Literature of Terror: A History of Gothic Fictions from 1765 to the Present Day*, London, Longman, 1980, and 'Social Relations of Gothic Fiction', in David Punter, David Aers, and Jonathan Cook (eds), *Romanticism and Ideology: Studies in English Writing 1765–1830*, London, Routledge, 1981, pp. 103–17. While gothic criticism in general has recently evolved from a psychoanalytic to a Marxist or feminist approach, Punter's work has developed in reverse.
78 For example, Day, op. cit., claims: 'The study of the Gothic illuminates the unbroken connections between our imaginative life and our economic, social, and political life' (p. 191).
79 Punter, op. cit., p. 425. See also Robert Miles, who claims that 'Gothic writing enters the aesthetic realm of cultural critique and itself offers self-conscious versions of the "subject", that nexus of self and power' (op. cit., p. 224).
80 Fred Botting, *Making Monsters: 'Frankenstein', Criticism, Theory*, New York, Manchester University Press, 1991, pp. 3, 4.
81 The gothic has often been attacked for suggesting that all authority and power is demonic, and so encouraging passivity. Tompkins, op. cit., pp. 59–61, notes how the gothic extended a sentimental interest in victims and the passivity of the cult of sensibility, arguing that: 'The passivity of heroines and sometimes heroes' is set in 'a world where initiative is too often a monopoly of the bad' (pp. 135–6). On the passivity of gothic figures, see also George Levine, *The Realistic Imagination: English Fiction from Frankenstein to Lady Chatterley*, Chicago and London, University of Chicago Press, 1981, p. 33. See also Tobin Siebers's attack on Romanticism in general as a cult of irresponsibility that makes being a victim a valued position, in *The Romantic Fantastic*, Ithaca and London, Cornell University Press, 1984.
82 Quoted from Summers, op. cit., p. 38.

Bibliography

Abel, Elizabeth, Hirsch, Marianne and Langland, Elizabeth (eds) (1983) *The Voyage In: Fictions of Female Development*, Hanover, NH, University Press of New England.

Abrams, M.H. (1960) 'The Correspondent Breeze: A Romantic Metaphor', reprinted in *The Correspondent Breeze: Essays on English Romanticism*, New York and London, W.W. Norton, 1984.

—— (1971) *The Mirror and the Lamp: Romantic Theory and the Critical Tradition*, New York, Oxford University Press.

—— (1971) *Natural Supernaturalism: Tradition and Revolution in Romantic Literature*, New York, W.W. Norton.

Allen, B. Sprague (1918) 'The Reaction Against William Godwin', *Modern Philology*, vol. 16, no. 5, pp. 57–75.

Ariès, Philippe (1962) *Centuries of Childhood: A Social History of Family Life*, New York, Vintage.

Armstrong, Nancy (1987) *Desire and Domestic Fiction: A Political History of the Novel*, New York, Oxford University Press.

Austen, Jane (1818) *Northanger Abbey*, Harmondsworth, Penguin, 1972.

Bakhtin, M.M. (1981) *The Dialogic Imagination: Four Essays*, trans. Caryl Emerson and Michael Holquist, Austin, University of Texas Press.

Baldick, Chris (1987) *In Frankenstein's Shadow: Myth, Monstrosity, and Nineteenth-Century Writing*, Oxford, Clarendon Press.

Barish, Jonas (1981) *The Antitheatrical Prejudice*, Berkeley, University of California Press.

Barker, Gerard A. (1974) 'Justice to Caleb Williams', *Studies in the Novel*, vol. 6, pp. 377–88.

Barker-Benfield, G.J. (1989) 'Mary Wollstonecraft: Eighteenth-Century Commonwealthwoman', *Journal of the History of Ideas*, vol. 50, pp. 95–115.

Bindman, David (1989) *The Shadow of the Guillotine: Britain and the French Revolution*, London, British Museum Publications.

Birkhead, Edith (1921) *The Tale of Terror: A Study of The Gothic Romance*, London, Constable.

Bloom, Harold (1973) *The Anxiety of Influence: A Theory of Poetry*, New York, Oxford University Press.

—— (1975) *A Map of Misreading*, Oxford, Oxford University Press.

Bibliography

Bogel, Fredric V. (1984) *Literature and Insubstantiality in Later Eighteenth-Century England*, Princeton, Princeton University Press.

Bordo, Susan R. (1987) *The Flight to Objectivity: Essays on Cartesianism and Culture*, Albany, State University of New York Press.

Botting, Fred (1991) *Making Monsters: 'Frankenstein', Criticism, Theory*, New York, Manchester University Press.

Boulton, James T. (1975 rpt) *The Language of Politics in the Age of Wilkes and Burke*, Westport, CT, Greenwood.

Bowerbank, Sylvia (1979) 'The Social Order vs. The Wretch: Mary Shelley's Contradictory-Mindedness in *Frankenstein*', *English Language Notes*, vol. 46, pp. 418–31.

Broadwell, Elizabeth P. (1975) 'The Veil Image in Ann Radcliffe's *The Italian*', *South Atlantic Bulletin*, vol. 40, pp. 76–87.

Brooks, Peter (1973) 'Virtue and Terror: *The Monk*', *English Literary History*, vol. 90, pp. 249–63.

—— (1985) *Reading for the Plot: Design and Intention in Narrative*, New York, Vintage.

Brown, Marshall (1987) 'A Philosophical View of the Gothic Novel', *Studies in Romanticism*, vol. 26, pp. 275–301.

Burke, Edmund (1757) *A Philosophical Enquiry into the Origin of Our Ideas of the Sublime and Beautiful*, ed. James T. Boulton, Notre Dame and London, University of Notre Dame Press, 1958.

—— (1790) *Reflections on the Revolution in France*, ed J.G.A. Pocock, Indianapolis and Cambridge, Hackett, 1987.

—— (1791) *An Appeal From the New to the Old Whigs*, ed. and intro. John M. Robson, Indianapolis and New York, Bobbs-Merrill, 1962.

—— (1791) *Letter to a Member of the National Assembly*, in *The Works of Edmund Burke*, 9 vols, Boston, Charles Little, 1839.

Butler, Marilyn (1980) 'The Woman at the Window: Ann Radcliffe in the Novels of Mary Wollstonecraft and Jane Austen', *Women and Literature*, vol. 1, pp. 128–48.

—— (1981) *Romantics, Rebels, and Reactionaries: English Literature and its Background 1760–1830*, Oxford, Oxford University Press.

—— (1982) 'Godwin, Burke, and *Caleb Williams*', *Essays in Criticism: A Quarterly Journal of Literary Criticism*, vol. 32, pp. 237–57.

Butler, Melissa A. (1988) 'Wollstonecraft versus Rousseau: Natural Religion and the Sex of Virtue and Reason', in Donald C. Mell, *et al.* (eds), *Man, God, and Nature in the Enlightenment*, East Lansing, MI, Colleagues, pp. 65–73.

Callahan, Patrick J. (1972) '*Frankenstein*, Bacon, and the "Two Truths"', *Extrapolation*, vol. 14, pp. 39–48.

Cantor, Paul A. (1984) *Creature and Creator*, New York, Cambridge University Press.

Carson, James P. (1988) 'Bringing the Author Forward: *Frankenstein* through Mary Shelley's Letters', *Criticism*, vol. 33, pp. 431–53.

Cassirer, Ernst (1963) *The Individual and the Cosmos in Renaissance Philosophy*, trans. Mario Domandi, Philadelphia, University of Pennsylvania Press.

Castle, Terry (1987) 'The Spectralization of the Other in *The Mysteries of*

Bibliography

Udolpho', in Felicity Nussbaum and Laura Brown (eds), *The New Eighteenth Century: Theory, Politics, English Literature*, New York, Methuen, pp. 231–53.

Cervantes (1614) *The Adventures of Don Quixote*, trans. J.M. Cohen, Harmondsworth, Penguin, 1950.

Chodorow, Nancy (1978) *The Reproduction of Mothering: Psychoanalysis and the Sociology of Gender*, Berkeley, University of California Press.

Claridge, Laura P. (1985) 'Parent–Child Tensions in *Frankenstein*: The Search for Communion', *Studies in the Novel*, vol. 17, pp. 14–26.

Clemit, Pamela (1993) *The Godwinian Novel: The Rational Fictions of Godwin, Brockden Brown, Mary Shelley*, Oxford, Clarendon Press.

Cobban, Alfred (ed.) (1950) *The Debate on the French Revolution*, London, Nicholas Kaye.

—— (1960) *Edmund Burke and the Revolt Against the Eighteenth Century: A Study of the Political and Social Thinking of Burke, Wordsworth, Coleridge, and Southey*, London, George Allen & Unwin.

Coleridge, Samuel Taylor (1936) *Coleridge's Miscellaneous Criticism*, ed. T.M. Raysor, London.

—— (1817) *Biographia Literaria*, in James Engell and W. Jackson Bate (eds) *Coleridge's Collected Works*, vol. 2, Princeton, Princeton University Press, 1983.

Cott, Nancy (1978) 'Passionlessness: An Interpretation of Victorian Sexual Ideology, 1790–1850', *Signs*, vol. 4, pp. 219–36.

Curtius, Ernst Robert (1963) *European Literature and the Latin Middle Ages*, trans. Willard Trask, Princeton, Princeton University Press.

Day, William Patrick (1985) *In the Circles of Fear and Desire: A Study of Gothic Fantasy*, Chicago, University of Chicago Press.

Deane, Seamus (1988) *The French Revolution and Enlightenment in England 1789–1832*, Cambridge, Mass., Harvard University Press.

DeLamotte, Eugenia C. (1990) *Perils of the Night: A Feminist Study of Nineteenth-Century Gothic*, New York, Oxford University Press.

De Man, Paul (1969) 'The Rhetoric of Temporality' in Charles S. Singleton (ed.), *Interpretation: Theory and Practice*, Baltimore, Johns Hopkins University Press, pp. 173–209.

DePorte, Michael (1984) 'The Consolations of Fiction: Mystery in *Caleb Williams*', *Papers in Language and Literature*, vol. 20, pp. 154–64.

Dickinson, H.T (ed.) (1974) *Politics and Literature in the Eighteenth Century*, London, J.M. Dent.

—— (1976) 'The Eighteenth-Century Debate on the "Glorious Revolution"', *History*, vol 61, pp. 28–45.

—— (1977) *Liberty and Property: Political Ideology in Eighteenth-Century Britain*, New York, Methuen.

Doody, Margaret Anne (1977) 'Deserts, Ruins, and Troubled Waters: Female Dreams in Fiction and the Development of the Gothic Novel', *Genre*, vol. 10, pp. 529–72.

Dumas, D. Gilbert (1966) 'Things as They Were: The Original Ending of *Caleb Williams*', *Studies in English Literature, 1500–1900*, vol. 6, pp. 575–97.

Duncan, Ian (1992) *Modern Romance and Transformations of the Novel: The Gothic, Scott, Dickens*, Cambridge, Cambridge University Press.

Durant, David (1981) 'Aesthetic Heroism in *The Mysteries of Udolpho*', *Eighteenth Century Theory and Interpretation*, vol. 22, pp. 175–88.

Bibliography

—— (1982) 'Ann Radcliffe and the Conservative Gothic', *Studies in English Literature, 1500–1900*, vol. 22, pp. 519–30.

Dussinger, John A. (1976) 'Kinship and Guilt in Mary Shelley's *Frankenstein*', *Studies in the Novel*, vol. 8, pp. 38–55.

Eagleton, Terry (1976) *Marxism and Literary Criticism*, Berkeley and Los Angeles, University of California Press.

Ellis, Kate Ferguson (1989) *The Contested Castle: Gothic Novels and the Subversion of Domestic Ideology*, Urbana and Chicago, University of Illinois Press.

Ezell, Margaret J.M. (1934) 'John Locke's Images of Childhood', *Eighteenth-Century Studies*, vol. 17, pp. 139–55.

Fawcett, Mary Laughlin (1983) 'Udolpho's Primal Mystery', *Studies in English Literature, 1500–1900*, vol. 23, pp. 481–94.

Finke, Laurie A. (1987) '"A Philosophic Wanton": Language and Authority in Wollstonecraft's *Vindication of the Rights of Woman*', in Robert Ginsberg (ed.), *The Philosopher as Writer: The Eighteenth Century*, Toronto, Associated University Press, pp. 155–76.

Fleck, P.D. (1967) 'Mary Shelley's Notes to Shelley's Poems and *Frankenstein*', *Studies in Romanticism*, vol. 6, pp. 226–54.

Fleenor, Juliann E. (ed.) (1983) *The Female Gothic*, Montreal, Eden.

Frankl, Paul (1960) *The Gothic: Literary Sources and Interpretations Through Eight Centuries*, Princeton, Princeton University Press.

Freud, Sigmund (1958) 'The Uncanny', in *On Creativity and the Unconscious*, New York, Harper & Row, pp. 122–61.

Froula, Christine (1983) 'When Eve Reads Milton: Undoing the Canonical Economy', *Critical Inquiry*, vol. 10, pp. 321–47.

Frye, Northrop (1982) *The Great Code: The Bible and Literature*, New York and London, Harcourt Brace Jovanovich.

Furbank, P.N. (1955) 'Godwin's Novels', *Essays in Criticism*, vol. 5, pp. 214–28.

Gilbert, Sandra, and Gubar, Susan (1979) *The Madwoman in the Attic: The Woman Writer and the Nineteenth Century Imagination*, New Haven, Yale University Press.

Godwin, William (1784) *Italian Letters or The History of the Count de St Julian*, intro. Burton R. Pollin, Lincoln, University of Nebraska Press, 1965.

—— (1793) *Enquiry Concerning Political Justice*, ed. and intro. Isaac Kramnick, Harmondsworth, Penguin, 1976.

—— (1794) *Caleb Williams*, ed. and intro. David McCracken, Oxford and New York, Oxford University Press, 1970.

—— (1797) *The Enquirer: Reflections on Education, Manners, and Literature in a Series of Essays*, New York, Augustus M. Kelley, 1965.

—— (1799) *Travels of St Leon*, London, Henry Colburn and Richard Bentley, 1831.

—— (1805) *Fleetwood, or The New Man of Feeling*, New York, Garland Publishing, 1979, 3 vols.

—— (1966) *The Letters of William Godwin and Mary Wollstonecraft*, ed. Ralph Wardle, Lawrence, Kansas, University of Kansas Press.

Gold, Alex (1977) 'It's Only Love: The Politics of Passion in Godwin's *Caleb Williams*', *Texas Studies in Literature and Language*, vol. 19, pp. 135–60.

Bibliography

Graham, Kenneth W. (1984) 'The Gothic Unity of *Caleb Williams*', *Papers on Language and Literature*, vol. 20, pp. 47–59.

—— (ed.) (1989) *Gothic Fictions: Prohibition/Transgression*, New York, AMS Press.

—— (1990) 'Narrative and Ideology in Godwin's *Caleb Williams*', *Eighteenth-Century Fiction*, vol. 2, no. 3, pp. 215–28.

—— (1990) *The Politics of Narrative: Ideology and Social Change in William Godwin's 'Caleb Williams'*, New York, AMS Press.

Griffin, Dustin (1986) *Regaining Paradise: Milton and the Eighteenth Century*, Cambridge, Cambridge University Press.

Grosse, Marquis of (1797) *Horrid Mysteries: A Story Translated from the German of the Marquis of Grosse by Peter Will*, London, Folio Press, 1968.

Guralnick, Elissa S. (1977) 'Radical Politics in Mary Wollstonecraft's *A Vindication of the Rights of Woman*', *Studies in Burke and His Time*, vol. 18, pp. 155–66.

Hagstrum, Jean H. (1980) *Sex and Sensibility: Ideal and Erotic Love from Milton to Mozart*, Chicago, University of Chicago Press.

Harvey, A.D. (1976) 'The Nightmare of *Caleb Williams*', *Essays in Criticism*, vol. 26, pp. 236–49.

—— (1980) '*Frankenstein* and *Caleb Williams*', *Keats–Shelley Journal*, vol. 29, pp. 21–7.

Hazlitt, William (1967) *Lectures on English Poets and The Spirit of the Age: or Contemporary Portraits*, intro. Catherine Macdonald Maclean, London, J.M. Dent & Sons Ltd.

Heller, Wendy Tamar (1992) *Dead Secrets: Wilkie Collins and the Female Gothic*, New Haven, Yale University Press.

Hennelly, Mark M., Jr. (1987) '"The Slow Torture of Delay": Reading *The Italian*', *Studies in the Humanities*, vol. 14, pp. 1–14.

Hill, Christopher (1958) *Puritanism and Revolution: Studies in Interpretation of the English Revolution of the Seventeenth Century*, Harmondsworth, Penguin.

Hirsch, Marianne (1989) *The Mother/Daughter Plot: Narrative, Psycho-analysis, Feminism*, Bloomington, Indiana University Press.

Hodges, Devon (1983) '*Frankenstein* and the Feminine Subversion of the Novel', *Tulsa Studies in Women's Literature*, vol. 2, pp. 155–64.

Holland, Norman N. and Sherman, Leona F. (1976–7) 'Gothic Possibilities', *New Literary History*, vol. 8, pp. 279–94.

Holmes, Richard (ed. and intro.) (1987) *Mary Wollstonecraft and William Godwin: A Short Residence in Sweden and Memoirs of the Author of 'The Rights of Woman'*, Harmondsworth, Penguin.

Homans, Margaret (1986) *Bearing the Word: Language and Female Experience in Nineteenth-Century Women's Writing*, Chicago and London, University of Chicago Press.

Howells, Coral Ann (1978) *Love, Mystery, and Misery: Feeling in Gothic Fiction*, London, Athlone Press.

Hume, Robert D. (1969) 'Gothic versus Romantic: a Reevaluation of the Gothic Novel' *PMLA*, vol. 84, pp. 282–90.

Hurd, Richard (1762) *Letters on Chivalry and Romance*, ed. Hoyt Trowbridge, Los Angeles, William Andrews Clark Memorial Library, 1963.

Bibliography

Jackson, Rosemary (1981) *Fantasy: The Literature of Subversion*, New York and London, Methuen.

Johnson, Samuel (1779) *Lives of the English Poets*, 2 vols, London, Oxford University Press, 1977.

Jones, Wendy (1990) 'Stories of Desire in *The Monk*', *English Literary History*, vol. 57, pp. 129–50.

Joseph, Gerhard (1975) 'Frankenstein's Dream: The Child is Father of the Monster', *Hartford Studies in Literature*, vol. 7, pp. 97–115.

Kahane, Claire (1985) 'The Gothic Mirror', in Shirley Nelson Gardener, Claire Kahane, and Madelon Sprengnether (eds), *The (M)other Tongue: Essays in Feminist Psychoanalytic Interpretation*, Ithaca, Cornell University Press, pp. 334–51.

Keily, Robert (1972) *The Romantic Novel in England*, Cambridge, Harvard University Press.

Keller, Evelyn Fox (1985) *Reflections on Gender and Science*, New Haven, Yale University Press.

Kelly, Gary (1975) 'Godwin, Wollstonecraft and Rousseau', *Women and Literature*, vol. 3, pp. 21–6.

—— (1976) *The English Jacobin Novel 1780–1805*, Oxford, Oxford University Press.

—— (1979) '"A Constant Vicissitude of Interesting Passions": Ann Radcliffe's Perplexed Narratives', *Ariel*, vol. 10, no. 2, pp. 45–64.

Kliger, Samuel (1952) *The Goths in England: A Study in Seventeenth and Eighteenth Century Thought*, Cambridge, Mass., Harvard University Press.

Kramnick, Isaac (1968) *Bolingbroke and his Circle: The Politics of Nostalgia in the Age of Walpole*, Ithaca and London, Cornell University Press.

—— (1977) *The Rage of Edmund Burke: Portrait of An Ambivalent Conservative*, New York, Basic Books.

—— (1977) 'Religion and Radicalism: English Political Theory in the Age of Revolution', *Political Theory: An International Journal of Political Philosophy*, vol. 5, pp. 505–34.

—— (1980) 'Children's Literature and Bourgeois Ideology: Observations on Culture and Industrial Capitalism in the later Eighteenth Century', in Perez Zagorin (ed.), *Culture and Politics from Puritanism to the Enlightenment*, Los Angeles, California University Press, pp. 203–40.

Langbauer, Laurie (1990) *Women and Romance: The Consolations of Gender in the English Novel*, Ithaca and London, Cornell University Press.

Levine, George (1981) *The Realistic Imagination: English Fiction from Frankenstein to Lady Chatterley*, Chicago and London, University of Chicago Press.

Levine, George and Knoepflmacher, U.C. (eds) (1979) *The Endurance of 'Frankenstein': Essays on Mary Shelley's Novel*, Berkeley, University of California Press.

Lévy, Maurice (1968) *Le Roman 'Gothique' Anglais: 1764–1824*, Toulouse, Association des Publications de la Faculté des Lettres.

Lewis, Matthew (1796) *The Monk*, ed. and intro. Howard Anderson, Oxford and New York, Oxford University Press, 1973.

Locke, John (1690) *An Essay Concerning Human Understanding*, 2 vols, New York, Dover, 1959.

—— (1690) *Two Treatises of Government*, Toronto, New American Library, 1963.

Bibliography

—— (1693) *Some Thoughts Concerning Education*, ed. and intro. John W. and Jean S. Yolton, Oxford, Clarendon Press, 1989.

London, April (1986) 'Ann Radcliffe in Context: Marking the Boundaries of *The Mysteries of Udolpho*', *Eighteenth-Century Life*, vol. 10, pp. 35–47.

Longueil, Alfred E. (1923) 'The Word "Gothic" in Eighteenth Century Criticism', *Modern Language Notes*, vol. 38, pp. 453–60.

Lovejoy, Arthur O. (1932) 'The First Gothic Revival and the Return to Nature', *Modern Language Notes*, vol. 47, pp. 419–46.

Lovell, Terry (1987) *Consuming Fiction*, London, Verso.

Lyndenberg, Robin (1979) 'Ghostly Rhetoric: Ambivalence in M.G. Lewis's *The Monk*', *Ariel: A Review of English Literature*, vol. 10, pp. 65–79.

MacAndrew, Elizabeth (1979) *The Gothic Tradition in Fiction*, New York, Columbia University Press.

Macaulay (1914) *The Works of Lord Macaulay* vol. 2, London, Longmans, Green & Co.

McCracken, David (1970) 'Godwin's Literary Theory: The Alliance between Fiction and Political Philosophy', *Philological Quarterly*, vol. 49, pp. 113–33.

—— (1970) 'Godwin's Reading in Burke', *English Language Notes*, vol. 7, pp. 264–70.

MacDonald, D.L. (1989) 'Bathos and Repetition: The Uncanny in Radcliffe', *Journal of Narrative Technique*, vol. 19, pp. 197–204.

McKeon, Michael (1987) *The Origins of the English Novel 1600–1740*, Baltimore, Johns Hopkins University Press.

McKinney, David D. (1990) 'The Castle of my Ancestors: Horace Walpole and Strawberry Hill', *British Journal for Eighteenth-Century Studies*, vol. 13, pp. 199–214.

McInery, Peter (1980) '*Frankenstein* and the Godlike Science of Letters', *Genre*, vol. 13, pp. 455–75.

Macpherson, C.B. (1962) *The Political Theory of Possessive Individualism: Hobbes to Locke*, Oxford, Oxford University Press.

Macpherson, Jay (1982) *The Spirit of Solitude: Conventions and Continuities in Late Romance*, New Haven and London, Yale University Press.

Marshall, David (1988) *The Surprising Effects Of Sympathy: Marivaux, Diderot, Rousseau, and Mary Shelley*, Chicago and London, University of Chicago Press.

Massé, Michelle A. (1990) 'Gothic Repetition: Husbands, Horrors, and Things That Go Bump in the Night', *Signs: Journal of Women in Culture and Society*, vol. 15, pp. 679–709.

Mellor, Anne K. (1989) *Mary Shelley: Her Life, Her Fiction, Her Monsters*, New York and London, Routledge.

Miles, Robert (1993) *Gothic Writing 1750–1820: A Genealogy*, London and New York, Routledge.

Miller, Jacqueline T. (1978) 'The Imperfect Tale: Articulation, Rhetoric, and Self in *Caleb Williams*', *Criticism*, vol. 20, no. 4, pp. 366–82.

Milton, John (1957) *Complete Poems and Major Prose*, ed. Merritt Y. Hughes, Indianapolis, Odyssey Press.

Moers, Ellen (1985) *Literary Women: The Great Writers*, New York, Oxford University Press.

Bibliography

Murrin, Michael (1969) *The Veil of Allegory*, Chicago, University of Chicago Press.

Myers, Mitzi (1972) 'Godwin's Changing Conception of *Caleb Williams*', *Studies in English Literature, 1500–1900*, vol. 12, pp. 591–628.

—— (1980) 'Unfinished Business: Wollstonecraft's *Maria*', *Wordsworth Circle*, vol. 11, no. 2, pp. 107–114.

—— (1981) 'Godwin's *Memoirs* of Wollstonecraft: The Shaping of Self and Subject', *Studies in Romanticism*, vol. 20, pp. 299–316.

—— (1982) 'Reform or Ruin: A Revolution in Female Manners', *Studies in Eighteenth-Century Culture*, vol. 11, pp. 199–216.

—— (1988) 'Pedagogy as Self-Expression in Mary Wollstonecraft: Exorcising the Past, Finding a Voice', in Shari Benstock (ed.), *The Private Self: Theory and Practice of Women's Autobiographical Writing*, Chapel Hill, University of North Carolina Press, pp. 192–210.

Napier, Elizabeth (1987) *The Failure of Gothic: Problems of Disjunction in an Eighteenth-Century Literary Form*, Oxford, Clarendon Press.

Newman, Beth (1986) 'Narratives of Seduction and Seductions of Narrative: The Frame Structure of *Frankenstein*', *English Literary History*, vol. 53, pp. 141–63.

Nicholl, Charles (1980) *The Chemical Theatre*, London, Routledge and Kegan Paul.

Ong, Walter (1967) *The Presence of the Word: Some Prolegemena for Cultural and Religious History*, Minneapolis, University of Minneapolis Press.

O'Rourke, James (1989) '"Nothing More Unnatural": Mary Shelley's Revision of Rousseau', *English Literary History*, vol. 56, no. 3, pp. 543–69.

Osler, Margaret (1970) 'John Locke and the Changing Ideal of Scientific Knowledge', *Journal of the History of Ideas*, vol. 31, pp. 1–16.

Ousby, Ian (1974) '"My servant Caleb": Godwin's *Caleb Williams* and the Political Trials of the 1790s', *University of Toronto Quarterly*, vol. 94, no. 1, pp. 47–55.

Paine, Tom (1791) *Rights of Man*, intro. Eric Foner, Harmondsworth, Penguin, 1984.

Parker, Patricia, A. (1979) *Inescapable Romance: Studies in the Poetics of a Mode*, Princeton, Princeton University Press.

—— (1987) *Literary Fat Ladies: Rhetoric, Gender, Property*, London and New York, Methuen.

Parreaux, André (1960) *The Publication of 'The Monk': A Literary Event*, Paris, Michel Didier.

Paul, C. Kegan (1876) *William Godwin: His Friends and Contemporaries*, 2 vols, London, H.S. King.

Paulson, Ronald (1983) *Representations of Revolution (1789–1820)*, New Haven and London, Yale University Press.

Peck, Lewis F. (1961) *A Life of Matthew G. Lewis*, Cambridge, Mass., Harvard University Press.

Philps, Mark (1986) *Godwin's Political Justice*, Ithaca, Cornell University Press.

Pocock, J.G.A. (1975) *The Machiavellian Moment: Florentine Political Thought and the Atlantic Republican Tradition*, Princeton and London, Princeton University Press.

—— (1989) *Politics, Language and Time: Essays on Political Thought and History*, Chicago, University of Chicago Press.

Pollin, Burton R. (1962) *Education and Enlightenment in the Works of William Godwin*, New York, Las Americas Publishing.

—— (1965) 'Philosophical and Literary Sources of *Frankenstein*', *Comparative Literature*, vol. 17, pp. 97–108.

Poovey, Mary (1979) 'Ideology and *The Mysteries of Udolpho*', *Criticism*, vol. 21, no. 4, pp. 307–30.

—— (1984) *The Proper Lady and the Woman Writer: Ideology as Style in the Works of Mary Wollstonecraft, Mary Shelley, and Jane Austen*, Chicago, University of Chicago Press.

Punter, David (1980) *The Literature of Terror: A History of Gothic Fictions from 1765 to the Present Day*, London, Longman.

—— (1981) 'Social Relations of Gothic Fiction', in David Punter, David Aers, and Jonathan Cook (eds), *Romanticism and Ideology: Studies in English Writing 1765–1830*, London, Routledge, pp. 103–17.

—— (1982) '1789: The Sex of Revolution', *Criticism*, vol. 24, pp. 201–17.

Radcliffe, Ann (1794) *The Mysteries of Udolpho*, ed. and intro. Bonamy Dobrée, Oxford and New York, Oxford University Press, 1966.

—— (1797) *The Italian or the Confessional of the Black Penitents: A Romance*, ed. and intro. Frederick Garber, Oxford and New York, Oxford University Press, 1981.

Radway, Janice (1981) 'The Utopian Impulse in Popular Culture: Gothic Romances and Feminist Protest', *American Quarterly*, vol. 33, pp. 140–62.

—— (1984) *Reading the Romance: Women, Patriarchy and Popular Culture*, Chapel Hill and London, University of North Carolina Press.

Railo, Eino (1927) *The Haunted Castle: A Study of the Elements of English Romanticism*, London, Routledge.

Rajan, Tilottama (1988) 'Wollstonecraft and Godwin: Reading the Secrets of the Political Novel', *Studies in Romanticism*, vol. 27, pp. 221–51.

Rawson, C.J. (1977) 'Cannibalism and Fiction: Reflections on Narrative Form and "Extreme Situations"', part 1, *Genre*, vol. 10, pp. 667–711.

Reeve, Clara (1785) *The Progress of Romance, Through Times, Countries, and Manners with Remarks on the Good and Bad Effects of it, on them Respectively, in a course of Evening Conversations*, 2 vols, Colchester, W. Keymer.

—— (1793) *Memoirs of Sir Roger de Clarendon*, 3 vols, London, Hookham & Carpenter.

Reiss, Timothy J. (1982) *The Discourse of Modernism*, Ithaca and London, Cornell University Press.

Richardson, Alan (1991) 'From *Emile* to *Frankenstein*: The Education of Monsters', *European Romantic Review*, vol. 1, no. 2, pp. 147–62.

Richter, David H. (1983) 'The Gothic Impulse: Recent Studies', *Dickens Studies Annual*, vol. 11, pp. 279–311.

—— (1987) 'Gothic Fantasia: The Monsters and the Myths; A Review Article', *The Eighteenth Century: Theory and Interpretation*, vol. 28, pp. 149–70.

—— (1988) 'The Reception of the Gothic Novel in the 1790s', in Robert W. Uphaus (ed.), *The Idea of the Novel in the Eighteenth Century*, East Lansing, MI, Colleagues, pp. 117–37.

—— (1989) 'The Unguarded Prison: Reception Theory, Structural Marxism,

Bibliography

and the History of the Gothic Novel', *The Eighteenth Century: Theory and Interpretation*, vol. 30, pp. 3–17.

Robbins, Caroline (1959) *The Eighteenth-Century Commonwealthman*, Cambridge, Mass., Harvard University Press.

Roberts, Marie (1990) *Gothic Immortals: The Fiction of the Brotherhood of the Rosy Cross*, London and New York, Routledge.

Rothstein, Eric (1975) *Systems of Order and Inquiry in Late Eighteenth-Century Fiction*, Berkeley, University of California Press.

Rousseau, Jean-Jacques (1761) *La Nouvelle Héloise*, trans. and abr. Judith H. McDowell, University Park and London, Pennsylvania University Press, 1968.

—— (1782) *Reveries of the Solitary Walker*, trans. and intro. Peter France, Harmondsworth, Penguin, 1979.

Rubenstein, Marc A. (1976) '"My Accursed Origin": The Search for the Mother in *Frankenstein*', *Studies in Romanticism*, vol. 15, pp. 165–94.

Sabor, Peter (1987) *Horace Walpole: A Reference Guide*, Boston, G.K. Hall.

—— (1987) 'Horace Walpole as Historian', *Eighteenth-Century Life*, vol. 11, pp. 5–17.

Sade, Marquis de (1966) 'Reflections on the Novel', in *The 120 Days of Sodom and Other Writings*, trans. Austryn Wainhouse and Richard Seaver, New York, Grove.

Sage, Victor (1988) *Horror Fiction in the Protestant Tradition*, London, MacMillan.

—— (ed.) (1990) *The Gothick Novel*, London, Macmillan.

Schiebinger, Londa (1988) 'Feminine Icons: The Face of Early Modern Science', *Critical Inquiry*, vol. 14, no. 4, pp. 661–91.

Schiller, Frederick (1853) *The Works of Frederick Schiller: Early Dramas and Romances*, trans. Henry G. Bohn, London, Henry G. Bohn.

Scott, Sir Walter (n.d.) *Scott's Lives of the Novelists*, London, J.M. Dent.

Sedgewick, Eve Kosofsky (1986) *The Coherence of Gothic Conventions*, New York, Methuen.

Sharrock, Roger (1962) 'Godwin on Milton's Satan', *Notes and Queries*, vol. 207, pp. 463–5.

Shelley, Mary (1818) *Frankenstein, or, The Modern Prometheus*, Oxford and New York, Oxford University Press, 1980.

—— [1819] *Mathilda*, Chapel Hill, University of North Carolina Press, 1959.

—— (1947) *Mary Shelley's Journal*, ed. Frederick L. Jones, Norman, Okla., University of Oklahoma Press.

Shelley, Percy Bysshe (1965) *The Complete Works of Percy Bysshe Shelley*, ed. Roger Ingpen and Walter E. Peck, New York, Gordian.

—— (1977) *Shelley's Poetry and Prose*, ed. Donald H. Reiman and Sharon B. Powers, New York and London, W.W. Norton.

Sherwin, Paul (1981) '*Frankenstein*: Creation as Catastrophe', *PMLA*, vol. 96, pp. 883–903.

Siebers, Tobin, (1984) *The Romantic Fantastic*, Ithaca and London, Cornell University Press.

Simms, Karl N. (1987) '*Caleb Williams*' Godwin: Things as They Are Written', *Studies in Romanticism*, vol. 26, pp. 343–63.

Small, Christopher (1972) *Ariel Like a Harpy: Shelley, Mary and 'Frankenstein'*, London, Gollancz.

Bibliography

Smith, Nelson C. (1973) 'Sense, Sensibility, and Ann Radcliffe', *Studies in English Literature, 1500–1900*, vol. 12, pp. 577–90.

Spencer, Jane (1986) *The Rise of the Woman Novelist: from Aphra Behn to Jane Austen*, New York and Oxford, Basil Blackwell.

Spitzer, Leo (1946) 'Notes on the Poetic and Empirical "I" in Medieval Authors', *Traditio*, vol. 4, pp. 414–22.

Stamper, Rexford (1973–4) '*Caleb Williams*: The Bondage of Truth', *The Southern Quarterly*, vol. 12, pp. 39–50.

Stanlis, Peter J. (1961) 'Burke and the Sensibility of Rousseau', *Thought*, vol. 36, pp. 246–76.

Starobinski, Jean (1971) *La transparence et l'obstacle*, Paris, Gallimard.

St Clair, William (1989) *The Godwins and the Shelleys: The Biography of a Family*, Baltimore, Johns Hopkins University Press.

Stein, Jess M. (1934) 'Horace Walpole and Shakespeare', *Studies in Philology*, vol. 31, pp. 51–68.

Stephens, Leslie (1902) *Studies of a Biographer*, vol. 3, second series, London, Buckworth & Co.

Stoker, Bram (1897) *Dracula*, Toronto and New York, Bantam Books, 1981.

Stone, Lawrence (1979) *The Family, Sex and Marriage in England 1500–1800*, Markham, Ont., Penguin.

Storch, Rudolph F. (1967) 'Metaphors of Private Guilt and Social Rebellion in Godwin's *Caleb Williams*', *English Literary History*, vol. 34, pp. 188–207.

Summers, Montague (1941) *A Gothic Bibliography*, London, Fortune Press.

—— (1964) *The Gothic Quest: A History of the Gothic Novel*, New York, Russell & Russell.

Swiggart, Ford H., Jr. (1969) 'Ann Radcliffe's Veil Imagery', *Studies in the Humanities*, vol. 1, pp. 55–9.

Swingle, L.J. (1973) 'Frankenstein's Monster and its Romantic Relatives: Problems of Knowledge in English Romanticism', *Texas Studies in Language and Literature*, vol. 15, pp. 51–65.

Sypher, Wylie (1945) 'Social Ambiguity in the Gothic Novel', *Partisan Review*, vol. 12, pp. 50–60.

Taylor, Charles (1989) *Sources of the Self: The Making of the Modern Identity*, Cambridge, Mass., Harvard University Press.

Thompson, G. Richard (ed.) (1974) *The Gothic Imagination: Essays in Dark Romanticism*, Pullman, Washington State Press.

Thorslev, Peter L., Jr. (1965) 'Incest as Romantic Symbol', *Comparative Literature Studies*, vol. 2, pp. 41–58.

—— (1984) *Romantic Contraries: Freedom vs. Destiny*, New Haven, Yale University Press.

Tobin, Patricia Drechsel (1978) *Time and the Novel: The Genealogical Imperative*, Princeton, Princeton University Press.

Todd, Janet (1982) 'Posture and Imposture: The Gothic Manservant in Ann Radcliffe's *The Italian*', in Janet Todd (ed.), *Women and Literature* vol. 2, Rutgers, Rutgers University Press, pp. 25–38.

—— (1988) *Feminist Literary History*, New York, Routledge.

—— (1989) *The Sign of Angellica: Women, Writing and Fiction, 1660–1800*, London, Virago.

Bibliography

Todorov, Tzvetan (1987) *The Fantastic: A Structural Approach to a Literary Genre*, Ithaca, Cornell University Press.

Tompkins, J.M.S. (1932) *The Popular Novel in England, 1770–1800*, Lincoln, Nebraska, University of Nebraska Press, 1963.

—— (1980) *The Work of Mrs. Radcliffe and Its Influence on Later Writers*, New York, Arno.

Varma, Devendra Prasad (1957) *The Gothic Flame: Being a History of the Gothic Novel in England; its Origins, Efflorescence, Disintegration, and Residuary Influences*, New York, Russell & Russell.

Veeder, William (1986) *Mary Shelley and 'Frankenstein': The Fate of Androgyny*, Chicago and London, University of Chicago Press.

Vickers, Nancy (1981) 'Diana Described: Scattered Woman and Scattered Rhyme', *Critical Inquiry*, vol. 8, pp. 265–79.

Walpole, Horace (1764) *The Castle of Otranto*, in E.F. Bleiler (ed.), *Three Gothic Novels*, New York, Dover, 1966.

Walzer, Michael (1965) *The Revolution of the Saints: A Study in the Origins of Radical Politics*, Cambridge, Mass., Harvard University Press.

—— (1985) *Exodus and Revolution*, New York, Basic Books.

Watkins, Daniel P. (1986) 'Social Hierarchy in Matthew Lewis's *The Monk*', *Studies in the Novel*, vol. 18, pp. 115–24.

Watt, Ian (1967) *The Rise of the Novel: Studies in Defoe, Richardson and Fielding*, Berkeley, University of California Press.

—— (1986) 'Time and Family in the Gothic Novel: *The Castle of Otranto*', *Eighteenth Century Life*, vol. 10, no. 3, pp. 159–71.

Weber, Max (1958) *The Protestant Ethic and the Spirit of Capitalism*, trans. Talcott Parsons, New York, Charles Scribner & Sons.

Webster, Charles (1982) *From Paracelsus to Newton: Magic and the Making of Modern Science*, London, Cambridge University Press.

Wehrs, Donald R. (1988) 'Rhetoric, History, Rebellion: *Caleb Williams* and the Subversion of Eighteenth-Century Fiction', *Studies in English Literature, 1500–1900*, vol. 28, pp. 497–511.

Wexelblatt, Robert (1980) 'The Ambivalence of *Frankenstein*', *Arizona Quarterly*, vol. 36, pp. 101–17.

Wilde, Oscar (1966) *The Complete Works of Oscar Wilde*, intro. Vyvyan Holland, London and Glasgow, Collins.

—— (1891) *The Picture of Dorian Gray*, ed. and intro. Isobel Murray, Oxford and New York, Oxford University Press, 1981.

Willey, Basil (1961) *The Eighteenth Century Background: Studies on the Idea of Nature in the Thought of the Period*, Boston, Beacon Press.

Williams, Ioan (ed.) (1970) *Novel and Romance 1700–1800: A Documentary Record*, London, Routledge.

Williams, Raymond (1973) *The Country and the City*, New York, Oxford University Press.

—— (1984) *Culture and Society 1780–1950*, Markham, Ont., Penguin.

—— (1984) *The Long Revolution*, Markham, Ont., Penguin.

Wilson, Anna (1989) 'Mary Wollstonecraft and the Search for the Radical Woman', *Genders*, vol. 6, pp. 88–101.

Wilt, Judith (1980) *Ghosts of the Gothic: Austen, Eliot, and Lawrence*, Princeton, Princeton University Press.

Bibliography

Wollstonecraft, Mary (1787) *Thoughts on the Education of Daughters* in Janet Todd and Marilyn Butler (eds), *The Works of Mary Wollstonecraft*, vol. 4, London, William Pickering, 1989.

—— (1790) *A Vindication of the Rights of Men*, Gainesville, Florida, Scholars' Facsimiles & Reprints, 1960.

—— (1792) *A Vindication of the Rights of Woman*, ed. Carol H. Poston, New York and London, W.W. Norton, 1975.

—— (1798) *Mary and The Wrongs of Woman*, ed. and intro. Gary Kelly, Oxford, Oxford University Press.

Woodcock, George (1989) *William Godwin: A Biographical Study*, Montreal and New York, Black Rose.

Index

Index

British nationalism 13–15, 21, 29, 56–7, 228 n.60
Brontë, Charlotte, *Jane Eyre* 34, 99
Brooks, Peter 39
Brown, Charles Brockden 12, 99, 144
Bunyan, John, *Pilgrim's Progress* 203
burial, premature, and closure 158
Burke, Edmund 13, 16, 24–30, 32–3, 38, 41, 62, 64, 78, 91, 96, 104, 113–14, 116, 125, 127, 130–1, 137, 139, 173, 176, 180, 184, 195, 214, 248 n.41; Godwin's relation to 47–53, 73–4, 98–9, 103, 107; *Reflections on the Revolution in France* 24–9, 74
Byron, George Gordon, Lord 3, 191, 204

Calvinism 50; *see also* determinism; Protestantism
canon: gothic and deconstruction of 221–2
Cantor, Paul 33
carnival 5, 8, 138, 174–5, 183–4
Carson, James 216
Castiglione, Baldesar, concept of *sprezzatura* 35
castle, image of 4, 10, 119–21
Catholicism 14; gothic's relation to 37, 99, 126, 139, 147–9, 173, 179; *see also* convent; cloister
causality 10–11, 19, 23, 28, 36, 39, 50, 57, 64, 72, 87, 174, 197, 211, 221
Cervantes, *Don Quixote* 192
change 10, 13, 20, 30, 39, 49, 53, 65–6, 80, 84, 91, 93, 106–9, 117, 124–5, 135, 138–41; in Burke 23–6, 33, 125; individual 66, 68; in Radcliffe 114, 123–5, 135, 138–41, 185; social 10, 23–4, 53, 57, 66, 74; *see also* development; past; progress; revolution
child 33–7, 129, 143, 166, 168–9, 190, 207; as artist 36
childhood 34, 114, 117, 128, 208; in Shelley 191, 200–2
chivalry *see* medievalism
Chodorow, Nancy 206, 232 n.102
class relations 19; in criticism 221; in

Godwin 62–3, 72; in Radcliffe 138–9; in Lewis 147, 164–5
Clemit, Pamela 138, 218
cloister, image of 143–4, 201–2; *see also* Catholicism; private sphere
closure, narrative 8–9; in Godwin 69–72, 107–9, 212; in Lewis 158, 160–4; in Radcliffe 32, 128–30, 140, 172, 183–5, 246; in Shelley 211–13; in Wollstonecraft 89–95, 212
Coleridge 3, 7, 30, 129, 165; 'The Rime of the Ancient Mariner' 74, 108, 197, 214
Commonwealthmen 40, 100
community, desire for 192–3, 206–7; narrative as model for 84; *see also* society
complementarity 79, 88, 96–7, 118; *see also* marriage, bourgeois ideal of
convent, image of 126, 135; *see also* Catholicism; cloister; private sphere
conventions, gothic use of 42–3, 56, 81–2, 85, 88, 93–5, 189
convergence, contusion ot opposites 20–1, 39–40, 63, 135–6, 160, 198, 205; gothic as 20–1; past and present 30–1; *see also* marriage
conversion narrative 71–2
creation 194, 215–16, 223; gothic models of 4, 168–9, 185, 190, 192, 194, 198, 206, 213, 217–23; *see also* art; author; science
creator and created 193, 200, 209, 211–12, 215–16; *see also* author; victor–victim
critic: as gothic villain 222; invidiousness of 167, 169; as necromancer vii, 218, 221; *see also* gothic, criticism of
curiosity 32, 58–9, 60, 63, 129
custom *see* habit

Dacre, Charlotte 202
dancing 35–6
Day, William Patrick 5, 10
defamiliarisation 9, 12, 15, 38, 189, 215, 220; *see also* alienation
desire and social duty, conflict

274

Index

Index

Sade, Marquis de 165
Sadlier, Michael 218
sailing, as metaphor for poetry 197
Satan, Milton's 40–1, 63, 79, 162–3, 176, 207–8
Schiebinger, Leonda 195
Schiller 4, 31, 40, 144, 156
science 47–8, 50–1, 57, 60–2, 74, 101–3, 109, 194–6, 204; and alchemy 196–8; and art 197–8; *see also* knowledge
scientist, figure of 194–8, 205–6, 220
Scott, Sir Walter 3, 7–8, 33, 113, 129, 169, 186
secret societies 104; *see also* private sphere
self-control 34–5, 51, 115, 120, 127; lack of 19, 22, 42, 60–1, 119, 127, 181, 202–3, 208–11, 216–17, 219–20
self-interest 11, 28–9, 49, 62, 88, 100–1, 103, 116, 120, 142, 177–8
self-scrutiny 50–1, 60; criticism as 221–3; gothic as form of 11, 70, 74, 77
sensationalism 189
sensibility 76, 78, 80, 83, 86, 88, 133
sentiment, sentimental 4, 56, 87, 114, 117, 122, 134, 172, 189, 193, 201, 209
separate spheres 37, 75–6, 78, 80–1, 86–9, 92, 96, 98–100, 116, 118, 145, 200, 203–4, 209, 213; *see also* private sphere
servants 19, 31, 59, 61–3, 68, 73, 83, 91, 123, 133, 180–4, 192–3; master–servant relation 19, 61–3, 180–4, 192–3
sexes, relations between the 12, 37, 75, 79–80, 85, 89, 103, 116, 118, 135–6, 216; *see also* complementarity; male identity; female identity; marriage; sexual difference
sexual difference 146, 216; *see also* complementarity
Shakespeare 4, 19, 21, 40, 53, 120, 132, 140, 145, 153, 181, 184–6
Shelley, Mary 4, 22, 33, 72, 75, 218; *Frankenstein* 4, 29, 33, 39–41, 51,

82–3, 93, 99, 185, 190–217, 223; relation to Godwin 190–2, 202, 216; relation to Percy Shelley 190–1, 193–4, 216; relation to Wollstonecraft 190–1, 216
Shelley, Percy Bysshe 113, 191, 193, 197–9, 204, 212, 216; 'Alastor' 197, 203
sincerity, Godwinian 51, 65
society 11–12, 25–9, 49–53, 107; alternatives to 84–5; as corrupting 15, 116–17; and individual 62–3, 70, 72, 74, 81, 84, 91, 143, 145, 179–80, 208; need for 66–7, 206–7; *see also* community; individual
solitary, romantic 41, 74, 107, 203–4; as explorer 198; female 79–80, 83, 193, 257; as scientist 195; *see also* alienation; outcast
spies, spying, 59–62; and 1790s politics 59, 104
Sterrenberg, Lee 217
Stevenson, Robert Louis 63; *Dr Jekyll and Mr Hyde* 145, 194
stoicism 66, 85, 115, 120
Stoker, Bram 4; *Dracula* 12, 31, 33, 36, 82, 202
sublime, the 4, 15, 17, 26, 30, 32, 40, 62, 113, 115–17, 119–20, 175, 198–9
subplots, functions of 123–4, 154–6
Summers, Montague 72, 218–19, 221
superstition 48, 101–2, 107, 120, 143–4, 152, 158–9, 196; as political weapon 27, 47, 49, 57, 62–3, 65–6
surrealism, and gothic 219–20
surveillance 6, 8, 59, 65; *see also* spies
suspense 32, 113, 130, 151, 153–4, 182, 189; *see also* narrative deferral
sympathy 67, 70–1, 87, 178, 196–7

theatrically, in gothic 145–6, 150–3, 156, 170, 186; *see also* Shakespeare
time, in Radcliffe 123–4
Todd, Janet 180–1
Tompkins, J. M. S. 5, 124, 218
tradition 13, 20–1, 24–8, 49, 65, 125, 139, 179–80
trunk, Caleb's 73–4

279

Index